THE SOLDIER

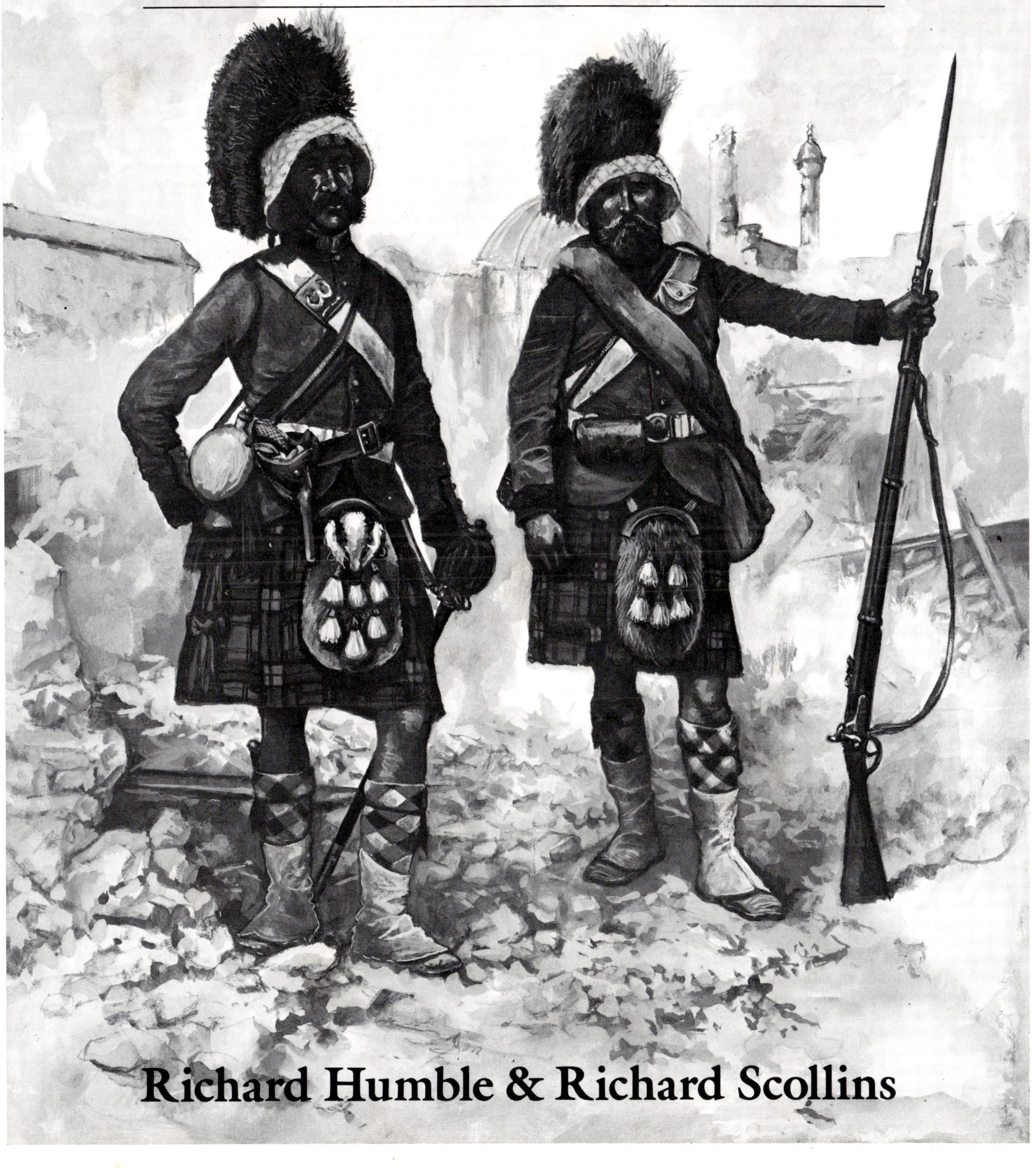

Richard Humble & Richard Scollins

THE SOLDIER

Richard Humble & Richard Scollins

ROYDON

Published by Roydon Publishing Co. Ltd.
London
England

Printed in Portugal

Produced by Talos Books Limited
Lincolnshire, Great Britain

Edited by Diane Moore
Book co-ordination John Moore
Designed by Brian Benson
Phototypesetting by Swiftprint Ltd, Stamford, Lincs
Origination by Four Color, London

Introduction

Hittite from the time of Kadesh: the great battle between the Egyptian and Hittite Empires in 1298 BC.

The dictionary definition of 'soldier' is clearly less than adequate; 'member of an army', is the usual bald formula. 'Army' tends to be rendered as 'organized body of men armed for war'. But no professional soldier would be likely to accept these all-embracing descriptions of their function. What of training? he will ask; what of discipline, of tradition, of regimental pride? Without these assets nobody could call himself 'a soldier', in anything like the full meaning of the word.

In the introduction to **A Matter of Honour,** his superb history of the Indian Army, Philip Mason goes deeper into the question:

'Weapons, equipment, training - these changed decade by decade. The ability to move quickly and bring force to bear on the enemy at the selected point - this was always needed though the means of achieving it changed. All these were ingredients of victory. But the one unchanging factor, the spirit which makes an army effective, was the confidence in each other of officers and men; this in its turn depends on those three virtues - loyalty, fidelity, courage.

How are they born? What makes a man cling with unbelievable tenacity and in the face of wounds and exhaustion to HONOUR - something that will send him out of cover into fire to bring back a wounded comrade, that will bring him to his feet when he is at the point of death and send him in a last charge to save a piece of coloured silk? Why should ***honour*** *inspire men whose homes are not threatened by invasion, to whom the cause for which they are fighting is remote and unintelligible? Why should they rise sometimes to heroic heights - and why sometimes should they angrily reject their oath, refuse obedience and even kill their officers?*

Officers, indeed, have usually had something to fight for. They have belonged to a society which rewards them, if they are successful, with titles, lands or pensions, which, even if they never rise to any great distinction, addresses them in terms of respect, and gives them rank and the means to live in tolerable comfort. But in most periods of history it is hard to see what the men have had to fight for...'

(Mason, Philip, **A Matter of Honour,** Jonathan Cape, London, 1974, p.14)

George MacDonald Fraser has put it another way, hardly less evocative:

I had just taken my final company orders in the office, and was sitting reflecting solemnly that tomorrow I would be a soldier no more, and from that my grasshopper mind started musing on how certain other military men must have felt when their tickets finally came through. Not the great martial names; not the Wellingtons and Napoleons and Turennes, but some of those others who, like me, had been what Shakespeare called warriors for the working day - the conscripts, the volunteers, the civilians who followed the drum and went to war in their time, and afterwards, with luck, picked up their discharges and back money and went home. Not soldiers at all, really, and quite undistinguished militarily - people like Socrates and Ben Jonson, Lincoln and Cobbett, Bunyan and Edgar Allan Poe, Gibbon and Cervantes, Chaucer and John Knox and Daniel Boone and Thomas Cromwell. (McAuslan was trouble enough, but I'd hate to take responsibility for a platoon consisting of that lot.)

And yet, I found it comforting to think that they too, like McAuslan and me - and perhaps you - had once stood nervously on first parade in ill-fitting kit, with their new boots hurting, feeling lost and a long way from home, and had done ablutions fatigue, and queued for the canteen and cookhouse, and worried over the state of their equipment, and stood guard on cold, wet nights, and been upbraided (and doubtless upbraided others in their turn) as idle bodies and dozy men, and thought longingly of their discharge, and generally shared that astonishing experience which, for some reason, men seem to prize so highly. Having been a soldier. It doesn't matter what happens to them afterwards, or how high or low they go, they never forget that ageless company they once belonged to...'

No match for the drilled legionaries and auxiliaries of Rome - Pictish warrior of the 1st Century AD, during the last Roman drive into Scotland.

(MacDonald Fraser, George, **McAuslan in the Rough**, Barrie & Jenkins, London 1974)

It was with similar thoughts that Richard Scollins and I set about the compilation of this book. We wanted to pay tribute to the universal soldier with the gloss off, not merely to present an array of immaculate figures for the delight of costume and uniform buffs. We have tried neither to glamorise the soldier in history, nor romanticise him. To an artist of Richard's quality, any such inclination is hardly possible, anyway.

As far as was possible, we wanted to give a picture of the evolution of the fighting man down the ages - comparing, say, the burdened Roman legionary on page 37 with the Falklands 'Para' on page 218; but we never believed it possible to restrict ourselves to the 'poor bloody infantry', much though they deserve such a tribute. We had to include mobile (i.e. non-foot-slogging) forces as well - chariot, cavalry, tank and airborne. In any case, the distinction between infantry and mobile forces has grown increasingly narrow when it comes to the crunch. To take just three modern examples at random, the crucial American Civil War Battle of

Gettysburg was opened by Union cavalry fighting dismounted; the Germans would almost certainly have achieved a decisive breakthrough at Ypres in October-November 1914 if the British cavalry had not been hurled dismounted into the thick of the action to help the infantry hold the line; and the mercifully quick knock-out victory over Argentina in 1982 would never have been possible without the amazing overland marches achieved by the two British parachute battalions.

5,000 years of soldiering

History, as preserved in pictorial and written records, began in the 3rd Millenium BC in Mesopotamia and Egypt; such records as have survived (including the earliest epic poetry) dealt copiously with soldiers and their achievements. One of the earliest (arguably **the** earliest) 'historical document' is a bas-relief on slate dating from around 3,000 BC; it hails the victory of Narmer, king of Upper (southern) Egypt over the Lower kingdom of the Nile Delta, and shows the king as victorious warlord. Its far more detailed Mesopotamian counterpart (from which Richard Scollins has depicted the troops shown on pages 14 and 15) is a fragment of another such victory memorial. It shows the army of the city of Lagash (in modern-day Iraq) marching to victory over a carpet of dead soldiers from the defeated neighbour-city of Umma. Both Egypt and Mesopotamia have served as battlefields throughout the 5,000 years since the wars of the 3rd Millenium BC, down to the last Arab-Israeli War of 1973 and the seemingly endless conflict still raging between Iran and Iraq.

Without labouring the point unduly, the history of warfare is as old as the history of mankind. Viewed as the darkest aberration of the human species, warfare is even older than history:

Forlorn hope at Culloden, 1746: Jacobite clansman with poleaxe.

'...lacking horns, tusks, fangs, claws, or a tough protective hide, the ability to burrow out of danger, fly, or out pace the fastest predator, primitive man was naturally thrown back on artificial aids. He learned to pick up rocks and throw them accurately, and to smite with clubs; he moved on to fashion spears and bows and arrows. Whether hunting for food or defending himself against predatory beasts, he also learned that teamwork in stalking and ambushing yielded much better results than individual action. In short, organization and weapons gave him, to use the lofty language of **Genesis**, *"dominion over the fish of the sea, and over the birds of the air, and over the cattle, and over all the earth, and over every creeping thing that creeps upon the earth". But there was one setback: it also applied to his fellow man. When the first primitive tribe discovered that organization and weapons could eliminate danger from rival tribes - that, surely, was when war was born.*

After thousands of years of recurrent conflict, "civilized" man emerged with his mind programmed for war ...'

(Humble, Richard, **Warfare in the Ancient World,** Book Club Associates, London 1980)

The modern soldier is the heir of the prehistoric warrior, the guardian and champion of the tribe. In action, he depends first and foremost on his mates. He is taught to live up to the glorious exploits of his predecessors. He follows rituals aimed at impressing the rest of the tribe with the values of past victories and present readiness to win more. Excellence in service and in combat is rewarded with greater authority and special decorations. In prolonged periods of peace, his privileges and the cost of his maintenance are naturally grumbled at by the rest of the tribe who have to pay for them. He knows that such resentment will vanish at a stroke and be replaced by hysterical adulation as soon as his services are needed. In all these and many other respects, soldiering in the 1980s has changed little since prehistoric times.

Neither the soldier nor the civilian has the slightest need to feel ashamed of the fact. Nobody deplores the waste and misery of war more than the soldier who has to fight it, and the civilian who denounces soldiers as homicidal mercenaries is not only ignorant but missing the point. To abolish aggression and the urge to fight wars would mean inflicting frontal lobotomy on the entire human race, abolishing those very instincts which have anabled our species to survive and develop. To accept this is neither to defend nor glorify war and the profession of arms. But it does help to understand them better.

Evolution of the soldier

If a graph is drawn to represent any human activity or achievement over the 5 thousand-odd years of recorded history, the usual result is a gradual upward incline for about 4.9 thousand years with a vertical leap over the past century, produced by the joint industrial, scientific and medical revolution which has led us to the age of nuclear energy, micro-chip technology, and heaven knows whither. Compiling data for the drawing of a similar graph on the evolution of the soldier, on the other hand, would be a virtually impossible task because there are so many overlaps. Take, for instance, the hackneyed historical usage of 'Stone Age', 'Bronze Age', and 'Iron Age', the latter usually referring to the later 1st Millenium BC. Only a hundred years ago it was possible to find stone projectiles being fired out of bronze guns by, and at, troops equipped with steel weapons. The idea that at recurrent periods the soldier was transformed by new tactics and technology is a myth.

In very basic terms, the soldier relied for some 4.4 thousand years on weaponry consisting only of spear (including thrusting pike and throwing javelin), sword, axe, club, bow and arrow, and slung missiles of stone or metal. By year 4.5 thousand, these mainstays were becoming supplemented by gunpowder-fired artillery and hand guns. By 4.7 thousand the spear, axe bow and arrow, and sling had been abandoned by the world's most advanced armies in favour of smoothbore muskets fitted with bayonets, and smoothbore artillery. This endured until about 4.82 thousand, when the adoption of rifled barrels in small arms and artillery ushered in a new era of accuracy instead of indiscriminate missile-projection at close range. By 4.9 thousand accuracy had been married to rate of fire with the perfection and continued development of breech-loading rifles and artillery, and the first automatic weapons or machine-guns.

This relentless increase in accuracy and rate of fire was accompanied by new phenomena in transport: motorised vehicles and heavier-than-air flight. Together, the three factors spelled the end of the mobile soldier's long reliance on horse and mule for battlefield mobility; gave him armoured fighting vehicles (armoured cars and tanks) to enhance his survivability; enabled him to reconnoitre from the air, attack enemy troops from the air, and land his own airborne troops, by parachute or transport aircraft, behind the enemy lines. All the changes described in the above paragraph have come into being in the last 70 years.

Ancient, medieval and modern

In the interests of balanced presentation we have reluctantly decided to cut across the line of evolution as outlined above, and fall back on the familiar if always misleading 'slicing' of history by period: Ancient, Dark Ages, Medieval, and Modern (for want of a better word, in the latter case). In sub-dividing the 'Modern' era, it has at least been possible to concentrate on the major changes in costume, weaponry and tactics which distinguished each period.

From the War of American Independence: infantryman of John Shire's Regiment.

The military supremacies which we have assigned to the 'Ancient' period range from the Sumerian wars of the later 3rd Millenium BC to the collapse of the Western Roman Empire in the early 5th Century AD. In sequence, the supremacies covered are the Sumerian, Egyptian, Hittite, Philistine, Assyrian, Persian, Greek and Macedonian, Carthaginian, Republican Roman and Imperial Roman. The main themes established in this opening section include the ousting of chariotry by horsed cavalry and the increasing supremacy over shock infantry pure and simple (massed pikemen) of infantry with a mixed shock and missile capability. By the end of the section the heavy-armoured lancer already appears as the forerunner of the medieval knight.

The term 'Dark Ages', properly used, should really be limited to the obscure decades of the 5th and 6th Centuries AD; but in purely military terms it is certainly appropriate to extend it to the rise of the Norman supremacy in the middle 11th. Opening this second section, Richard Scollins offers his view of what the 'real' King Arthur and his 'knights' looked like: armoured cavalry of the later Roman type. This is followed by the warriors who beat down the Roman West in the opening decades of the 5th Century - Vandal, Goth and Hun; the 'all-rounder' Byzantine cavalry used in the campaigns of the Eastern Empire in the 6th Century; and the Arab warriors who overran the Middle East, southern Mediterranean, and Spain in the 7th and early 8th Centuries. Also included

British private of 44th foot, retreat from Kabul, 1842.

are the Carolingian Franks who carved out the 'Holy Roman Empire', the Scandinavian Vikings and the Saxon English, and the dreaded Magyar horsed archers of the 10th Century.

We open our section on the 'Middle Ages' with a close look at the military machine of the Normans, whose extraordinary career took them not only north to England but south to Italy and Sicily and ultimately, in the Crusades of the late 11th and 12th Centuries, to Syria and Palestine. The supremacy of the armoured knight, once established by the Normans, was destined to endure for the next 400 years, and we duly show the developments in knightly armoured protection from the 12th Century to the 15th. The knight's supremacy was, however, repeatedly challenged with startling effect - by the Mongol horsed archers in the 13th Century; by the pike-wielding infantry of the Scots and the Swiss in the late 13th and early 14th Centuries; and by the English longbowmen in the 14th and early 15th Centuries. Though by the middle 15th Century artillery and hand-guns were ushering in the 'age of gunpowder', the pikemen of Switzerland remained the élite troops of Europe until the general use of field artillery in the opening decades of the 16th Century. One answer to the prowess of the Swiss pikemen was offered by the German **landsknechte:** mercenary specialists in hacking pike formations apart.

Though English longbowmen (at Flodden in 1513) were still savaging enemy armies a century after their destruction of the French knights at Agincourt, it was already obvious that the hand-gun and cannon had come to stay. The only question was how long it would take the new to oust the old. It was a prolonged and cautious process to which we have devoted a complete section: 'The 16th and 17th Centuries', a vital chrysalis-period for both infantry and cavalry. In a sense this was the true end of the Middle Ages, giving place to the first professional standing armies in European history which appeared in the later 17th Century. It saw the end of the uneasy co-existence between musketeer and pikeman, their roles blended with the adoption of the musket bayonet; and the supplanting of the fully-armoured horsed lancer by faster types of cavalryman relying on speed in manoeuvre and the charge, of which had already appeared by the time of Waterloo in 1815: the rifled barrel and the explosive shell. By 1914 the universal shift to magazine-fed breech-loading rifles and artillery had yielded potential fire-power undreamed-of in the musket and solid-shot days. The colonial wars of the 19th Century, which we cover in our seventh section, had made this new destructive potential hard to set in a European context. On the first day of the Somme in 1916, British casualties alone exceeded the total number of dead left on the field by all three armies at Waterloo.

The two World Wars added three main elements to land warfare: the tank, air power, and motorised transport. All three combined to bring about the final redundancy of horsed soldiers after more than 4.9 thousand years. And yet, as we have tried to show in our tenth and final section, mere superiority in matérial and fire-power has never been, and still is not, a guarantor of victory in itself. In the final analysis the only such guarantors are the troops on the ground, with their will and ability to march, fight, endure and win. And this applies both to the soldier of the 'high-tech' armies of East and West and the ragged guerrilla braving the resources of either:

'...There is nothing to distinguish their generals from their private soldiers except the star they wear on their collars. Their uniform is cut out of the same material, they wear the same boots, their cork helmets are identical and their colonels go on foot like privates. They live on the rice they carry on them, on the tubers they pull out of the forest earth, on the fish they catch and on the water of the mountain streams. No beautiful secretaries, no pre-packaged rations, no cars or fluttering pennants ... no military bands. But victory, damn it, victory!'

(Roy, Jules, **The Battle of Dienbienphu**, Harper and Row, New York, 1965)

Private of Princess Patricia's Canadian Light Infantry, 1915.

c.3000 bc

THE ANCIENT WORLD

-410 ad

War, the most destructive activity contrived by the human species, has never been possible without two essential artificial aids: weapons and organization. Both were forced on primitive man by the urge to survive, whether hunting for food or defending himself against predatory beasts. When the first primitive tribe discovered that weapons and organization could also eliminate danger from rival tribes, war was born.

After long millenia of conflict, 'civilized' man emerged with his mind programmed for war. The retreat of the ice-caps, warming of the climate, growing dependence on agriculture as well as hunting – all failed to erase the programme. Now the prize was the best pasture and ploughland, drawing hungry nomads like a magnet. When not directly threatened by hostile aliens from the wild lands, the growing city-civilizations taking shape in the fertile plains bickered and fought with each other over their conflicting spheres of interest. And they fought with armies of soldiers – with organization and uniform weaponry.

Such is the story told by the earliest written and pictorial records, dating from the early 3rd Millenium BC and relating to the city-states of Sumer, the lower reaches of the Mesopotamian 'land bridge' between the Rivers Tigris and Euphrates, in modern-day Iraq. How ironical it is that 5,000 years after these earliest of all known wars, the former 'land of Sumer' is still the cockpit for one of the bloodiest and most futile conflicts on the planet: the Iran/Iraq 'Gulf War' of the 1980s.

This, the opening chapter in the long history of THE SOLDIER, takes his story from the Sumerian wars through the successive military supremacies of Egypt, the Hittite Empire, Assyria, Persia, the Greek city states, Carthage, Macedon, and the Roman Republic and Empire. It ends in 410 AD with the defeat not only of the Roman West, but of the former capital of the world: the collapse of the greatest military power the world had ever seen.

The first armies: city-state wars of

From the 'Stele of the Vultures'. . .
One of the earliest known visual 'close-ups' of troops in battle array dates from the city-state wars of Sumer - the civilization centered on the Rivers Tigris and Euphrates in lower Mesopotamia - in the 3rd Millenium BC. A fragment of a victory monument known as the 'Stele of the Vultures', it shows soldiers of the city of Lagash advancing into battle, led by their governor-general Eannatum. These troops are spearmen equipped with close-fitting helmets, ranked in close formation and advancing behind a wall of deep rectangular shields. The latter are studded with what must have been rows of circular bronze bosses.

. . . and the 'Standard of Ur'
Another invaluable 'visual document' from 3rd Millenium Sumer is a colourful mosaic known as the 'Standard of Ur', from the city of that name where it was discovered. This provides even more detailed evidence of the sophisticated range of troops and weaponry with which the Sumerian city-states fought their wars in this remote era. There are helmeted and cloaked infantry spearmen, in close formation but without shields; a king or governor flanked by what are obviously elite guards spearmen armed also with axes; and war chariots rolling into action over the bodies of the enemy dead. From some 5,000 years ago, here we have proof of regular and guards infantry 'regiments', and even fighting vehicles in action.

The chariots of Sumer
The chariots depicted on the 'Standard of Ur' seem to have been cumbersome, 'boxy' affairs on four solid wooden wheels, drawn by a team of four mules (the distinctive ears and tails of the beasts are stressed). It would seem most unlikely that they were built for speed, even over level ground; they most probably advanced at a modest pace to give the enemy the impression

the Sumerian era, c.2850-2300 BC

of unstoppable momentum. There is a crew of two: a driver and a spearman, the latter able either to hurl javelins from the moving chariot or dismount and fight on foot. Each chariot is fitted with a built-in 'magazine' at the front, holding a replacement store of javelins.

Though we know, from the heroic Sumerian 'Epic of Gilgamesh', that the Sumerians practised archery, neither the 'Stele of the Vultures' nor the 'Standard of Ur' shows archers on the battlefield. This hardly proves that the Sumerians never included archers among their skirmishing light infantry, but can be taken as indicating that they relied on javelins rather than arrows for missile fire-power. If this was the case, it was an anticipation by some 2,000 years of the javelin-throwing legions of Rome **(pp. 29-35)**.

Troop roles at the dawn of history

To sum up, this early evidence from the Sumerian wars establishes basic types of soldier which have endured down the ages. The Sumerians used **light infantry,** to draw out the enemy and, after the main action, keep him on the run in retreat. Their tactical mainstay, the core of the order of battle, was most probably **heavy shock infantry** manoeuvered in **close formation.** This was the menacing hedge of levelled spears or infantry **phalanx** which, employing longer and heavier spears or pikes, was destined to appear and reappear until the advent of the bayonet in the 17th Century AD. As for the decisive infantry charge in close formation, this would not become fully redundant until rendered obviously suicidal by rapid rifle and machine-gun fire in the First World War.

Menace of the shield-wall

The close-knit **shield wall** favoured by the Sumerians also had a long future ahead of it; the shield wall was last used by the formidable Zulu army in the 19th Century. To be fully effective it would have required good **close-order drill,** particularly when advancing over broken ground. It had the obvious advantage of offering protection from enemy fire when holding ground as well as during the advance, and also had a most intimidating appearance. The bronze discs shown on Sumerian shields must have made the phalanx glitter in the sun like a reptile's scales.

Heyday of the

war chariot: c.1700-609 BC

The chariot was the medium for the first adoption of the horse in war, which seems to have been achieved around 1800 BC by the Hurrian kingdom of Mitanni (east of the upper Euphrates) and by the Hittites of Asia Minor. The superior power of draught horses led rapidly to the development of a lighter, two-wheeled chariot with a rear-slung axle, the latter feature greatly increasing manoeuvrability by permitting sharp course changes to be made at speed.

Even in its clumsy Sumerian prototype form, the chariot was a device to give an army mobile hitting-power: a fast platform from which enemy forces could be harrassed by hit-and-run doses of archery or javelin fire. When used in mass the chariot could also serve as an infantry personnel carrier, conveying 'instant' groups of spearmen or archers to points of crisis on the battlefield.

The chariot eventually became extinct because horsed cavalry was faster, more manoeuvrable, and could cope with a wider variety of terrain. For all that the horsed chariot had a long 'service career' : 1800 BC to the 1st Century AD, its last real exponents being the Celtic tribes in Britain **(see pp 38-39).** Though as useless as cavalry in frontal attacks on steady infantry, chariots in mass had a frightening appearance and would usually panic an enemy low in training, morale or both. Chariots could inflict great slaughter against disorganised troops in open terrain.

Designed to harrass and pursue enemy infantry, chariots were not suited to fighting enemy chariots but there was one famous exception: the great chariot v. chariot battle at Kadesh on the Orontes (1298 BC) between the armies of the Hittite King Muwatallis and the Egyptian Pharaoh Ramesses II ('The Great'). The Hittite chariots **(below)** drove in the Egyptian right wing but the day was saved by a counterattack led in person by Ramesses (depicted **opposite, top**). Closely derived from the Hittite model, the lighter Egyptian chariot was ideal for the superior fire-power of archers.

The heavier, larger Assyrian chariot ***(opposite, below)*** *embarked shield-bearers to protect its marksman, in this case King Assurbanipal (669-c.627 BC).*

The Egyptian kingdoms:- c.2615-332 BC

The unlikely combination of the Bible and the Hollywood 'epics' have created a widespread impression of Egypt as one of the greatest imperial military powers of the Ancient World. In fact Egypt, geographically isolated from the mainstream of military evolution in western Asia, remained amazingly backward as a military state for much of its recorded history. Throughout the centuries spanning the Egyptian 'Old Kingdom' (c.2615-1991 BC), 'Middle Kingdom' (c.1991-1570 BC) and 'New Kingdom' (c.1570-332 BC), less than 250 years all told were devoted to successful wars of conquest or defence.

The Old and Middle Kingdoms

The early Egyptian wars of the 3rd Millenium BC derived from the struggle to unite the kingdoms of Upper Egypt (from the Nile's 1st Cataract at Aswan upstream to Cusae) and Lower Egypt (from the 1st Cataract downstream to the Delta). For over a thousand years, these wars were fought by armies of semi-naked spearmen, supplemented by archers recruited from the savage Nubians of the northern Sudan. Other weapons were simple maces and light axes of bronze, the latter featuring sheet-metal rather than heavy cast blades.

The Hyksos wars and after

Radical change only came because of the need to defeat and expel the Hyksos, a warrior people from Syria/Palestine who conquered Lower Egypt and held it from c.1678-1550 BC. It was the Hyksos, driven south by Hittite pressure, who introduced the horse and chariot into Egypt. In a fundamental reorganisation brought about by the struggle against the Hyksos, Egyptian armies also adopted body armour and a wider variety of side-arms : clubs, pole-axes, hand-axes and swords. Above all, archery with the powerful composite bow (chariot and infantry) became the most potent weapon in the arsenal of the Egyptian New Kingdom.

Zenith and long decline

At its height the New Kingdom dominated Palestine and southern Syria, abutting with the Hittite Empite **(see p. 18)**. From 1232-1190, however, Egypt was repeatedly invaded by the 'Sea Peoples' **(pp. 20-21)** Though saved by the victories of Ramesses III Egypt steadily declined, finally being conquered successively by Assyria (663 BC), Persia (343 BC), Macedon (332 BC) and Rome (30 BC).

The Hittite Empire, c.1600

The Hittites were one of the most important military supremacies of the Ancient World: the first master-practitioners of chariot warfare and the use of iron weapons in preference to bronze. The latter skill gave the Hittites a tremendous initial advantage in hand-to-hand combat against their bronze-armed neighbours and led to the creation of an empire stretching from the Aegean Sea to the upper Euphrates.

The early Hittite wars

Unlike Egypt, which normally had to contend with only one foreign foe at a time (and that rarely) the Hittite Kingdom was ringed with enemies in east and northern Asia Minor as well as the Hurrian kingdom of Mitanni, its biggest rival to the east. The original Hittite kingdom was centered on Khattusas (modern Boghazköy) on the Halys river in Asia Minor and the first Hittite campigns, in the early 16th Century BC, were west and south towards the Mediterranean. Hittite expansion then turned east into northern Syria. Though briefly checked by Hurrian Mitanni, these early Hittite wars produced one outstanding military feat: a 500-mile advance down the Euphrates to sack Babylon (c.1531). But this dramatic raid into southern Mesopotamia was followed by decades of domestic unrest. It was not until the middle 14th Century, under a secure ruling dynasty, that the great years of Hittite conquest began.

A brief-lived empire

As with the Egyptians and the Hyksos, the Hittites survived and prospered by improving on the most effective weaponry and tactics of their leading enemies, most notably a chariotry superior to that of Mitanni. The biggest flaws in the otherwise tough and well-armed Hittite infantry - insufficient body armour and archery fire-power - did not inhibit the triumphant campaigns of King Suppiluliumas (c.1380-1346 BC), who created a Hittite Empire by conquering Mitanni and the minor kingdoms of northern Syria.

After meeting and holding the Egyptian challenge in the great chariot battle at Kadesh (1298 BC) the Hittites remained masters of northern Syria after their homeland was overrun (c.1240-1230) by the eruption of the 'Sea Peoples' from the Aegean: a formidable soldiery overborne by sheer numbers.

OPPOSITE: *Egyptian soldiers of the 'New Kingdom', from the time of Ramesses III (c.1198-1156) - infantry spearman, Sherden mercenary brandishing sword (recruited from one of the most formidable of the 'Sea Peoples'), and guardsman with axe.*

BELOW: *Hittite infantrymen from the late 14th Century BC, showing a much more formidable array of weapons - mace, sword, heavy double-headed axe - than their Egyptian counterparts, but with notably less attention to protection.*

Warriors from the sea; the Philistines, c.1180-980 BC

Of the otherwise-mysterious swarm of 'Sea Peoples' who pulled down the Hittite Empire and briefly threatened the conquest of Egypt, only one branch has retained any credible documentation. This was the warrior race of the Philistines, the foremost enemies of Israel in the Old Testament chronicles of **Judges** and **Samuel**.

The Philistine heartland

After the repulse of the 'Sea Peoples' from the Nile Delta by Ramesses III (1190 BC) the Philistines descended on the southern Palestinian coast about 1180 and rapidly settled the coastal strip from Gaza to Mount Carmel. Philistia became a confederation of five city-states: Gaza, Gath, Ashkelon, Ashdod and Ekron, each under a warlord. The Philistine League was far and away the most formidable enemy to the disunited Twelve Tribes of Israel, who only paid dubious allegiance to a succession of charismatic 'judges' and whose most ambitious idea of a national muster (as laid down by Moses) was 'of every tribe a thousand'.

The conquest of Israel

Against such feeble opposition, the Philistines fielded well-drilled spearmen and archers, soundly equipped with body armour **(right)** who for most of the late 12th and 11th Centuries BC appeared invincible. Around 1050 BC the Philistine League rallied behind the warlord of Gath for the outright conquest of Israel, duly accomplished with a blend of ruthlessness in combat and shrewd political judgement.

After a shattering defeat at Aphek the Israelites remained utterly cowed by the Philistine capture of the sacred Ark of the Covenant, withheld as a hostage for seven months. During this time the Philistines studded Israel with garrison towns and, to prevent the beaten Israelites from secretly amassing stores of weapons, outlawed the smithying of iron in Israel. By Philistine decree, 'every one of the Israelites went down to the Philistines to sharpen his ploughshare, his mattock, his axe, or his sickle' - but only on payment of a humiliating scale of charges.

Even when the Israelites sought unity under the leadership of their first king, Saul (c.1020-1000 BC) their chronic lack of weapons made the opening of a guerrilla war of resistance a long and costly sequence of inevitable early defeats, for which the national temper was ill adapted. Though one of the first on record, they were not the last people to attempt the tricky evolution from guerrilla tactics to regular warfare before they were truly ready.

After King Saul and his sons died in battle with the Philistines on Mount Gilboa, the respected guerrilla leader David became the second King of Israel. It was under his inspired generalship that the Philistine hold on Israel was broken at last, and the Philistines were forced back to their original coastal strip. Finally, around 980 BC, David conquered Philistia and incorporated it as a province in his splendid but brief-lived united Kingdom of Israel.

One of the most famous Old Testament stories from the Philistine wars is that of the young David's single combat with the fearsome giant Goliath, whose gleaming armour and mighty weapons are rendered null and void by a well-aimed slingstone between the eyes.

This is much more than a dutiful parable about the repayment of faith in God. It may for instance be taken as a classic example of the potency of missile fire-power against armoured infantry equipped only for hand-to-hand combat - there is nothing incredible about the encounter, or its outcome (though, we are told, Goliath's 'shield-bearer went before him', and seems to have been remarkably incompetent at his job).

There is also a fascinating parallel between the detailed description of Goliath in I **Samuel** 17, and the Bronze Age Mycenean warriors described by Homer in his epic poem of the Trojan War - the **Iliad.** Goliath

> *'had a helmet of bronze on his head, and he was armed with a coat of mail'*

- presumably bronze scale armour, not mail, for which bronze is too soft a metal:

> *'and he had greaves of bronze upon his legs, and a javelin of bronze slung between his shoulders. And the shaft of his spear was like a weaver's beam, and his spear's head weighed six hundred shekels of iron'.*

Compare this with Homer's Ajax, preparing to fight Hector of Troy in Book VII of the **Iliad:**

> *'Ajax was putting on his flashing bronze. When all his armour was slung on, he sallied out . . . brandishing his long-shadowed spear as he strode forward . . . carrying a shield like a tower, made of bronze and seven layers of leather.'*

Certainly Goliath and Ajax could have changed places without exciting undue comment. Though the 'real' Trojan War would have been fought about 200 years earlier, here is a direct reminder of the Philistines' 'Sea People' origins in the Aegean world.

Masters of fire-power and mobility:

Assyrian heavy archer, clad in a calf-length tunic of scale armour, with head protection consisting of an armoured coif topped by a pointed helmet. In addition to his main weapon, the composite bow, he also carries a sword for close-quarter combat. He is attended by his shield-bearer (also armoured) whose task is to position the tall wicker shield or ***gerrhon.***

The empire of Assyria, centered on Nineveh in Upper Mesopotamia, was one of the most ferocious and successful military supremacies of the Ancient World. Its expansion began in the vacuum created by the Hittite defeat of Hurrian Mitanni (c. 138 BC) and reached its peak in the 'new Kingdom' of c. 935-612 BC. Under such capable military monarchs as Shalmaneser III, Tiglathpileser II, Sargon II and Sennacherib, the Assyrians beat down the civilizations of Babylon, Syria, the Jewish kingdoms in Palestine, and even overran Lower Egypt. The Assyrian Empire finally collapsed in civil war and general revolt after the death of Assurbanipal (c. 627), with Nineveh itself falling in 612 BC.

Highly specialised troops

The keynote of the Assyrians' long military supremacy was the method which they brought to the waging of war, particularly with regard to the training and use of specialised troops. Assyrian monuments show an extraordinary range of troop types. The light, medium, and heavy infantry consisted either of **missile troops** (slingers and archers equipped with the powerful composite bow) or **shock troops** (spearmen armed with shields and swords).

Chariots and cavalry

The Assyrians were the first to perfect the marriage of mobility and fire-power represented in the modern era by the armoured car and the tank. They made extensive use of **chariots** for the conveyance of archers (p.16), as lamented in the Old Testament: 'Their land is filled with horses, and there is no end to their chariots' (**Isaiah** 2: 7-8). But their greatest and most successful innovation was **horsed cavalry:** lancers and mounted archers.

At first the Assyrians seem to have regarded horses as economical substitutes for chariots: mobile seats for moving missile troops about the battlefield. Their first horsed archers were accompanied by armoured grooms who held the horses when the archers dismounted to shoot - mounted infantry rather than true cavalry. But Assyrian methodology soon exploited the full potentialities of horsed troops, the most obvious advantage being that a horse and rider can go places where a chariot cannot, and a good deal faster than a chariot anyway. This naturally cast horsed troops in the reconnaissance role, as the eyes of the army - a task which cavalry was to retain until the coming of aircraft 3,000 years later. Their superior pace also made horsed troops better than chariots when it came to pursuing a beaten enemy, harrying fugitives and preventing them from rallying.

But the best use to which the Assyrians put their horsed troops in battle derived from their basic tactic of relying on, and hence protecting, the central mass of infantry archers and spearmen. This meant using chariot and cavalry attacks to deter the enemy from swift advances which might, regardless of losses, get in among the Assyrian foot archers and cut them down.

Versatility of the mounted archer

Though Assyrian cavalry remained a 'service department' for the foot archers, it used the mobility of the horse to keep the enemy at a range where massed arrow fire could be most effective. By the 8th and 7th Centuries BC, Assyrian horsed soldiers no longer depended on mounted attendants and had replaced the chariot as the most numerous mobile arm in the Assyrian battle array. The Assyrian horsed archer **(right)** achieved a near-perfect blend of the **mobility** provided by the horse, and the **fire-power** provided by the bow.

The reverse applied to the other vital Assyrian innovation, the horsed spearman or lancer - a soldier type destined still to be riding into action in the Second World War. Assyrian lancers came into their own during the pursuit of broken armies, harrying fugitives at close ranges where archers were not only less effective but vulnerable to desperate counter-attacks.

The Assyrians, c.1380-612 BC

A notable Assyrian trait was the attention given to protection: body armour (even for normally light troops such as slingers) and a lavish allocation of shield-bearers. The generous size of the Assyrian chariot **(p.16)** was designed to accomodate up to four shield-bearers for the protection of the chariot archer. Infantry archers used the tall standing wicker shield or **gerrhon (opposite).**

To the Assyrian supremacy in field tactics was added a mastery of siege warfare, in four main stages. First the beleaguered force was isolated, and its water supply shut off if possible. Second, the approach to the walls was prepared by levelling work. Third, the wall was breached by picks and rams mounted in protected siege-engines, and if possible by mining under the wall. Engineers and miners were protected at all times by squads of shield-bearers. The decisive assault was covered by concentrated archery fire to suppress defensive fire from the walls.

The 'land bridge' between the Caspian Sea and the head of the Persian Gulf was the homeland of the Medes and Persians, whose alliance with Babylonia was instrumental in bringing down the Assyrian Empire in the late 7th Century BC. The submission of the Medes and Persians to the joint rule of Cyrus in 550 was the prelude to the creation of a mighty empire stretching from the Aegean Sea to India and south-west to Lower Egypt.

In its early years, the Median/Persian army triumphed, like that of the Assyrians, by the exploitation of joint mobility and hitting-power. Horsed cavalry was the prime arm - with the accent on horsed archers - plus chariotry and infantry formations of unarmoured spearmen. As the Persian Empire grew, its rulers took to recruiting the most effective warrior subject races until, by about 500 BC, the Empire's armies were no more 'Persian' than those of the British Empire and Commonwealth were 'British' in 1939.

Loss of combat efficiency

The new result was a vast increase in manpower at the expense of fighting efficiency. This came about because of the Persian ban on subject peoples from fighting with their most effective weapons. Thus Assyrian troops in Persian service were phalanx spearmen with tall shields, not horsed or even heavy infantry archers. Nor were archers recruited from subject Egypt, only light spearmen from Libya and Ethiopia. The huge armies recruited by the expanding Persian Empire came to rely more and more on the daunting effect of sumptuous display and sheer numbers, rather than on genuine fighting efficiency. The method and application which had characterised the Assyrian military machine was sadly lacking in that of Persia.

The splendid Immortals

The same applied to the famous Persian household corps, the Immortals: crack spearman/archers maintained at a strength of 10,000. They could have done with less ostentation and more body armour for the rigours of close-quarter combat.

The Persian Empire c. 550-330 BC

LEFT: *Persian mounted spearman/archer, with his cased bow slung at his back. The Persian combination of the roles of lancer and horsed archer was less successful than the clear distinction preferred by the earlier Assyrians. Rather like the early 20th Century tanks in which the commander also had to serve as gunner, it asked too much of the rider.*

CENTRE: *Median archer/spearman the best of the Persian army's 'line' infantry. As with all costume of the Persian Empire, military clothing tended to be brightly coloured and rich with embroidery. One important detail not revealed by contemporary accounts is how quickly a formation of such infantry could down spear and shield and commence effective archery fire. No less important would have been the reverse drill: casing bows and reassuming spear and shield to repel a sudden charge.*

RIGHT: *A Persian Immortal, one of the crack soldiers from the elite corps of the Persian Army, with the combined bowcase and quiver slung over the left shoulder. The ornate silver pomegranate decorating the butt of the long spear prevented the weapon from being jammed into the ground to create a spear-hedge behind which the archers could shoot.*

The Hoplites of Greece:

Archaeology has now confirmed that the 'Greece' of Homer's epics, the heroic age of Bronze Age Mycenae, was in the last quarter of the 2nd Millenium BC. Like the Hittite Empire, the splendid civilization of Mycenae went under to a prodigious surge of warrior race migrations around 1100 BC and a 'dark age' ensued on the Greek mainland and islands. Lasting at least 300 years, this dark age gradually gave place to a painfully evolving scatter of Greek city states, the largest with their own defence forces and the smaller combining in defensive alliances when occasion demanded.

By the 6th Century BC the city states of the central and southern Greek mainland had perfected a new ideal type of soldier: the citizen warrior or **hoplite,** whose political duties were inseparable from the duty of military service when his state was in danger.

Sparta's iron code

The duties and conditions of hoplite service varied widely from state to state. They were taken to their most draconian extreme in the state of Sparta in the Peloponnese, which evolved as the only true military state in all Greece. In Sparta there was compulsory military training for all male citizens from the age of seven, with life in barracks and communal meals (notable throughout Greece for the hardness of the regime and the utter foulness of the cuisine) for all men of military age.

This self-imposed iron discipline was prized by Spartans simply as a means to and end: the survival of the state to fight tyranny. Not that hatred of tyranny, a common Greek ideal, prevented the Spartan state from depending on the labours of **helots** (serf labourers), while the society of every other Greek **polis** or state

c.550-400 BC

depended unashamedly on slave labour.

Like Japanese **bushido,** Spartan discipline was not merely a means towards achieving invincibility in battle: it was a state of mind, a conduit of virtue. Plutarch preserved the story of the old man at the Olympic Games, unable to find a seat and jeered at until he came to the Spartan benches, whereupon every Spartan rose as one man to offer him a seat - the moral being that 'All Greeks know what is right, but only the Spartans do it'.

Certainly the main aim, the training of unbeatable armies, was amply achieved by Sparta's iron code. Throughout the wars with Persia (499-478 BC) and the exhausting Peloponnesian War which followed between Athens and Sparta (460-404 BC) Spartan forces retained a legendary and awesome reputation which was, in the main, upheld. When beaten Spartans surrendered at Sphacteria in 425 instead of fighting to the death, it was remembered as a major historical event.

The hoplite and his weapons

Of all the Greek states, only Thessaly and Boeotia produced horsed soldiers; for the rest, the military strength of Greece in the late 6th and 5th Centuries BC was measured in hoplite infantrymen, each with armour and weapons of his own provenance. The armour consisted of helmet, round shield, cuirass, stiffened apron, and greaves; the weapons were a thrusting spear which could be thrown like a javelin if need arose, and a sword.

The tendency in the 5th Century BC was a general lightening of the more antique body armour, with the antique back-and-breast 'bell cuirass' of bronze giving place to body protection of leather or stiffened linen and metal greaves going out of fashion. By the end of the Peloponnesian War, Spartan hoplites had abandoned armour altogether, helmets included, but this was exceptional.

Hoplite tactics

In their spells of compulsory military training, hoplites learned to manoeuvre and fight in close formation, with intricate drills for converting the line of march to the order of battle - line, echelon, or 'hedgehog' phalanx. The hoplite **tour de force,** seen to classic advantage in the battles of Marathon and Plataea in the Persian War, was a swift and disciplined charge, crashing into the enemy line with minimum delay and breaking it up with spear-thrusts and expert close-quarter swordplay.

The hoplite hefting his spear for an 'overarm' thrust is equipped in a style already becoming antique by the dawn of the 5th Century BC: ornate solid bronze back-and-breast cuirass (known as the 'bell' cuirass from its elegant and functional flare at the waist). He is shown with his successor: a Spartan hoplite of the Persian War. Richard Scollins has depicted one of the immortal '300 Spartans' who died holding the Pass of Thermopylae against the Persian march on Athens in 480 BC. His shield carries the Greek letter ***lamda*** *(an inverted 'V') for* ***Lakedaimon,*** *the correct name of the Spartan state. At his feet lies his main weapon, the spear, now broken and useless, showing the grip used for throwing and the spike at the butt enabling the spear to be rammed into the ground when presenting a hedge of spears against cavalry attack. He wears the stiffened linen cuirass which replaced the heavier 'bell cuirass' in the early 5th Century BC.*

Hannibal's War (218-201 BC): Carthage . . .

In the late 3rd Century BC one of the decisive power-struggles of the Ancient World settled the mastery of the western Mediterranean: the 2nd Punic War (218-201 BC). In the 1st Punic War (264-41 BC) the Roman Republic had established itself as a central Mediterranean rival to the trading empire of Carthage; the second conflict saw Rome shatter the Carthaginian empire and reduce Carthage to an isolated North African city state.

Led by the master-tactician of the age, Hannibal Barca, the main Carthaginian field army marched from Spain to invade Italy in 218 BC. Though Hannibal won several shattering victories in Italy (most notably at Cannae in 216 BC) he failed to take Rome, which adopted the strategy of avoiding battle in Italy while knocking away the props of the Carthaginian empire overseas. Expeditionary forces under Publius Scipio conquered Spain and finally (204 BC) invaded Africa, compelling the recall of Hannibal's army from Italy. After Scipio's victory over Hannibal at Zama in 202 BC Carthage had no choice but accept humiliating terms from Rome.

Carthage: a polyglot host

Lacking the manpower which served Rome so well in Italy, Carthage recruited troops from every province under her control and made the fullest possible use of warrior tribal allies. The best of these were Spanish infantry and light cavalry from neighbouring Numidia **(centre and left)**; luring the Numidians onto his side was the immediate prelude to Scipio's victory at Zama.

The Romans had first encountered Carthaginian war elephants **(top centre)** during the 1st Punic War, and in the 2nd War elephants proved as doubtful an asset as ever against steady infantry. Only a handful survived Hannibal's crossing of the Alps in 218, and at Zama his attempted frontal 'tank attack' by 80 elephants was foiled by deployment of the Roman ranks into lanes, down which the elephants harmlessly charged.

Clearly Hannibal's greatest asset was as a leader of multi-national troops. Mere conscripts or mercenaries could never have endured or achieved so much.

. . . and the Roman Republic

Traditionally founded in 510 BC, the Roman Republic's first armies of citizen-soldiers had been graded according to the individual's wealth and social status. The poorest classes had manned the front rank as light infantry, backed by better equipped middle-class troops and finally by armoured infantry with long spears. First steps towards the professional standing army created in the 1st Century BC began in the late 4th Century, with the building of the first military roads and regular payment of troops required for long-term service far from home. But much of the original system was still discernible at the time of the 2nd Punic War, in particular the grading of the infantry into front-rank **hastati,** second-rank **principes,** and third-rank **triarii.**

Infantry of the battle line

The first Roman troops into action would usually be the **velites** or light-armed skirmishers **(centre left)**, closely backed by javelin-throwing **hastati (centre)** and **principes.** If the battle hung in the balance the decisive push would be given by the heavy **triarii (right foreground)** who could also sustain **principes** and **hastati** in the event of a setback.

Legion, maniple, century, cavalry

The legion's basic building-block was the century, each commanded by a centurion **(centre right)**. Tactical flexibility was improved by grouping the centuries in maniples (usually of two centuries each). At Zama, hastily deployed in unwonted line-ahead, Scipio's maniples ushered Hannibal's charging elephants safely to the rear, then redeployed laterally to avoid being outflanked.

After Cannae in 216, when the Roman legions were trapped and cut to pieces by Hannibal's brilliant use of flanking cavalry, the Roman cavalry arm was substantially improved. By the time of the final showdown at Zama, Scipio's victories owed much to the prowess of his trusted commander of cavalry, Gaius Laelius - a military partnership fit to rank with that of Marlborough and Prince Eugene, or Robert E. Lee and 'Stonewall' Jackson.

Swansong of

The massed phalanx of long pikes perfected in the 4th Century BC by King Philip of Macedon, father of Alexander the Great, was the most spectacular shock infantry formation of the Ancient World. It was developed as a refinement of the traditional hoplite 'hedgehog' formation which, deepened and used in close conjunction with cavalry, won several decisive victories over Sparta for the Thebans under their great general Epaminondas between 371 and 362 BC. Impressed by the tactics of Epaminondas, Philip transformed the close-order drill of the Macedonian infantry, ordered the adoption of the long pike or **sarissa** (c.16-18ft), and created a military machine which had

the Macedonian phalanx, 323-146 BC

made Macedon supreme on the Greek mainland by the time of Philip's death in 336 BC.

Heyday of the long pike

Developed to beat hoplite formations by a nation which had no hoplite caste of its own, the Macedonian phalanx was the ultimate use of massed infantry in depth. Its basic element was the battalion or **syntagma** of 256 men; its commander, the **syntagmatarch,** led from the right-hand end of the front rank, with his deputy in the centre. Each **syntagma** file of 16 men could be subdivided into half-files or quarter-files during complex manoeuvering; crescent, wedge and half-square formations were used as well as line-abreast. Four **syntagma** made a **chiliarchy,** four chiliarchies formed the basic phalanx of 4,096 men; the Grand Phalanx, of four phalanxes in two divisions, was 16,384 strong.

When the long pikes were lowered for the advance or in defence, the pikeheads of the first four ranks formed a dense hedge extending some 12ft beyond the front rank - well outside the 'reach' of enemy infantry equipped with conventional thrusting spears. The phalanx was designed for an irresistible line attack at a steady pace; unlike hoplite forces, it was unable to launch sudden attacks, and was in fact highly vulnerable to surprise attack from flank or rear. But it was never intended to operate unsupported; it was screened by medium infantry **(hypaspists)** and was intended to fix the attention of enemy infantry while flanking cavalry cleared the decks for a decisive advance.

Defeat by the legions of Rome

The phalanx was at its best against the vast but brittle armies of the Persian Empire **(pp. 24-25)** and survived the futile civil wars after the death of Alexander in 323 BC. But the phalanx infantry of King Pyrrhus of Epirus was badly mauled by the Roman and allied Italian army in the campaigns of 280-272 BC. Outright defeat of the phalanx by the more flexible legion came in the early 2nd Century BC, when Rome moved in to exercise direct control over the Greek mainland: at Cynoscephalae (197 BC) and finally at Pydna (168 BC), after which Macedon was reduced to the status of a client state.

Celtic Warrior

Broadly speaking, the Celtic warrior tribes of western and central Europe were to the expanding Roman Republic what the Sikhs and Afghans were to the expanding British Empire in India. They were the biggest menace of the north-west frontier, fiercely determined to maintain their independence and glorying in battle. Yet once beaten and attracted to Roman service and discipline, Celtic recruits provided excellent auxiliary troops for the Roman Army, earning battle honours second to none.

The old enemy

The Roman Republic never forgot its traumatic introduction to Celtic valour in the early 4th Century BC. To the Romans the Celts were known as **Galli** - 'Gauls' - whose homeland was split by the Alps. In 390 BC the Celts of the Po valley or 'Nearer Gaul' embarked on a mass raid against the cities of Italy, routing the Roman citizen army and sweeping on to occupy the city itself, with the exception of the Roman citadel garrison on the Capitoline Hill.

Though the invaders were out for loot, not conquest, and were readily bought off, the experience taught Rome that superior discipline and tactics offered the only antidote against the Celts' natural ferocity and overwhelming numbers. A steady sequence of improvements in the Roman army created the fighting force able to take on and eventually beat Carthage - which made extensive use of Celtic tribal recruits - in the following century.

Virtues and vices

The Celts were adept at creating hill-top fortifications of great strength, 'sculpting' natural contours into formidable ramparts. Celtic tenacity also took readily to guerrilla warfare, enforcing new techniques of entrenchment and field fortification on the Roman Army. The history of the Roman world would have been very different if the Celts had overcome their tribal disunity and achieved a similar military evolution to that of Rome. They never learned how to counter the deadly javelin volleys and stabbing swordplay of the Roman infantry, but retained the traditional thrusting spear and long sword ***LEFT:*** Nor, though natural horsemen, did the Celts renounce the obsolete war chariot **(pp.38-39)** in favour of horsed cavalry.

v. Roman Legionary

Rome's defeat of Carthage in the 3rd Century Punic Wars won the Republic its first overseas provinces: Sicily, Corsica and Sardinia, and coastal Spain. This new imperial role continued to expand in the 2nd Century, with deepening involvement east of the Adriatic; an enduring distrust of Carthage in Africa; and the immensely difficult task of reducing the warrior tribes of inland Spain. By 110 BC the tally of Roman provinces included Macedonia and Achaea in Greece, Tunisia in Africa (after the brutal liquidation of Carthage in 146 BC), most of inner Spain apart from the mountainous north-west, and the Balearic Is. A direct land link with the Spanish provinces had been established with the new province of Narbonese (transalpine) Gaul in 121 BC.

The impact of empire

Reluctant though it was in the main, with one new overseas commitment tending to lead to the next, Rome's rise to empire inevitably required the maintenance of an enlarged standing army. This in turn eventually spelled the death of the old Roman constitution. By the middle 1st Century BC the reality of political power was controlled by the leading army commanders rather than with the Republic's traditionally elected magistrates. What mattered now was which general commanded the personal allegiance of how many legions, not the political complexion of the two consuls elected each year.

The transformation of the Roman Army began with the reforms of Gaius Marius, himself a soldier risen from the ranks, hero of the 'people's party' and elected consul for the first time in 107 BC: the fifth year of an inconclusive war against King Jugurtha of Numidia. Denied a regular army command by an apprehensive Senate, Marius appealed directly to the people and raised his own volunteer force, scrapping the long-standing property qualification for military service. Its eventual victory over Jugurtha in 105 BC was the prelude to the reconstruction of the whole Roman Army by Marius, enabling the poorest citizen to become a paid professional soldier who trained and fought with standardised equipment and weaponry.

The new legionary

The Marian reforms abolished the old distinctions between **hastati, principes** and **triiarii.** All legionaries now carried the short stabbing sword and improved **pila** or javelins, greatly adding to the legion's fire-power as it advanced to the attack. Standard armour consisted of a bronze helmet with a neck-protecting flange and cheek-pieces, and a mail shirt.

These were the drilled professionals who enabled Julius Caesar - in 59 BC a middle-aged politician who had never commanded a field army before - to conquer the tribesmen of Gaul in less than four years, bridge and cross the Rhine, and fight two campaigns in Britain. In 52 BC came their greatest triumph: destroying the Gallic rising of Vercingetorix at Alesia, 65,000 Romans besieging 80,000 Gauls, while fighting off 250,000 more.

Soldiers of the Empire

1st Century AD

*LEFT: Auxiliary of late 1st Century AD, with bronze helmet, issue sword and boot-sandals **(caligae)** and mail shirt.*
*FAR LEFT: Legionary of same period, with cuirass of segmented plate-armour **(lorica segmentata)**, and **pilum** weighted with lead ball for extra range. Both soldiers from reign of Trajan (98-117).*

The Roman Civil Wars which followed the assassination of Julius Caesar in 44 BC ended with his adopted son Octavius Caesar master of the Roman world in 30 BC. Himself a mediocre general served by excellent lieutenants, Octavius (who took the honorific title of 'Augustus' in 27 BC) owed his triumph mainly to his illustrious surname, which the legions held in reverence.

Learning from Julius Caesar's ill-judged acceptance of the state of life dictator, Augustus contented himself with the modest political title of **princeps** or 'first citizen'. Though he claimed to be no more than the instrument and servant of the Republican Senate, it was a total sham. The power of Augustus as the first effective Roman emperor rested solidly on the personal loyalty of the Roman Army; the very word 'emperor' is derived from **imperator** - the honorific title of a Roman army commander-in-chief.

The Army and the Empire

Augustus assumed personal control of all provinces which required the permanent presence of army garrisons, and left the Senate to run the others. Of course, the military provinces were the ones that mattered. In the east the most important was Syria, on the frontier with the formidable Parthian Empire whose horsed archers had destroyed or captured seven Roman legions during a disastrous invasion in 53 BC. One of Augustus' first acts (20 BC) was to negotiate a peace treaty with Parthia in which the standards captured in 53 BC were returned to Rome. The other key 'Imperial' frontier provinces were Egypt (annexed after the defeat of Cleopatra and Marcus Antonius in 30 BC), Galatia in Asia Minor, Illyricum, Gaul and Spain.

Augustus made only one attempt to secure the Empire's frontiers by a war of aggression, and this proved as disastrous as the Parthian venture had been. In 9 AD he tried to conquer Germany as far as the Elbe, creating a buffer province for the security of Gaul; but his lacklustre general Varus, marching through the **Teutoburgerwald,** was slaughtered with the loss of three legions by ably-led guerrilla attacks. After this disaster Augustus fell back on a strategy of 'natural frontiers' for the Empire - the Atlantic, the Rhine, the Danube, and the Euphrates.

The Army, swollen to 70 legions by the end of the Civil Wars, was cut down to under 30 by the death of Augustus in 14 AD. It now became a professional long-service force, with discharged veterans receiving a pension and land allotment from a state fund. The troops took an oath of allegiance to Augustus as commander-in-chief, and the renewal of this oath became one of the first acts of his successors. Far more important than the 'peacetime' role of the legionaries was the entirely new status of the auxiliary forces: non-Roman recruits trained and equipped for service with the heavy infantry of the regular legions.

Role of the auxiliary

Auxiliary troops had first been raised by Caesar in Gaul, to increase his manpower. Under Augustus auxiliary recruitment was systematised to provide half of the Empire's defence forces, the guiding rule being that auxiliaries never served in their country of origin. They were recruited in the imperial provinces in cohorts of 500 for the infantry and **alae** ('wings') of 500 for the cavalry.

By the late 1st Century BC the auxiliary cohorts were so capable that they were able to win battles without the support of the regular legionaries. This happened during the battle of Mons Graupius in 85 AD, the victory which sealed the Roman conquest of northern Britain. Dutch and Belgian auxiliaries **(Batavi** and **Tungri)**, 8,000 all told, advanced uphill to rout 30,000 Caledonians without the legions stirring a foot, supported by cavalry.

The splendid Praetorians . . .

Though Caesar and Augustus completed the transformation of the Roman Army into a professional long-service force, there was a price to pay for the enhanced status of the soldier in the new imperial Roman state. This was the creation of the Praetorian Guard by Augustus, a force which, though brought into being to secure the emperor's hold on Rome and central Italy, soon became one of the biggest menaces to imperial authority at times of disputed succession or unpopular rule.

A favoured military elite

The blueprint of the Praetorians had been drawn by Julius Caesar in his unique relationship with the Roman Army. Caesar had been an inspirer of loyalty, **esprit de corps** and fighting spirit second to none, and he made his beloved 10th Legion the envied elite of the Army. For all its favoured status and weapons rich with gold and silver inlay, the 10th Legion nevertheless remained a fighting unit which considered that it had the right to be given the most hazardous assignment in battle - as it was in Caesar's showdown battle with Pompey at Pharsalus in 48 BC.

Always quick to exploit his reputation as Julius Caesar's true heir, Augustus had two main motives in creating the Praetorian Guard. The first, and of course the most ostensible, was to keep alive the precedents set by Julius Caesar with the 10th Legion. The Praetorian Guard was conceived as an elite force of the best troops in the Roman Army, bound if anything even closer to the reigning heir of the Caesar family than the regular troops of the legions. For the rank and file of the Roman Army, an appointment to the Praetorians was to beckon as the ultimate reward for a career of exemplary service, with splendid equipment and excellent conditions of pay and duty.

The Republican constitution, to which Augustus paid such careful lip-

***LEFT:** Three Praetorians in parade dress – guardsman, officer, and **signifer** or standard-bearer, the latter with his distinctive leopard-skin cape and eagle standard bedecked with decorations. Each cohort had its own eagle and individual battle honours. The plumed helmet, distinct from the plain headgear of the 'line regiment' legions, was the hallmark of Praetorian troops.*

. . . and the legionary foot-slogger

service, forbade the presence of troops within the city limits of Rome (other than during triumphal processions). Accordingly the Praetorian Guard, originally of nine cohorts of 1,000 men each, were stationed outside the city. In the reign of Augustus' successor Tiberius (14-37 AD) there was built the great Guards barracks or **Castra Praetoria.** (The site is still used by the modern-day Rome garrison of the Italian Army.) This ploy gave the reigning emperor, in time of unrest, all the force he needed - but the dangerous potential of the Guards as a political force was soon demonstrated.

The emperor-makers

The first emperor to fall victim to the Praetorians was the unstable Caligula in 41 AD, assassinated by Guards officers. The Guards then chose Caligula's uncle Claudius as their new emperor; backed the young Nero as Claudius' successor in 54 AD; and in 68 AD 'made' two of the four emperors who seized power that year. From then on until their liquidation by Constantine in 312, the Guards remained the biggest domestic threat to the imperal power. It was always vital for the reigning emperor to retain the support of the Praetorian Prefect - the Guards commander. Claudius was the first of the 'Guards candidate' incoming emperors to begin his reign with a large cash payment to buy the loyalty - always fickle - of the Praetorians. It was a fateful precedent which, by the end of the 2nd Century AD, had been extended to the legions by ambitious generals with their sights set on the imperial title.

The episode which did most to tarnish the splendour of the Praetorian Guard came in 193 AD. After assassinating the Emperor Pertinax the Praetorians put the Empire up to auction between the richest millionaires of Rome, finally giving their support to Didius Julianus for a 'bid' of 6,250 drachmae per man.

After this shameful episode, the resulting civil war of 193-194 AD was the most widespread since the 'year of the four emperors' (Galba, Otho, Vitellius and Vespasian) in 68 AD. With no other military backing apart from the shaky support of the Praetorians, Julianus was promptly challenged by three contenders. These were Clodius Albinus with the legions of Britain, Pescennius Niger with the legions of Syria, and Septimius Severus with the legions of Pannonia (the frontier province of the middle Danube, a training-ground famous for the excellence of the troops it produced). Severus, the closest contender to Italy, wasted no time in marching on Rome. A lightning march intimidated the Praetorians and Senate into abandoning Julianus, who was deposed and executed after a reign of only 66 days.

*BELOW: One of the 'mules of Marius', as the legionaries were nicknamed after the Marian army reforms at the beginning of the 1st Century BC. Full marching order included armour, weapons and three days' rations, plus the tools which made the legionary self-supporting in the field – saw, pickaxe, sickle and bucket. It was all a far cry from the glitter and comfort of the **Castra Praetoria.***

The first act of Severus as emperor was to disarm the Praetorian Guard and disband its troops in disgrace. He then invaded Asia Minor and crushed Niger at Issus before settling accounts with Albinus in southern Gaul, with a hard-fought battle at Lyons. Once established as undisputed master of the Roman world, however, Severus made no attempt to resume the pretence, upheld since the days of Augustus, that the emperor was merely the first citizen and servant of the Senate. Instead Severus became the first emperor to flaunt his total dependence on the loyalty of the Army, which he showered with unheard-of pay rises and increases of privilege.

The Praetorian Guard restored

To repay the frontier legions who had made him sole emperor, Severus not only raised legionary pay but extended public land grants to auxiliaries. Though he had cleverly exploited the traditional resentment of the frontier troops against the pampered Praetorians of Italy, he still needed a guards corps. The new Praetorian Guard of Severus was not only recruited from every province and race in the Empire (the original Guard had been recruited from Italians only) but expanded from 10,000 to 50,000. Once again the Praetorian Prefects became the Empire's virtual prime ministers.

Swansong of the war chariot:

Julius Caesar's famous account of the conquest of Gaul reveals one extremely interesting fact. This was that the Celtic and Germanic tribes defeated by Caesar's legions in Gaul had virtually abandoned the war chariot

the conquest of Britain, 43-84 AD

by the middle 1st Century BC. But this ancient weapon of war was still very much in use across the Channel in Celtic Britain, and it came as an unwelcome surprise to Caesar's veterans when they first landed on the Kentish coast in 55 BC.

The British chariot was little more than a two-wheeled, wicker-sided platform, drawn at disconcertingly high speed by a pair of horses. Ground clearance was good, and Caesar's assault troops as they struggled ashore found themselves attacked from chariots driven without hesitation right into the surf. Again we find an undeniable parallel with the combat described in Homer's **Iliad.** From Caesar's account it is clear that British chariot tactics were much the same as those attributed to Homer's Greeks and Trojans: to launch elusive hit-and-run attacks and serve as a high-speed personnel carrier, conveying warriors to where they could dismount and fight on foot, and if necessary re-embark and withdraw at speed.

Caesar's own description of British chariot tactics cannot be bettered. 'First they drive in every direction, hurling their javelins. Very often the sheer terror inspired by the galloping horses throws their opponents into a state of confusion. They then make their way through the squadrons of their own cavalry, leap down from the chariots, and fight on foot. Meanwhile the drivers retire a little from the battle and halt the chariots in a suitable position so that, if those who are now fighting on foot are hard pressed by the enemy, they will have an easy means of retreating to their own lines. So in their battles they combine the mobility of cavalry with the stamina of infantry. Daily training and practice have brought them to a remarkable state of efficiency. They are able, for instance, to control their horses at full gallop on the steepest slopes, to pull them up and turn them in a moment, to run along the pole, stand on the yoke, and dart back again into the chariot.'

Caesar frankly admits that on his first British expedition, undertaken without adequate cavalry support, 'our men were quite unnerved by this kind of fighting, which was so unfamiliar to them'. He had personally to advance to the aid of the 7th Legion, 'bounced' by a surprise chariot attack while foraging; 'and I came to their rescue just in time. For the enemy halted when they saw us coming and our men recovered from their terror'. The whole episode is very reminiscent of the first contract of Guderian's XIX Panzer Corps with Polish cavalry in September 1939. On this occasion, too, the general's personal intervention was required to steady troops momentarily brought to the verge of panic by contact with the unforeseen: an antique novelty to which the familiar 'book' had no reply.

55 BC: the chariot's last victory?

The unforeseen problem posed by the British chariots was not the only reason why Caesar abandoned his first cross-Channel foray in 55 BC. There were others, the most important being the unpredictable Channel weather and the threat it posed to the fleet of transport ships. But in 55 BC Caesar certainly had to accept that the high mobility of the British chariots, and his own lack of cavalry with which alone a successful battle could be joined and won, meant that he had no chance of achieving any positive result by staying in Britain. Caesar's withdrawal to Gaul can, therefore, without too much exaggeration, be taken as the last tangible victory won by war chariots in their long history.

Easy antidote: Roman cavalry in force

No further lesson was needed, and Caesar brought 2,000 cavalry with his five legions when he returned to Britain in 54 BC. This proved ample for neutralising the chariot menace, which could do no more than shadow the invasion force as it advanced on the Thames. The south-eastern tribes duly submitted and Caesar withdrew to Gaul after a comparatively easy campaign.

The lessons of 55/54BC were also heeded in the following century during the Roman conquest of Britain, launched in 43 AD. The last mention of British chariots - scattered as usual by the Roman cavalry - was at Mons Graupius in 84 AD, fought in Scotland.

Years of crisis: the 3rd Century AD

As the 3rd Century Ad opened it was clear that the original imperial system established by Augustus 200 years before had been shattered for good. Emperors no longer troubled to pose as 'first citizens' executing the will of the Roman Senate and people, and choosing the best available candidates as successors in preference to their own offspring. Instead, emperors gained and held their power by no other agency but the goodwill of the Praetorian Guard, or of the legions they commanded, or both. When he died in 211 AD after precariously restoring the Empire to unified rule, the main legacy of Severus to his sons was the brutal advice to 'Stick together, pay the troops, and to hell with the rest'.

Even this counsel of basic realism was not enough. In the first Century AD, six of the 12 ruling emperors had been assassinated or raised to power by military coups. In the 2nd Century, thanks to the easy transfer of supreme power from Trajan to Hadrian, Antoninus Pius and Marcus Aurelius (117-161 AD), the ratio dropped to three out of eight. But in the 3rd Century every one of the 17 emperors between Severus (193-211 AD) and Diocletian (284-305 AD) was elevated or deposed by whim of the Praetorians or the legions. At no other time in history have the fortunes of a world empire been decided to such an extent by soldiers.

Overload on the frontiers

The resultant civil strife which racked the Empire in the 3rd Century AD would have been bad enough on its own, but it coincided with a redoubled surge of external pressure on the Empire's frontiers. This was no longer limited to the Rhine and Danube but came also from the East, where the resurgent Persian Empire of the Sassanid dynasty posed a recurrent threat from 227 AD. The result was a strategic overload beyond the normal capacity of the traditional, infantry-oriented Roman Army. The frontiers ceased to hold, with barbarian invasions drivng deep into the Empire and obliging cities to be given fortified defences. Rock bottom was reached in the late 250s when the Emperor Valerian, after a string of defeats on the Rhine and Danube, was captured on the Syrian frontier and ended his life as a living freak at the Persian court.

Exceptional skills of generalship were required to compensate for this overload on the frontiers. The Empire only survived because from 268 AD the Danubian frontier provinces produced a string of military emperors who were so gifted. These were Claudius Gothicus (268-270), Aurelian (270-275), Claudius Tacitus (275-276), Probus (276-282), Carus (282-283) and Diocletian, the latter uniquely surviving to abdicate in favour of a chosen successor in 305 AD.

More mobility for the Roman Army

It was under these capable 'Illyrian emperors', most notably Aurelian, that the Roman Army underwent its greatest reconstruction since the days of Marius. The accent was now on cavalry: enhanced mobility to enable the main Roman field army to race from one frontier trouble-spot to the next.

***LEFT:** Centurion of the Praetorian Guard, one of the influential company commanders whose voice could help topple an emperor or maintain him in power. His promotion would be carefully vetted by the Praetorian Prefect, the power behind the throne for nearly 300 years until the abolition of the Guard by Constantine the Great (312-337 AD).*

RIGHT:** Forerunner of the medieval knight - armoured lancer or* ***cataphract. *Awesome in aspect, with an irresistible onset against unprepared troops, cataphracts were the most effective enemy troops encountered by the Roman Army during Aurelian's bitterly-fought war in the East against rebel Palmyra (267-273 AD). After the defeat of Palmyra, cataphracts were recruited for the Roman cavalry as the army's mobile arm continued to expand.*

***LEFT:** Light cavalryman of the later Roman Empire, early 4th Century AD.*
***RIGHT:** Frankish warriors of the middle 4th Century. The warrior at far right is armed with the **francisca** or throwing hatchet, an unpleasant missile weapon but usually good for little more than one damaging volley during the charge.*

Fall of the Roman West 377-410 AD

The Roman Army of the 4th Century AD bore little resemblance to the military machine of the 1st and 2nd Centuries. Until the Empire's population was savagely reduced by plague in the late 2nd Century, the infantry legions operating from their fortified bases had been more than a match for the barbarian opposition outside the Rhine and Danube frontiers. By the 4th Century, however, mounting barbarian pressure along the whole length of the northern frontier between the North and Black Seas required nothing less than the remodelling of the Roman Army to rely on cavalry rather than infantry: a highly mobile fire-brigade to race from one trouble-spot to the next.

Under the new system only light troops - **limitanei** - were permanently stationed along the frontier. These were backed by the mobile field army under the emperor's command, the **palatini:** five cavalry regiments (**vexillationes palatinae**) and five infantry regiments (**legiones palatinae**). The old legionary establishment was never formally abolished, but legionary strengths were greatly reduced to permit the creation of new units: a process reflective of the Empire's growing shortage of manpower for military service.

The Empire weathered its first major external crisis when the massive Gothic invasion of the Balkans was routed by Claudius at Nish in 269 AD. Though the battle was won by the 'new-look' Roman cavalry, Claudius lacked the manpower to achieve more than a partial encirclement of the Gothic host.

In 378, however, the Goths finally avenged Nish by destroying the main Roman field army at Adrianople, exploiting their superior numbers and the inept manoeuvering of the Roman emperor Valens. After Adrianople the Empire was never granted sufficient respite to raise and train a new regular army, and there was nothing for it but to rely on large-scale recruitment of barbarian allies and mecenaries. In the early reign of Honorius (395-423) the last 'Roman' victories of the Western Empire were won by largely barbarian levies commanded by Stilicho, a Vandal in Roman service. But after the political murder of Stilicho in 408 opposition to the Goths under Alaric collapsed. Alaric invaded Italy in 409 and captured Rome in the following year.

c.410–

THE DARK AGES

1000 ad

The leading barbarian kingdoms which collaborated in the destruction of the Western Roman Empire all had the same basic motive. They had been driven west against the fragile frontiers of the Empire by the surge of the Huns out of Asia, and were determined to conquer new, safe homelands from the provinces which the dwindling armies of Rome were no longer able to protect.

The 5th and 6th Centuries were the true 'Dark Ages' an obscure interregnum in which the kingdoms of the Franks, Visigoths, Ostrogoths and Vandals were established over the former provinces of the ruined Western Empire. In these barbarian kingdoms were planted the seeds of medieval feudalism: military service on the demand of one's lord, rather than defence by a standing army paid for by state taxation.

The latter system lived on in the Eastern or Byzantine Empire, which in the 6th Century managed to reconquer Africa from the Vandals and Italy from the Ostrogoths. An exhausting series of Byzantine wars with Persia, however, left neither empire in a fit state to survive the great eruption of Arab expansionism in the 7th Century, which by the early 8th was threatening Francia across the Pyrennes. But the Arabs' high-water mark was reached by their defeat by the Franks at Tours in 732.

The swollen kingdom created by the Frankish kings Pepin and Charlemagne had already begun to split into Easy Franks (German) and West Franks (French) when, in the 9th Century the first Viking attacks out of Scandinavia broke on north-west Europe. Saxon England, all but overrun by Danish invaders in the 870s survived under Alfred the Great to counter-attack under his heirs. Meanwhile, central Europe fell victim to the destructive raids of the Magyar horsed archers, a menace not broken until the middle 10th Century.

This second chapter examines the fighting men of the Huns, Vandals and Goths; the Byzantine Empire and the Arabs; the Carolingian Franks, the Vikings, the Saxon English and the Magyars.

Source of the legends of Arthur

PREVIOUS PAGES:* *The collapse of the Western Empire left Roman Britain to sink or swim after 406 AD but British *resistance to Teutonic invasion seems to have been far more effective than is usually believed, with the Saxon invaders unable to break out from the south and east until the middle 6th Century. Medieval legends of King Arthur and his knights probably derived from the exploits of Romano-British armoured cavalry (p.46) led by a military governor: a 'real' Arthur (p.47) who could have wielded a king's authority in defence of Christian civilization.*

Settlement of the West, 395-455 AD

The massive race migrations which culminated in the collapse of the Western Roman Empire in the early 5th Century AD were triggered off by the western surge of the Huns out of Asia in the late 3rd Century. Recoiling from the onset of these ferocious horsed archers, the Gothic tribal confederations (Ostrogoths and Visigoths) could only seek accomodation within the Roman Empire, or failing that the forcible invasion and conquest of Roman provinces. And with Asian Minor largely shielded from direct assault by the natural barrier of the Black Sea, barbarian pressure in the late 4th and 5th Centuries came heaviest to bear on the Western provinces.

Neglect of potential allies

In the century after the death of Constantine (337 AD) the Western Empire could only have saved itself by a fundamental reappraisal of its problems. It could have been done by enlisting the barbarian confederations immediately outside the frontiers, settling them inside the frontier provinces and encouraging them to fight for their new lands as **federati** (allies) of Rome. But this policy was only feebly attempted on the lower Rhine, in the case of the Salian Franks; no such accommodation was attempted with the Vandals and Goths pressing on the upper Rhine and Danube. As a result these numerous and able warrior confederations, both of which produced cavalry capable of a high degree of disciplined training, remained blood enemies of the Western Empire.

The Roman West's downfall was heralded by the Goths' acceptance of Alaric as their joint overlord after 395 AD. For over ten years the Western Empire survived by the victories of the Vandal Stilicho, **magister militum** or commander-in-chief until 408 AD. He kept Alaric at bay by widespread recruitment of barbarian mercenaries (favouring Huns for his bodyguard) and playing off one concentration of barbarian tribes against the other. But after fear and jealousy at the imperial court led to Stilicho's judicial murder in August 408, Alaric was left without an effective rival and led the Ostrogoths to sack Rome in 410.

When the Visigoths under Alaric's brother-in-law settled southern Gaul, then pushed the Vandals ahead of them through Spain and into Africa. A Vandal kingdom of Africa was recognised in 435, four years before its King Gaiseric took Carthage for his capital. Gaiseric's Vandals took naturally to sea power and conquered the Balearics, Corsica and Sardinia before sacking Rome again, with thoroughgoing ferocity, in 455. This was four years after the Huns, under their leader Attila, had been smashed in Gaul by Romano-Gallic and Visigothic allies at the battle of the Catalaunian Fields, near Troyes (June 451) - the last flicker of resistance by the Roman West.

LEFT TO RIGHT: *Hunnish archer-mercenary in Roman service; Ostrogothic lancer; Vandal warrior (all c.405 AD).*

The Byzantine Empire and the Arab

Byzantine lancer of the reign of Justinian (527-565 AD).

Geographically screened from the disasters of the Roman West save in the Balkans, the Eastern Roman or Byzantine Empire not only survived the upheavals of the 5th Century AD but emerged to take the offensive in the 6th, reconquering North Africa and Italy in the reign of Justinian (527-565 AD). But this illusory re-creation of Roman imperial power was shattered in the early 7th Century by the phenomenal pace of the Arab conquests after 632. These stripped the Byzantine Empire of its African and eastern Mediterranean provinces and restricted imperial power to Asia Minor and the southern Balkans.

Unlike its doomed counterpart in the West, the Byzantine Empire was never obliged to rely on extensive barbarian recruitment. The East retained an indigenous army, featuring the most effective elements of late Roman military science.

In the late 5th and early 6th Centuries the best troops of the Byzantine army were cavalry, to which missile poower was added. Though Hunnish cavalry continued to serve with the imperial army as mercenaries, the Byzantine Empire - as the old Roman Empire had never done - recruited its own horsed archers.

The Byzantine cavalry arm

Like the Assyrians and Persians before them, Byzantine horsed archers rode with combined bowcase and quiver. The bow was not carried by light or heavy cavalry units, but these still had the use of missile power in the form of weighted darts, useful at close range against enemy infantry. These darts (**martiobarbuli** in Latin, **marzobaboula** in Greek) were carried by infantry as well as by Byzantine heavy and light cavalry. They were poised for throwing by being held at the feathered end, and a clutch of them could be held in the belt or shield-hand.

Serving mainly on the Persian front, the Byzantines also deployed 'super-heavy', Persian-style **clibanarii:** armoured lancers with the head protected by helmet and mail hood and the forearms by overlapping splint armour, riding armoured horses.

Screened by a well-balanced cavalry arm, the foot archers and spearmen of the Byzantine infantry went into action with a new confidence. Foot archers carried a useful light axe and small shield or target for close-quarter defence. Byzantine heavy spearmen blended the best features of the ancient Greek hoplite, Macedonian phalangite, and early imperial Roman legionary. Protection consisted of helmet, mail cuirass and large oval or circular shield. A long thrusting-spear lent itself well to forming bristling phalanxes for attack or defence. The heavy spearman's other weapons were the long sword or **securis**, with limited missile power provided by a clutch of **marzobaboula** darts.

Over-ambitious strategy

In general the Byzantine army of the early 6th Century AD was economic in manpower and admirably suited to the defence of the Empire on all fronts. Too much was asked of it, however, when Justinian made his bid to re-establish the old Roman Empire by conquering the barbarian kingdoms of the West, for which enormous reserves of manpower and finance would have been required. The army was well able to win victories, and some of those won by Justinian's excellent generals Belisarius and Narses remain classics of the military art - but it was far too small to garrison and hold the conquered territories. Waging wars of conquest with an army best suited to defensive strategy resulted in a strategic overload similar to that which racked the Western Empire to pieces in the early 5th Century.

In the 50 years after Justinian's death (565) wars between the Byzantine and Persian Empires reached an exhausting climax, while at the same time both empires had to cope with wars on other fronts. The result, by the second quarter of the 7th Century AD, was a state of mutual exhaustion exploited with shattering effect by the Arabs.

conquests, c.500-650 AD

The Arab phenomenon
The Arab conquests began after the death of the Prophet Mohammed in June 632, and owed absolutely nothing to Arab superiority in military organization, strategy or weaponry. The latter was of the crudest - straight sword or **saif**, spear for infantry and lance for cavalry, and the simple stave bow supplemented by slingers. Helmets and mail armour were adopted later - after the conquest of Syria and Persia. What the Arabs did have were sufficient numbers, a rapid succession of ferociously able leaders, and an amazing capacity for adopting the best of their enemies' techniques. The Arabs' biggest tactical asset were speed of movement and horsemanship, relying on the superior manoeuvrability of the light horseman over more heavily armoured opponents. Horses and mules were a prized spoil of war. When the Arabs beat the Spanish Visigoths on the Lakka river in 711 they captured so many horses that they were able to mount nearly all their Berber infantry and overrun Spain before the year was out. With this technique, one Arab victory led rapidly to the next. Masters of the pursuit, the Arabs excelled in beating the enemy field army at the earliest opportunity, relieving them of the need to develop orthodox siege tactics against walled cities.

Arab cavalryman and infantryman of the early wars of conquest, c. 640 AD.

Champions of the Christian West:

In the 6th Century Ad the Frankish kingdoms stretching from the Pyrenees to the Rhine and beyond had been welded into an unwieldy realm under the Merovingian dynasty, which by the 8th Century was far gone in decay. A seemingly unending succession of boy-kings and weaklings presided over an assortment of Frankish sub-kingdoms and dukedoms - Austrasia, Neustria, Alamannia, Burgundy, Aquitaine, Gascony - all too frequently at odds with each other. And the powerful Frankish provinces had a record of successful resistance to the Merovingian official styled 'mayor of the palace' - an echo of the old Western Roman **magister militum** - who governed in the king's name.

By the early 8th Century, however, despite the feebleness of the so-called ruling dynasty, Francia's weaknesses were less marked than they had been in the middle 7th. The Austrasian mayors of the palace, Pepin II and his son Charles, had reunited the kingdom and were able to put up a spirited resistance to Arab encroachment from across the Pyrenees.

Soldiers of the Franks

Frankish military recruitment in the 8th Century was based on a levy system of military service in return for land tenure. This followed a pattern familiar since ancient times, with poorer tenants providing the infantry and the richer the cavalry. The Franks relied mainly on unarmoured infantry spearmen carrying round shields, with the **seax** or long knife for close-quarter work. The battle line of spearmen could be packed close to form a shield wall perfectly capable of withstanding Arab cavalry, and was covered on the flanks by mail-clad cavalry lancers. The latter, during a foray across the Pyrenees by an Arab force in 721, enabled Duke Eudo of Aquitaine to surround the invaders with gratifying speed at Toulouse and break them, with the Arab governor of Spain being killed in the battle.

Frankish victory at Tours

The great Frankish victory of the early 8th Century was the defeat of the Arabs at the battle of Tours in 732, which gained for Mayor Charles the nickname of Martel - 'the hammer'. This battle, remembered as one of the decisive combats of the Western world, saw the Franks blunt the Arab attacks with infantry before unleashing a decisive cavalry counterstroke. It would seem that the Frankish infantry had been stiffened by an increased archer component. Charles, who commanded the Frankish muster in person, deployed his infantry on rising ground and beat off repeated Arab cavalry charges. He then aimed a cavalry charge at the Arabs 'Achilles' heel: their plunder-laden baggage train. The Arab flexibility in tactics was markedly lacking on this occasion; the threat to the baggage train prompted an immediate Arab withdrawal, which degenerated into flight when word spread that the Arab commander, Abd ar-Rahman, had been killed. Content to return to Tours with the spoil recovered from the invaders, Charles left the beaten Arabs to evacuate Aquitaine virtually unmolested. From this reluctance to pursue a beaten enemy it would certainly appear that the cavalry resources available to Charles were still strictly limited in numbers, reliability or both.

Improving the Frankish muster

Ten years after Charles Martel died in 741, his son Pepin 'The Short' achieved the transition from hereditary court official to ruling monarch when he was elected king by the magnates of Francia, founding the Carolingian dynasty. The new king's ambitions were restricted by the tenacious limitations of the Frankish levy system. His available military power was provided by the **Heerban,** the provincial call-up of land tenants for the military service they owed their lords, and which the lords in turn owed the king. By tradition the counts of Francia assembled with their contingents at an annual national muster known as the **Marchfeld** or 'Field of March'. Though unspecified, the actual period of military service was necessarily limited by the seasonal tug of agriculture: if the provinces were starved of manpower at harvest-time, there would be no crops and no tax revenue. As a result the counts tended to arrive at the **Marchfeld** ready to oppose any long-term military adventures which the king might be contemplating. Thus the true strength of a 'strong' king was measured by his success in persuading his vassal lords to fall in with his plans.

The Franks, c.730-760 AD

The Franks in Italy

Perhaps the most impressive achievement of Pepin 'The Short' (747-768) was the repeated mustering of Frankish armies for service at unheard-of distances from home. In his two campaigns in northern Italy (754 and 756) Pepin championed the struggling Roman Papacy against the powerful kingdom of the Lombards. In so doing he established Latin Francia as the successor to the remnants of the Byzantine 'Exarchate' of Italy established back in Justinian's time, compelling the Lombard King Aistulf to hand over Ravenna (conquered from the Byzantines in 751) to the Papacy. Pepin's immediate

aim was the Papal blessing and support for his family's new status as kings of Francia. This he achieved, but the unseen price was eleven hundred years of war-torn Italian history set in motion by the creation of the central Italian Papal State, the survival of which depended on military power from beyond the Alps.

Apart from this new 'Italian front', Pepin found his other wars comparatively easy to 'sell' to the Frankish warlords at the **Marchfeld.** The first of these was the conquest of Septimania, the coastal strip of Provence between the Rhone and the Pyrenees. Septimania had been the last foothold of the Visigoths in southern Gaul before its conquest as a convenient bridgehead of Arab territory north of the Pyrenees. Pepin led Frankish armies to conquer Septimania after repeated campaigning between 752 and 759, posing as the liberator - in one of the first discernible crusades against the Moslem 'infidel' - of the local Visigothic population.

The least successful of Pepin's wars were against the defiant Duke Waifar of Aquitaine, who held out against campaign after campaign launched against him every year from 760 to 768. In the end the Aquitainian nobles only submitted when Waifar died, a few months before Pepin himself - but even then Pepin had to offer the Aquitainians generous privileges to make sure of their allegiance to the Frankish kingdoms.

Search for secure frontiers

When Pepin died in September 768, Francia had been set on a course of expansionism from which there could be no immediate turning back. There were no 'natural frontiers' such as the Roman Empire had once enjoyed. To the north-east lay heathen Frisia and Saxony; to the east the Duchy of Bavaria (a German counterpart of Aquitaine, no less resistant to Frankish overlordship); to the south-west lay the still-formidable Moslems of Spain.

These encircling commitments led to a significant change in the Frankish army. Almost exactly like the imperial Roman army back in the 3rd and 4th Centuries, for former dependence on slow-moving infantry had to go; the need for intensified campaigning on a wide range of fronts demanded an expansion of the cavalry force. One of the most significant military/social reforms of Pepin's reign was postponing the date of the **Marchfeld** annual muster from March to May, to allow the growth of enough grass to feed the army's horses - transport animals as well as cavalry mounts.

Though Pepin left his realm partitioned between his sons Carloman and Charles, the interregnum was cut short by Carloman's death in 771. The Frankish dominions were thereupon reunited under the sole rule of Charles 'The Great' - Charlemagne (771-814).

War on all fronts: the conquests of Charlemagne, 771-814

At first sight there seems little in common between the empire won by Alexander the Great and that created by Charlemagne in the later 8th Century AD. Alexander's empire fell apart as soon as he died; that of Charlemagne endured (at least in name) until its formal demolition by Napoleon. This, in fact, was the First or 'Thousand-Year Reich' whose fame Hitler vowed to surpass. Yet there is one important parallel between Alexander and Charlemagne. In each case the conquests of the son were achieved by a military machine created by the father. The increased mobility given to the Frankish army by the expansion of its cavalry element under Pepin 'The Short' enabled Charlemagne to wage virtually non-stop campaigns on one front after another - Italy in 773-74, Saxony in 775-77, Moslem Spain in 778; Saxony in 782-85; Italy in 786; Bavaria in 787; The Danube in 791; Saxony in 792-95; the Danube in 796. Here was a grandiose sequence of constant redeployment and conquest unknown in western Europe since the collapse of the Western Roman Empire.

The Pattern of Frankish conquest

These were the main campaigns which moulded Charlemagne's empire on to the firm base of united Francia created by Pepin. Looked at in detail, there was little to distinguish them from earlier Frankish campaigns in that the army was mustered in May, campaigned through the summer months, dispersed for harvest and winter, and reassembled for the next campaign in the following spring. As Pepin had found against the Aquitainians, and as Charlemagne found against the Saxons, this season parttern meant that several years were required for the reduction of a really determined enemy. During the European wars of the Roman Empire, winter campaigns had been known, though the summer months were

naturally preferred for the greater ease which they lent to the movement of armies. In medieval Europe, however, summer campaigning became accepted as the norm and remained so until the Revolutionary Wars at the end of the 18th Century.

Similarly, Chjarlemagne's empire-building was no less opportunist than his father's had been; yet it was by no means entirely haphazard. In so far as Charlemagne had a 'grand strategy', it consisted of surrounding Francia with a comfortable belt of conquered or allied territory - exactly like the basic policy of the Soviet Union since the end of the Second World War. The most notable feature of Charlemagne's empire at zenith was the ring of new frontier provinces, or **marks** - the Spanish Mark against the Moslems, the Breton Mark against the Bretons (no less resistant to Frankish expansionism than their Cornish and Welsh kinfolk across the Channel, blood foes of the expanding Anglo-Saxon kingdoms), the Pannonian Mark against the Avars of the Danube valley, the Friulian Mark against the Illyrian Croats.

Resources and strategy

In the wars which culminated in the establishment of these territorial buffers Charlemagne usually acted as his own commander-in-chief, reviewing the army as each spring's 'Mayfield' muster and leading it on campaign. He never attempted to plant fortresses and leave costly garrisons all over the territories he conquered; he did not have a professional, long-service army, and the provinces could not endure the withdrawal of farming manpower which prolonged foreign service demanded. Instead he tried, wherever possible, to seal each successful offensive with a **political** settlement, reaching an accomodation with the defeated magnates. Throughout the Middle Ages, other victors tended to pursue the same policy; in the first two years after Hastings, for example, William of Normandy held out the most generous terms to the surviving leaders of Saxon England. There was nothing generous or humanitarian about this policy: it was common sense, a coat designed very much by the shortage of military cloth.

Roland and the rearguard

In many ways Charlemagne's least successful campaign - the Spanish foray of 778 - was the most important he ever fought, because of its enduring legacy. It followed three years of hard fighting, which Charlemagne believed had left the Saxons sufficiently cowed to permit Frankish exploitation of a promising opportunity south of the Pyrenees. This was a civil war between Ibn ar-Arabi of Saragossa, who solicited help from Charlemagne, and the Emir Abd-ar-Rahman. Though Charlemagne's army reached the Ebro he failed to take Saragossa; his western flank and communications were menaced by the Christian Basques of Navarre (isolationist then as now) and Abd-ar-Rahman advanced against him in disconcerting strength. News that the Saxons had risen left Charlemagne with no choice but to evacuate Spain, during which the Frankish rearguard under Count Roland was cut off and slaughtered by Basques in the Roncevaux pass.

Virtually nothing is known about Roland other than the fact that he was Count of the Breton Mark, but stories of the alleged glory of his last stand endured and grew. Some 200 years later they were enshrined in the epic poem **Chanson de Roland,** extolling the idea that Roland's respect for his knightly reputation had prevented him from summoning aid. This poem, exaggerated out of measure though it undoubtedly was, remains a master-document to understanding the so-called 'age of chivalry', with its first attempt at civilized rules for warfare. It was said that the **Chanson de Roland** was chanted by the first man to strike a blow at Hastings in 1066: the Norman minstrel Taillefer.

Though the Saxons produced no troops capable of standing up to the Frankish armoured lancers **(left)** the effective guerrila tactics they persistently waged forced Charlemagne to break Saxon resistance by population deportations rather than conventional operations. But only two major campaigns were required for the Frankish cavalry to break the Avar cavlary of the middle Danube (791, 796), who had menaced Constantinople itself at the height of their power 150 years before.

9th/10th Centuries:

The momentous Scandinavian expansion remembered as the 'Viking era' spanned the 9th and 10th Centuries and took the form of two distinct surges, one in each. Both featured isolated raids followed by attacks by roving armies, then attempts at outright conquest and settlement. The mastery of the sea which enabled Scandinavian settlers to cross the Atlantic to Greenland, Labrador and Newfoundland also enabled their warriors to strike where they chose at any enemy coast, but this was not all. The wonderful versatility of their oared, shallow-draught longships enabled them to penetrate as far up the rivers of Europe as there was enough water in which to float. At this point they would beach their ships, protect them with a rampart and garrison, then take off to ravage the surrounding hinterland before returning to embark with the spoils.

Target: the wealth of Christian Europe
This skill afloat gave the Vikings a tremendous range and choice of targets. In 860, for instance, Viking raiders were active in every river of Francia - Rhine, Scheldt, Somme, Seine, Loire, and Garonne - the coasts of Moslem Spain, Provence, and Italy, plus the Irish Sea, North Sea and English Channel, whence one raiding army plunged confidently inland to plunder Winchester, capital of the strongest kingdom of Saxon England. Initial objectives were always the same: the loot of all portable riches, the capture of slaves, and the extortion of protection-money ('Danegeld') for a promise, rarely kept, to go away and not return.

***LEFT:** A West Saxon thegn or estate-holding nobleman-warrior of the time of Alfred of Wessex (871-899). He summoned the local fyrd levy and led it to join the royal army, or commanded in local operations under the direction of the regional ealdorman or even bishop. According to individual means his sword and spear – the main English weapons against the 'heathen men' from the sea – would be inlaid, and were often family heirlooms.*

Saxon and Viking

Viking tactics

A Viking ship could hold up to 50 men (taking the famous 'Gokstad ship' as a norm) which means that even a modest fleet of 20 ships could land a force of a thousand expert fighting men capable of inflicting immense damage in a very short period. A Viking force wanting to extend its range would 'horse' itself with rounded-up local mounts, though Vikings always fought on foot. They were expert in the use of terrain and field fortification and were highly disciplined infantry capable even of fighting off Frankish cavalry from behind their tenacious shield-wall formation.

Saxon England at bay

England, open to seaborne attack from all sides, was a natural target. The shires of the English kingdoms were governed by **ealdormen** - the equivalent of the Frankish counts - who in emergency raised the shire **fyrd** or levy of freemen. Though basic **fyrd** armament and deployment was probably little more than a hedge of spears and hatchets, its fighting value was surprisingly high. Of seven pitched battles fought between Viking armies and Saxon **fyrdmen** between 840 and 851, the **Anglo-Saxon Chronicle** records that the English won four. In 866, however, the 'Great Army' of the Danes began the piecemeal conquest of East Anglia, Northumbria and central Mercia. By 875 only Alfred's southern kingdom of Wessex remained to continue the fight against the invaders, surviving by the narrowest of margins.

RIGHT: *Viking warrior of the 9th Century, wearing a helmet with built-in 'spectacle' eye-protectors. Armour, when worn, consisted of a mailshirt or byrnie to protect the trunk, to which mail sleeves might be added. Viking axes, usually a one-handed weapon, were often richly inlaid with precious ornamentation. The Scandinavian axemen recruited in the elite Byzantine 'Varanger Guard' were regarded as the foremost infantry of Europe.*

Saxon England breaks the Viking menace

Viking assault on an English stockade, one of the many which took place during the last 15 years of the 9th Century. Having saved his kingdom of Wessex by his great victory over the East Anglian Danes at Edington in 878, Alfred set to work to devise a workable defence strategy against future invasions by Viking armies. His new system involved a field army recruited for long-term service, with the fyrd levies serving on a rota basis; and fixed bank-and-stockade defences at key sites and existing towns - the **burhs.**

When an existing town was converted into a burh (the most prominent was London, taken and fortified by Alfred in 886), each citizen was required to help maintain the defences and defend his own sector of the stockade when the burh was attacked. The net result was that Viking raiders, encountering unexpected resistance at a burh, would settle down for a siege. This gave the English field army time to march to the burh's relief, catching the attackers between hammer and anvil. The first success with the burh system was Alfred's relief of besieged Rochester in 885.

Alfred's son and successor, Edward 'The Elder' (899-924) turned the formerly defensive burh system inside out, using it **offensively** to reconquer East Anglia and the southern Midlands. His technique was to march deep into Danish territory and establish a new burh, which the local Danish ruler would feel compelled to attack and eliminate. The English field army would then advance to crush the Danish force thus conveniently concentrated and immobilized. It was with this highly effective strategy that the Midlands and North Country were reconquered (910-940), creating the kingdom of England.

The Magyar hordes

In the late 9th Century the westward surge of the Magyars from the Ukraine forcibly reintroduced the Christian West to a menace it had not known since the heyday at Attila the Hun, 400 years before: the mounted horde of horsed archers, only this time wearing armoured protection equal to that of Western cavalry, and using fluid tactics which were not misapplied imitations of Western models.

The seven Magyar **voivode** or hordes were made up of clans, about 10-15 clans per **voivode,** and each clan consisting of up to 2,000 warriors at maximum strength. Estimating the strength of a Magyar horde is almost as impossible as estimating that of a Viking army; both varied widely, and were almost certainly never as great as the totals recorded by their victims' chroniclers. Certainly the Magyars never relied on numbes alone. Their tactical specialities were a screaming charge to unleash an arrow-storm, followed if necessary by feigned flight to lure the incautious enemy off his chosen ground into enfilade fire. Like the Arabs, the Magyars always tried to meet the only effective enemy field army at the outset of the campaign and eliminate it, meeting no resistance during the subsequent rampage.

Tremendous operational range

Endurance in the saddle, boosted by the practice of riding with spare mounts, gave the Magyars a tremendous speed and range of operations. In the half-century 895-955, Magyar hordes set off from their chosen homeland north of the middle Danube on devastating annual expeditions, spanning half Europe in their career. In 899 they broke into the Po valley and drove as far west as Pavia; in 907 they reached the Rhine, crossed it, and advanced south into Provence; in 947 they raided Italy as far south as Apulia.

No effective answer to the Magyars was found until the German kingdoms - like the English against the Danes - repaired their city fortifications and recruited defence forces trained to fight on horseback. Once denied the sort of battle they liked, and opposed by disciplined troops, the limitations of the Magyars' repertoire were soon revealed. Their united **voivode** were finally shattered at the battle of the Lechfeld (August 955) by a German army consisting almost entirely of armoured cavalry, and well-judged tactics.

Allies for the Norsemen: the Scots

As the English reconquest of the Midland and northern shires from the Danes got under way in the early 9th Century, the hard-pressed Viking warlords naturally turned to the Scots for aid. Here we show two Scottish warriors of the epic campaign of 937, when King Constantine of Scotland invaded England in alliance with Olaf Guthfrithson, one of the last Norse kings of York. The upshot was a triumphant English victory at a place called **Brunanburh,** one of the most celebrated events in the history of Saxon England. As an unknown English poet recorded, 'five young kings lay on that field of battle, slain by the swords, and also seven of Olaf's earls, and a countless host of seamen and Scots . . . the aged Constantine, the hoary-headed warrior . . . was shorn of his kinsmen and deprived of his friends at that meeting-place, bereaved in the battle, and he left his young son on the field of slaughter.' The victor of **Brunanburh** was the English King Athelstan, grandson of Alfred 'The Great'.

c.1000

THE MIDDLE AGES

-1500

Amid the turmoil of 10th-Century Europe, an event took place which was to have the most profound effect on the history of the medieval world. This was the creation of the Duchy of Normandy (911) by a group of Scandinavian adventurers, enlisted under treaty by the West Frankish kingdom to secure the French Channel coast from Viking raiders.

A unique blend of the best in Scandinavian and Frankish military techniques, the Norman duchy had by the middle 11th Century evolved the most disciplined martial state since the long-vanished Roman Empire. Adept at mounted warfare, superb at the control of terrain by well-sited castles, the mail-clad knights of Normandy became the master soldiers of the Western world. They carved out Norman duchies in Italy and conquered England; they crossed to the Balkans and assaulted the failing Byzantine Empire. And their crowning triumph was the First Crusade of 1097-99, which briefly conquered Turkish Syria and Palestine for the Christian West.

For the next 400 years the military history of the Middle Ages was dominated by the career of the armoured knight and attempts to find an antidote to it. The knight's commanding role in feudal society survived shattering defeats by the invading Mongol horsed archers (1241); by pikemen at Courtrai and Bannockburn (1302, 1314); and by massed arrow fire at Crécy, Poitiers and Agincourt (1346, 1356 and 1415).

By the middle 15th Century well-drilled shock and missile infantry had established themselves as irreplaceable troop types, but the armoured knight could not be replaced in the role of heavy cavalry. As the 16th Century dawned, it remained to be seen what lasting effect the newest element in war – gunpowder-fired cannon and infantry firearms – would have on the armies of Europe.

The Normans' war machine,

Norman history began in 911 with a treaty between the embattled King Charles 'The Simple', of the West

***OPPOSITE:** Norman knight of the middle 11th Century, with spear hefted for throwing from the saddle in a hit-and-run missile attack.*
***BELOW:** Similar in basic equipment (note the same helmet and 'kite' shield carried by the knight) but immediately below the knight in military/social status: a **vavasseur** or minor tenant, who fought on foot as the backbone of the Norman heavy infantry.*

Franks (or French); and the Viking chieftain Rolf 'The Ganger', one of the most powerful raiders along the Channel coast. This treaty, signed at St Clairsur Epte, granted Rolf and his followers the province of Rouen, subsequently extended west to include the Cotentin peninsula. Charles was thus buying the services of a tough new ally who might be capable of repelling future Viking attacks where Charles himself could not. Just as Charlemagne had done, Charles needed a powerful buffer between central France and Briottany. The Norman duchy was thus born as a 'Northman's Mark', intended to contain the Bretons as well as shield Paris from more Viking attacks.

No previous deal of this nature had remained stable for long, but this one did. As Viking expansionism continued to wane, the settlers were not exposed to sustained pressure from other would-be conquerors. The Normans - as the descendants of Rolf and his followers are known - turned out to have an uncanny knack of making things work, usually to their own advantage. The result, by the early 11th Century, was a highly efficient amalgam of all that was best in the Scandinavian and Frankish social and military orders.

The Norman formula

Along with the language of the West Franks, the Normans rapidly adopted the Frankish aristocratic structure, with counts holding land from the duke and owing him military service in return. Also from the Franks, the Normans learned all the advantages of fighting as well as riding to battle on horseback, developing a cavalry capable of fighting on foot if necessary. This cavalry was formed by the knights whose small manorial holdings or **fees** formed the broad base of the landholding pyramid with the duke at its peak.

The knight's manorial revenue paid for the weapons and equipment not only of himself but of the men he was required to bring to his lord's service on demand. The latter included the petty sub-tenants or **vavasseurs**, immediately below the manorial knights in status, plus rank-and-file infantry - spearmen, archers and later crossbowmen.

Armour and weapons

The most expensive item of the knight's equipment was the mail **hauberk** of linked iron rings: a long-sleeved tunic ending in a loose skirt which could be secured behind each knee with straps. The better-off could afford mail extensions for the lower leg (**chausses**).

Until the later 11th Century head protection seems to have been limited to the simple conical helmet with its nose-guarg or **nasal**. There is strong evidence that the Normans adopted neck protection as soon as they came up against professional infantry axeplay - the Byzantine Varanger Guards in the Mediterranean, and English house-carles in 1066. (The lower margin of the Bayeux Tapestry frankly shows several decapitated Norman knights.) The new neck protection took the form of a mail **coif,** perhaps best described as a long-necked 'balaclava helmet' of mail, enclosing both head and neck and worn under the helmet.

Versatility in the saddle

Hardly less important was the war-horse or **destrier,** a highly-trained beast fed when possible on expensive grain fodder to keep him in peak condition. A knight whose destrier could not be relied on to charge straight and wheel at the precise moment of command was a useless liability on a battlefield. The destrier provided the platform for the knight's attack, which usually took two forms. There was the **shock attack,** pressed right home with the lance couched or tucked firmly under the right arm; and the **missile attack,** a galloping approach followed by a volley of javelins at the enemy before wheeling and retiring. Apart from the lance or javelin, the Norman knight's main weapon - in the saddle or on foot - was the heavy tapering **longsword.**

911-1066

Hastings, 1066: Norman knights checked by elite infantry

The great myth of the Norman Conquest of England is that it was achieved by the absolute supremacy of the Norman knight on the battlefield, but this was not the case. At Hastings in 1066 the charging knights were repeatedly checked by the English house-carles - paid professionals, armoured 'all-rounders' expert with spear, axe and sword - in their disciplined close formation. Such enemies were rarely encountered by the Norman military machine and the Bayeux Tapestry admits as much, showing the house-carles standing firm under frontal charges. The knights are shown using their spears as flung javelins more than couched lances, the point clearly being that their horses refused to 'charge home' into the waiting hedge of spears and axes. At one moment the Normans showed signs of panic, forcing William to rally them in person (also shown in the Tapestry) Until William switched to attacking the English fyrdmen **(pp. 68-69)** the battle was running in favour of the English. The house-carles held firm even when their decimation by archery fire began after the destruction of the fyrdmen on their flanks.

In his high-speed march from York to Sussex, to meet Duke William's invading Norman army, the basic strategy of King Harold was sounder than his tactics. As Rommel knew very well while awaiting the Allied invasion of France in 1944, it is a vital principle to hit invading troops before they can establish themselves properly ashore. But Harold had an almost impossible task, in that the distance was too great. In his eagerness to bring on a decisive action in the South, he threw away his best chance of victory: raising an infantry force from the English **fyrd,** or general call-up, which could in time be drilled to withstand attacks by Norman knights.

The point was that the Norman expeditionary force was, for the immediate future, finite: William did not have - as the Allied assault troops had in June 1944 during the invasion of Normandy - limitless reinforcements at his back. Until he had broken the main English field army, the Normans would control only the ground they rode over. Harold gave William the chance of a quick kill, by advancing to battle with rough-and-ready fyrd support dangerously lacking in steadiness and training.

Luring out the fyrdmen

William exploited the weakness of the English fyrdmen to the full, but only after his opening charges had failed to break the shield wall of the house-carles. William then switched tactics and, like Auchinleck at the first battle of Alamein in June-July 1941, concentrated on cutting away the inferior flanking troops from the enemy's hard core. The battle began to tip in the Normans' favour as soon as William began the decimation of the fyrdmen, luring them out of their sole defensive formation with feint attacks and feigned flight, then wheeling to cut down the fyrdmen in the open. As depicted here, a trained swordsman (mounted, no less important, on a trained war-horse) was more than a match for an amateur spearman - surprised by the sudden turnabout of his enemy, caught off guard and without the steadying support of steady troops who knew their business.

Hastings, 1066: defeat of the Saxon fyrd

BELOW, CENTRE: English peasant soldier of the 'Great Fyrd', the general manpower yield of the summons to arms. Unarmoured, his main role was to provide a spear-hedge in line formation, relying mainly on the knife in close-quarter work during the advance.

BELOW, RIGHT: A select fyrdman, the invaluable auxiliary to the house-carle elite, of which Harold did not give himself time to collect enough before Hastings. Recruited from the better-off farmer-householders, select fyrdmen could afford basic armour and round shield, and would also have had the rudiments of swordsmanship. In Old English society the sword was not – as it was in the iron military society of Normandy – the badge and prerogative of the knightly caste. The greatest long-term weakness of all grades of fyrdmen, however, was their reluctance to be committed to lengthy field service with the army – particularly during the approach of the all-important harvest season back on the farm.

The Crusaders: Western mass versus

The most effective field troops of the Western European armies, fighting in Syria and Palestine in the wars of the Crusades (late 11th, 12th, and early 13th Centuries) were the knight and the crossbowman.

The knight **(right)** provided mass for the standard Western field combat tactic: the charge of armoured cavalry, intended to sweep away all in its path. This remained effective against any enemy either prepared to meet it, or trapped in terrain which prevented a timely retreat or dispersal. 'A charging Frank could smash a hole in the walls of Babylon', was one rueful Turkish comment.

Western armies on the march, however, were always vulnerable to surprise attacks by the fast-moving cavalry of the Saracens **(centre)**. The Saracens were effective horsed archers and, being more lightly protected and

Eastern mobility

faster mounted, were extremely hard to ride down.

The best defence against such attacks, able to provided marksmanship at long range, was the crossbowman **(left)**, whose principal weapon was accurate and extremely hard hitting. The crossbowman was usually recruited as a well-paid professional, suitable for castle garrison service as well as service with the field armies. The biggest weakness of the crossbow was its low rate of fire and its indifferent performance in wet weather. Though a cocked crossbow would perform well enough when fired by any individual able to point it, it was a cumbersome and intricate weapon for its day, requiring constant expert maintenance. For all that, soundly posted crossbowmen could usually be relied on as the best deterrent to punishing surprise attacks against a Western army on the march.

The 'poor bloody infantry' in the

The role of the rank-and-file infantry in medieval warfare is frequently discounted, eclipsed by the more glamorous exploits of knights and specialised infantry such as axemen, archers or cross-bowmen. This tendency is misleading, because no army in any age has been able to operate without foot soldiers. Ground can be commanded by artillery (catapults or guns) or overrun by cavalry, but it can only be taken and held by the infantry. As the British General Weavell was to put it in the 20th Century, 'Sooner or later the time will come when Private Snodgrass must advance straight to his front.'

In the Middle Ages, 'Private Snodgrass' and his comrades were represented by the feudal levy, the spearmen who formed the main line of battle. They were the most numerous manpower yield from the feudal summons to arms in time of war, peasantry drawn from every farm on every manor. This was particularly true in the high age of European feudalism, from the 11th Century to the early 14th, before the drift towards a specialised infantry establishment began in the 14th Century.

Tinchebrai, 1106: a case history

The Battle of Hastings in 1066 opened Saxon England to conquest by the Duchy of Normany, but by no means signified the total eclipse of the traditional peasant infantry by the Norman Knight. Fifty years after Hastings the youngest son of the Conqueror, King Henry I of England, crossed to Normandy to reconquer the Duchy from his elder brother, Duke Robert. The decisive battle was fought at Tinchebrai on 28 September 1106, and is remarkable for having been fought predominantly on foot. The reason given by the chronicler Henry of Huntingdon is interesting: 'The King and the Duke, with great part of their troops, fought on foot that they might make a more sustained attack'.

No less revealing is the composition of King Henry's army. 'In the first line were the men of the Bessin, the Avranchin and the Cotentin, and these were all on foot. In the second line was the King with his very numerous barons and these likewise were on foot. Seven hundred mounted knights were placed with each line; and besides these the Count of Maine, and Alan Fergaunt, Count of Brittany, flanked the army with about a thousand mounted knights. All the camp followers and servants were removed far to the rear of the battle. The whole army of the King may be reckoned as having consisted of about 40,000 men.'

Peasant infantry to the fore

Assuming these figures to be reasonably correct, the following picture emerges. King Henry's front line consisted of his infantry of the feudal levy, 18,800 strong, and supported by 350 knights on each flank. In close support was an armoured second line, the King and his barons, in similar strength; while out on the flanks of the whole array was an indeterminate force of mounted knights, maybe 500 strong on each flank.

Accounts of the actual fighting are confused, but indicate that Duke Robert attacked the King's stronger array, with the confidence born of his experience gained in the First Crusade (1096-99). Apparently the battle began well for Duke Robert, who seems to have driven the hapless front line of the King's army back on the second. Even after the rival lines of armoured infantry came to grips the outcoume hung in the balance, being finally settled by a charge of King Henry's Breton knights which ripped open the whole left flank of Duke Robert's army. It was all a far cry from the sequence of events at Hastings 50 years before.

Allowing for all the uncertainties, it is clear that Tinchebrai was an infantry collision resolved by cavalry flanking attack, and that at least 50 per cent of the victorious infantry force had been yielded by the feudal levy. King Henry used his feudal infantry as a shock absorber to take the brunt of the enemy attach and stabilise the action. Their casualties must have been heavy but are unknown; medieval chroniclers and-eye witnesses tended nearly always to concentrate on the deeds of the upper-crust fighting men, their potential patrons. The priest who gave the above description of King Henry's order of battle recorded as a 'marvel' that the King's casualties amounted to two men killed and one wounded - 'men', in this instance, clearly referring to the armoured knights of the second line.

Tenacity under attack

Cynics will doubtless argue that the hapless Royalist infantry at Tinchebrai had no choice but to fight hard, with a line of armoured knights at their back; but feudal infantry were capable of brave resistance even when fighting completely unsupported. This happened at Lincoln in 1141 during the protracted civil wars ('the Anarchy') of King Stephen's reign,the last Norman king of England. Counterattacked at Lincoln, Stephen again chose to fight on foot, 'wielding his gread two-handed battle-axe'. The rebel cavalry drove Stephen's knights from the field and drove in on the King and his depleted infantry hard core, which fought on with great gallantry until the King himself was captured.

The infantry's effectiveness

All contemporary accounts indicate that feudal infantry naturally tended to fight all the harder when supported by armoured infantry (as at Tinchebrai) or by professional missile troops - archers or crossbowmen. It is certainly wrong to regard feudal infantry as an ill-armed rabble prone to dissolve in rout at the first shock. Such collapses invariably occurred when the infantry centre was left exposed and without heavy infantry support, either as a result of faulty deployment before the action, or the defeat of the flanking cavalry, or by the flanking cavalry forgetting its vital task of protecting the infantry and losing touch in a reckless advance.

Another point in favour of the fighting efficiency of the feudal infantry - again, one often overlooked - is the infantryman's startling increase in combat efficiency during the press of battle or **mêlée** when the struggling armies interlocked. Two similarly equipped knights with equal technique could do little rapid damage to each other. But a light infantryman who kept his head and picked his chance well could easily lug an embattled knight from his saddle, pin him down by sitting on his chest, and finish him off with a quick dagger thrust. Moreover, peasant infantry lacked the knight's natural reluctance to cripple enemy horses which, if captured, would provide valuable remounts or hard cash in sale price. A foot soldier armed with a pole-axe would have little compunction in mowind down a knight's horse, then pouncing on the capsized knight before he could struggle to his feet.

As a final testimony to the combat value of the humble infantryman in the Middle Ages, it is worth considering the steady improvements in knightly armour made between the 11th and 15th Centuries: the evolution from mail to plate armour. This was not prompted solely by the attempt to give knights maximum protection in combat with each other. The early provision of plate protection for knee, leg and foot was a telling admission of the crippling injuries which peasant infantry, with their motley armament of spears, billhooks and knives, could inflict on their knightly overlords.

Here we show two typical infantrymen of the feudal levy from the ,middle 13th Century. Both are from the English baronial wars of Simon de Montfort versus King Henry III, in 1264-65. They fought on opposite sides during the battle of Lewes (May 1265) in which the royalist army was defeated by de Montfort and the King himself was captured. (King Henry owed this humiliation to the over-successful cavalry charge led by his son, Prince Edward, which left the royalist infantry exposed. The spearman of de Montfort's army *(opposite)* wears the quilted tunic or *gambeson* to which metal plates could be sewn for additional protection. The royalist *below* is armed with both short sword and anti-cavalry pole-axe.

1241: Mongol archers crush European

The Middle Ages were remarkable for three great 'flood surges' of horsed warriors from the wastes of central and eastern Asia, all of which shook the foundations of the civilized world. The first of these eruptions had been the Huns in the 2nd Century; the second was the Magyars in the late 9th and early 10th Centuries. The third and greatest onslaught was the landslide of Mongol conquests in the 13th Century, which in the space of 50 years struck at every focus of civilization in Eurasia.

In military history the Mongols may be seen as the last and easily the most effective exponents of a soldier type first perfected by the Assyrians **(pp.22-23)** some 2,500 years before: the horsed archer. Mongol hardihood, horsemanship, and proficiency with the powerful composite bow had of course existed for centuries before the time of Temujin (c.1154-1227), but it was Temujin who united the Mongol tribes under his rule and disciplined their martial talents into a world-beating military machine. It was in 1206, at a **kuriltai** or assembly of Mongol vasals, that Temujin assumed the title of Jenghiz Khan, 'all-mighty lord', the immediate prelude to an astonishing career of conquest across Eurasia.

To their enemies the Mongols seemed an elemental, almost supernatural force, able to ride, fight and butcher in all extremes of climate and terrain. (The Mongols are still the only military invaders on record to have coped successfully with the Russian winter.) On a world in which the idea of waging war according to chivalrous rules (written and unwritten) was beginning to emerge, the Mongols forced the reality of TOTAL WAR in a manner destined only to be surpassed 700 years later, in the anti-civilian bombing raids of two world wars.

The Mongol system

Reinforced by ferocious discipline, Mongol military organisation was constructed on a decimal basis: the basic **arban** of ten men, **jagun** of 100,

Mongol horsed archer.

minghan of 1,000, **tuman** of 10,000, **tuk** of 100,000. 'They are all obedient to the word of command', noted the Venetian Marco Polo, 'more than any other people in the world'. Mongol armies rode unencumbered by baggage train, the warriors sustained by dried rations (in emergency, they drank their horses' blood) and sheltered by one-man 'dog tents'. Herds of spare mounts, riding with the troops, carried supplies of spare bows, bowstrings, quivers, arrows, harness, and armour, the latter for the most part of tough but light boiled leather.

The Mongols did not rely solely on their horsed archers, which made their military machine far less lightweight than that of the Magyars had been. Mongol tactics favoured a five-deep formation, the front two ranks being armoured and carrying lance and sabre as well as the great composite bow. The rear three ranks were unarmoured, and it was they who had the task of softening up the enemy, advancing firing and retiring behind their armoured comrades until the time was ripe for the latter's decisive charge

Invasion of Europe, 1236-1241

Under Jenghiz Khan the Mogols' main effort was directed against China, but in 1236 his successor Ogadai entrusted the conquest of the West to his nephew Batu Khan and the great general Subotai. After overrunning central Russia (1236-1240) Batu and Subotai invaded eastern Europe, shattering the German-Polish host at Liegnitz (March 1241) and the Hungarians at Mohi. The Danube had been crossed and Wiener Neustadt, south of Vienna, had been reached when (December 1241) the Mongol armies heard that Ogadai Khan was dead, and evacuated Europe to elect his successor. Fortunately for Europe they never returned, subsequent campaigning in the West being levelled against the Moslem rather than the Christian powers

Outclassed representative of European chivalry - German knight of the time of Liegnitz.

Bannockburn, 1314: Scottish pikemen

In the late 13th and early 14th Centuries, two widely separated wars of resistance - fought by the Scots against England, and by the Swiss against Austria - produced the same phenomenon. This was the high effectiveness of dense formations of pikemen against mouted knights: a revelation after the knight's supremacy on the battlefield, which had endured for some 250 years.

The Scottish schiltrons

The use of shock infantry in close formation was not, of course, a new discovery: it had been widely practised in the Ancient World and had reappeared in modified form with the 'shield walls' of axemen in the Dark Ages. But these new pike formations did not use the wide-front, massed phalanx of the Macedonian era; instead they deployed in smaller, inter-dependent units known to the Scots as **schiltrons.** The standard battlefield deployment - like Roman maniples - was the **quincunx:** the schiltrons in the rear filling the gaps between those in the front line.

The primary function of the schiltron was to frustrate the charge of the enemy's chivalry, the armoured knights. As the English house-carles had demonstrated at Hastings, horses will always refuse to charge home into formations of steady infantry holding their ground. This would endure until the age of the machine-gun; one of the most basic manoeuvres in infantry drill, right down to the end of the 19th Century, was assuming defensive formation to 'receive cavalry'. The ideal position on which to deploy pike infantry was along the top of a forward ridge, forcing the enemy to charge uphill.

From defensive to offensive

Once the enemy's horses had shied away from the awaiting hedge of pikes, only rarely did they withdraw in good time and re-group in good order. A well-timed downhill advance by the pike formations, disabling horses and

rout the knights of England

bringing down knights by the score, could then convert a frustrated enemy charge into a disaster, with the capsized knights being finished off by knife-wielding light infantry advancing with the pikemen. And this, broadly speaking, is what took place at Bannockburn in 1314, when the over-confident army of King Edward II of England was routed by the Scottish schiltrons led by King Robert the Bruce.

The schiltron's big advantage was that it combined the mass of the old-style phalanx, or shield wall, with much of the flexibility enjoyed by the Roman infantry maniples. An army of pikemen deployed in schiltrons was far less likely to lose formation when advancing across broken terrain. Deployed in good time on the right ground, the schiltron of the early 14th Century was as good a 'cavalry-stopper' as were the British squares at Waterloo 400 years later. And, also like Wellington's infantry, schiltron formations could pass instantly from the strict defensive to the attack.

A short-lived supremacy

When all this is admitted, however, the success of the new pike tactics was bound to be short-lived. The Scottish triumph at Bannockburn exploited English slowness to re-learn an ancient military truth: that the most economical way to overcome enemy infantry holding ground in close formation is by missile fire, not frontal charges. The English had excellent missile infantry in their archers equipped with the longbow, but at Bannockburn the English archers were deployed behind the knights, not in the front line. Twenty years later, with English tactics drastically re-cast to exploit the rapid fire of their archers to the utmost, it was a very different story; in 1333 an English longbow army shot the Scottish schiltrons to pieces at Halidon Hill. Final nemesis for the schiltron would come in the early 16th Century, at Flodden (**pp. 86-87**).

The English Longbow, 14th Century: infantry fire-power triumphant

In the so-called 'Hundred Years War' with France (c.1340-1453) the classic English longbow victories of Crécy (1346) Poitiers (1356) and Agincourt (1415) were all achieved by exploiting the worst excesses of French military snobbery. The latter weakness prevented the French from accepting that low-born infantrymen armed with high fire-power missile weapons were best tackled with care - particularly when they had had time to deploy on ground of their own choosing. All the English longbow victories depended on having enough time to deploy on terrain chosed to channel the enemy into a frontal assault. For a moment, at Agincourt, it seemed that the massed French knights were not going to oblige. King Henry V therefore took the enormous gamble of ordering his archers - who, he knew, had only one good fight in them aftern an exhausting march - to uproot their protective hedge of stakes and advance deliberately into archery range of the French front line. Once stung by this insolence, and the first volleys of clothyard shafts, the French dutifully went into their lemmings-over-a-cliff act and charged to destruction.

It took the blunt but revelatory common sense of Joan of Arc (1429) to convince the French military establishment that the supremacy of the English longbow was a myth - when correctly tackled. It is small wonder that the English burned Joan for a witch. Under her direction, after nearly a century of military suicide, the French suddenly began to scout intelligently, to refuse battle at first contact - and, worst of all, to attack before the English were ready. At Patay (14th June 1429) the French caught the English archers before they had established their line and planted their usual anti-cavalry defences, and overwhelmed them with a smartly-executed assault on foot. Joan's most famous feat, the raising of the siege of Orleans, was a similarly intelligent use of new military technology hitherto neglected by the French: the potency of cannon against 'soft' targets.

From Joan of Arc the French learned three great lessons which ended the heyday of the longbow: that knights were most effective when they operated as versatile heavy cavalry, switching from mounted to dismounted action as circumstances required; that longbowmen were easy meat when attacked in the right manner; and that troops as well as fortifications were highly vulnerable to well-laid guns. After Joan's death the French continued to perfect their cavalry training and field artillery, expelling the English from France (with the exception of Calais) by 1453.

***OPPOSITE:** English archer with dismounted man-at-arms in support.*
***RIGHT:** French knight of the late 14th Century, showing the continuing improvement in 'tailored' plate armour intended to deflect blows rather than absorb them.*

The 14th and 15th Centuries:

Long known in the East, gunpowder seems first to have been 'discovered' in Europe in the 13th Century, but the first successful attempts to use its explosive properties in war date from the 14th. What has been called the 'age of gunpowder' lasted from the early 14th Century to the late 19th, when more efficient explosives - dynamite, cordite, lyddite - were developed.

Explosives in war have always had two basic functions: either to propel missiles (bullets, solid shot or explosive shell) or, exploded in packed charges, to demolish enemy fortifications. Solid metal or stone shot ruled supreme until the 17th Century, when the first successful explosive missiles were developed; shells, bombs and grenades, as often as not with a cheerful if confusing indiscriminate use of words. (Even in the First World War, the official term for throwing hand grenades was 'bombing'.) In general shells are fired from guns, mortar-bombs are lobbed on a high trajectory from a low-velocity projector or mortar, and grenades are usually thrown by hand. In all three cases the missile is detonated by a fuse to ensure that the explosion discomforts the enemy, not the dispatcher.

The first guns

From the early 14th Century to the early 17th gunpowder in war was used mainly in the missile-propellant role, with the use of explosive demolition charges secondary but steadily increasing. Once the idea of using a controlled explosion to throw a missile out of a tube or barrel was grasped, it took some 200 years before metal-casting technology caught up and produced gun barrels which were both effective and safe. Recognizable guns were used at the siege of Metz in 1324, and two years later were ordered by the **signoria** of Florence for the defence of the city. These proto-cannon were known as **vasi** or **pots-de-fer:** bottle-shaped containers of gunpowder intended to fire barbed darts, which can hardly have been very successful because of the difficulty of making the narrow bore long enough and strong enough. By 1340, however, wrought iron was being used to make simple short tubes capable of firing spherical stone or cast iron shot: the **bombard,** named for the buzzing hum made by the projectile in flight.

'Cracys' and 'great gunnys'

These early 14th-Century guns were far to cumbersome to be of any real use in the field, but by the end of the century their use in the siege train was assured. It was usual to 'back up' guns with old-style spring and counter-weight siege artillery because of the distressing frequency with which the guns blew up. In Henry V's bombardment of Harfleur (August-September 1415) the English 'cracys' and 'great gunnys' fired millstones, huge tumbling missiles that gouged great chunks out of masonry and sprayed lethal fragments when they broke up on impact. The English gunners poured tar over the gunstones to set alight woodwork in the defences and provide a 'tracer' effect at night.

The English, however, neglected artillery development in the early 15th Century; the French, under King Charles VII, remembered the precepts of Joan of Arc and produced the best artillery arm in Europe. As the admiring chronicler Monstrelet recorded, 'never in living memory has there been such an assemblage of large bombards, heavy cannon, veuglaires, serpentines, mortars, culverins and ribaudekiṅsand these were amply provisioned with powder, protective coverings known as cats, a great number of carts to transport them, and everything else necessary for the capture of towns and castles, and well provided with men to operate them all.'

Ancestors of musket and pistol

The first handguns, small cannon set in a wooden holder for operation by

a new source of fire-power

one man, also appeared in the 14th Century but their development was slow. It was the same problem of lagging technology: the initial inability to cast a barrel long enough and strong enough - yet at the same time sufficiently portable - to give the soldier a firearm superior in range to the familiar bow and crossbow. By the middle 15th Century, however, handgunners were valued mercenaries and could deliver damaging volleys, if hardly at a high rate of fire. Germany took the lead in developing a firearm with a stock for bracing against the user's chest or shoulder and a trigger mechanism which could jam a burning length of slow match into the touch-hole while the user sighter along the barrel. The German word was **hâkenbüsche** or 'hookgun'; **arquebuse** in French, **arcebus** or **harcebus** in English.

OPPOSITE: *Burgundian mercenary handgunner of the 1470s.* ***BELOW:*** *Hussite wagenburg of c.1425, with wagons linked in defensive formation.*

The Hussite battle-wagons

In the 1420s and 1430s the revolt of the Czech Hussites against the Empire produced the most startling and effective use of the new fire-power. Hussite war leader Jan Zizka trained his people to travel with guns mounted in groups of four or more heavy wagons, which at the word of command could be wheeled together and joined by reinforced wooden boards. The result was the **wagenburg** or 'wagon stronghold', bristling at all angles with guns and capable of shattering all conventional attacks on it. Here was a blend of mobility and fire-power which even the Mongols in their heyday would have found a disconcerting if not impossible prospect. To conventional chivalry and infantry the **wagenburg** must have been as frightening an apparition as the first tanks on the Somme in 1916. The **wagenburg** units were accompanied by a strong artillery train including the heaviest bombards then in service (45 kilogram projectiles).

The essence of Zizka's system was centuries ahead of its time: getting the biggest possible concentration of gunners to the right point at the right moment - or, as the inimitable Nathan Bedford Forrest was to put it in the American Civil War, moving 'fustest with the mostest'. The Hussite order of march was an even bigger prodigy and would not be seen again until the first mechanized and armoured divisions in the 20th Century. As it was vital for all arms to fight together, all arms therefore moved together, in five parallel columns: cavalry and field artillery in the centre, flanked by two outer columns of wagons with their infantry. By 1430, riding at will through Germany in bitter parody of the traditional medieval **chevauchée** of armoured knights, the Hussites had proved that they could raid as far as the Baltic if they chose.

The pikemen of Switzerland

If the English longbowmen were the supreme missile infantry of the 14th Century, the Swiss pikemen were the supreme shock infantry. Almost exactly like the Scots in their war of independence from English rule, the rebel Swiss cantons who broke with Austria in 1291 found themselves fighting orthodox feudal armies of knights and light infantry. The Swiss, like the Scots, adopted close pike formations as the answer to Austrian chivalry. By th 1300s the Swiss national army featured massed formations of light pikemen, wearing little armour and capable of movement at great speeds. This restored a true offensive role to the pike phalanx and it flourished mightily, because in their formative years Swiss - unlike the hapless Scottish schiltrons - never came up against effective missile troops.

If the French had ever hired a Swiss army to fight the English archers, it is hard to see a decisive advantage for either side; but at the very least the high mobility of the Swiss would have exposed the longbowmen to unpredictable and highly dangerous attacks, launched from positions and pressed with a speed impossible to formations of armoured knights, whether mounted or dismounted. All the classic 14th-Century Swiss victories - Laupen (1338) and Sempach (1386) - were battles won against out-matched and out-dated feudal armies unable to find an answer to the pike phalanxes, even when the knights fought dismounted with shortened lances.

By the end of the 14th Century nearly a quarter of the Swiss army consisted of light troops armed with missile weapons - crossbows at first but, from the 1380s, handguns. The Swiss used their light missile infantry to save the pike phalanxes from premature commitment, skirmishing and generally 'setting up' the enemy for the decisive charge of the pikemen. The Swiss infantry reached a peak of excellence not matched by other armies until the early 16th Century, and by the last quarter of the 15th were hiring themselves out as mercenaries, serving in most European wars of the period.

The splendid career of the Swiss pikemen only serves to highlight the military backwardness of Germany in the later Middle Ages, where the old feudal nature of armies survived the longest. The German tendency of continued reliance on the armoured knight was not helped by the fact that southern Germany, as one of Europe's major ironworking centre, was also a focus of armour development and manufacture. Nuremberg, Innsbruck, Augsburg, and Landshut were the most famous German armour-producing centres, matched across the Alps by Milan and Pisa in Italy. It was from these centres that the final refinements of plate-armour development, as displayed by the 15th-Century German knight at **left** were taken to their peak of practical excellence and beauty in the early 16th Century.

Landsknechte and ritter: German

The German **landsknechte** (literally 'servants of the land', a hilarious misnomer more often than not) were a paradoxical blend of colourful individuality and iron professionalism. They were mercenaries, first recruited in the 1470s as a reply to the apparently unstoppable Swiss citizen infantry. They fought for the highest bidder and proved so effective that they were hired to fight not only throughout Germany but in Spain, France, Italy and even England, where a brigade of **landskenechte** helped crush the Robert Kett rising in 1549.

The German Emperor Maximilian (1493-1519) transformed the **landsknechte** into a disciplined **corps d'elite** , inviting the German nobility to join their formations. **Esprit de corps** permitted the individual to retain his unique choice of outrageous, multi-coloured garb, but was underpinned by hard training in regimental formations. They excelled in hand-to-hand fighting against enemy pike formations, with commoners wielding a heavy short sword known as **katzlaber** or 'cat ripper' and the noblemen swinging the long, two-handed **zweihander (left).** In battle formation the front-rank **landsknechte** used the **zweihander** and long-handled chopping halberds to mow a breach in the enemy pike formation, then carve deep into the enemy ranks with cut and thrust weapons.

By their very nature it was never practicable to impose uniform equipment on the **landsknechte**, each of whom provided his own gear. Many favoured breastplate and/or thigh armour; many fought unarmoured. Flamboyance in dress was always a **landsknecht's** point of pride - huge plumed hats, slashed doublet and hose in vivid, contrasting colours, ribbons and bows. But the **landsknechte** did not neglect modern fire-power; their ranks included arquebusiers and the latest field artillery on wheeled carriages. Their success, under such commanders as Georg von Frundsberg, sprang from an intelligent use of all arms in co-ordination.

The **landsknecht** ethos included an eve-of-the-battle ritual intended to cow the enemy; kneeling for prayers followed by a leap in the air with a defiant yell, throwing down a handful of soil in token of the **landsknecht's** determination to conquer or die where he stood. Unashamed mercenaries throughout their heyday, the **landsknechte** thought in terms of 'Good Wars' and 'Bad Wars'. A 'Good War' was against an enemy who would yield a rich crop of prisoners who could be held for ransom. A 'Bad War'usually referred to a clash with the blood enemies of the **landsknechte:** the Swiss, who could only be killed and not captured for ransom.

Mercenaries on horseback

The **ritter** was the mounted contemporary of the **landsknecht:** a mercenary armoured cavalryman, recruited in Spain, Italy, Germany and France throughout the Wars of Religion in the 16th Century. At the outset of their career there was nothing to distinguish the **ritters** in equipment or tactics, from conventional armoured chivalry at the

mercenaries of the 16th Century

dawn of the 16th Century. Their weapons were lance, sword and axe or war-hammer (a spike-headed sidearm specially developed for cracking enemy plate armour); they wore full plate armour and they rode heavy mounts which were also armoured (the **chanfron** for the horse's face, **peytral** for the chest,**crinet** for the neck, **flanchards** for the flanks, the latter fitted to the saddle). Later, however, the **ritters** discarded the lance in favour of the pistol, carried in twos or even threes.

The result was an innovation in cavalry tactics with the formation of squadrons of 20-30 ranks. Attacks were now carried out at a steady trot, each rank discharging its pistols as it came into range, then wheeling smartly to the rear to reload. This became widespread until the Swedish 'cavalry revolution' of the early 17th Century (pp.94-95).

PLAIN ET
SURE
VERIAS VINCIT

Flodden, 1513: pikes, longbows, cannon

The bloody clash between the Scottish and English armies at Flodden (9 September 1513) provides a fascinating case-history of how the roles of the most prominent later medieval types of soldier had changed by the early 16th Century.

As at Bannockburn 200 years before, the bulk of the Scottish infantry was massed in pike schiltrons. This time, however, the schiltrons were backed by the powerful artillery train built up by the Scottish monarchy since the middle 15th Century. Scotland in the later Middle Ages was a classic example of how domestic history assisted military develpment, for the Scottish kings welcomed artillery as an aid to crushing rebel castles rather than to enhance the efficiency of the main field army. (This interest in the new weaponry had cost King James II dear; he had been killed in 1460 when one of his new guns burst.) At Flodden, the Scottish guns were ranged behind the schiltrons, which as usual were deployed atop a hill facing the enemy position. But too many of the trained gunners, costly to hire and maintain in service, were at sea with the equally new Scottish fleet, and as a result the Scottish guns at Flodden were indifferently served.

In the English ranks, the main infantry missile weapon was still the longbow, which had torn the schiltrons to pieces at Halidon Hill in 1333; but the English infantry deployment in 1513 was very different to what it had been at Agincourt in 1415. Instead of forming the bulk of the English infantry with their formations 'corseted' by stiffening links of armoured infantry, the longbowmen at Flodden were outnumbered by nearly two to one by the English strength in halberdiers and billmen, equipped and trained to tackle pikemen at close quarters. The painful experience of the later French wars had taught the English the inadvisability of always deploying archers in a fixed position. At Flodden the English archers displayed a mobility which they had never had to use in the great longbow victories of the 14th Century, and reaped the benefit.

Halberds versus pikes

The action at Flodden began while the English army was still deploying across the Scottish front, with a wild charge by the Highland pikemen and Border horse stationed on the Scottish left flank. This had the effect of driving back the English right-wing division, but the Scottish horse was not kept in hand to operate against the English flank and rear, as the main advance of the Scottish pikemen was unleashed down the hill. After a few volleys at the advancing schiltrons the English archers deployed smartly to the left flank, leaving the halberdiers and billmen to bring the Scottish pikemen to an abrupt halt at the foot of the hill.

The resultant deadlock in the centre was resolved by the rearmost English division moving out to the left, lapping round the flank and rear of the Highland pikemen on the Scottish right and savaging them with archery. The Scottish left was similarly enveloped, assisted by a well-judged charge on the part of the English horse. The battle ended in a slaughter of the hemmed-in schiltron infantry, which fought bravely but unavailingly against the English halberdiers and billmen carving deeper and deeper into the Scottish ranks; the Scottish casualties included King James IV, fighting to the last with his men.

Flodden therefore ranks as the last great longbow victory, but was really won by the new anti-pike tactics developed in the later 15th Century.

OPPOSITE: *English and Scottish banners and troops at Flodden.*
BELOW: *Battle of Flodden.*

c.1500

THE 16th and 17th CENTURIES

-1700

The soldier of the later Middle Ages had changed very little, in terms of weaponry and equipment at least, since Sumerian and Egyptian times. He still fought primarily with edged, pointed and clubbing weapons and archery against which armoured clothing offered varying degrees of reasonable protection. Much the same applied to the cavalry, of which the armoured lancer remained the epitome. But that was before the ascendancy of gunpowder firearms was confirmed beyond question in the wars of the Renaissance and Reformation. From the late 15th Century 'Brother Lead', delivered by musket and cannon, advanced relentlessly against 'Sister Steel'. By the late 17th Century there could be no doubt that 'Brother Lead' was now the boss.

The advent of firearms liquidated many types of combat troops which had been familiar as long as war itself. Of these the most prominent was the pike phalanx or spear-hedge which had enjoyed its last period of ascendancy in the 13th and 14th Centuries. The creation of halberdiers, who could chop open pike formations at close quarters, was a temporary expedient; volleys of musketry proved the real killer. As the most effective form of shock infantry, the pikeman co-existed with the musketeer until the 17th-Century invention of the bayonet, which made the pikeman wholly redundant at last.

The 16th and 17th Centuries may also be thought of as the last years of individual armour: the period when the dynamic virtues of mobility and fire-power took precedence over the static virtue of armoured protection. But perhaps the most far-reaching change was the evolution of standing armies with uniform clothing and weapons – unknown since the Roman Empire. By the 1690s the unarmoured infantryman stood forth with musket and bayonet, the arbiter of battle for the next 200 years.

From knight to cavalry trooper

Though it is nearly always a mistake to look for natural 'partitions' in history, the wars of the Renaissance and Reformation can certainly be considered a watershed in the history of the soldier. Powder firearms had come to stay - no longer merely used in siege artillery, to batter down the stone defences of castles and towns, but as the main element of infantry fire-power. Halberdiers armed with pole weapons were no longer the sole defence against fast-moving shock infantry formations of pikemen. Though still in its infancy, musketry fire had proved its superiority over longbow and crossbow.

Viewed merely in terms of its efficiency as a firearm, the muzzle-loading arquebus and its successor the musket never exceeded the longbow in rate of fire and killing range; both were grossly inferior weapons. The vital difference was in practicality. Proficiency with the longbow could only be attained through constant practice from early manhood; proficiency with an arquebus could be attained in a matter of weeks. The longbow had been the ideal weapon for the peasant armies of the feudal era, but the arquebus and musket were far better suited to the slowly emerging new professionalism in soldiering.

Pavia, 1525: musketry triumphant

The shape of things to come was revealed by the Battle of Pavia on 24 February 1525, when the chivalry of France and their hired Swiss pikemen were torn apart by the fire-power of the Spanish arquebusiers. This was the first successful challenge of shock infantry - the pike phalanx - by professional missile infantry armed with powdered firearms, backed by artillery.

Pavia did not, of course, result in an overnight transformation in the composition of armies, any more than Bannockburn or Crecy, some 200 years earlier, had resulted in the immediate abandonment of the armoured knight. After Pavia, shock and missile infantry continued to co-exist as separate entities until the latter 17th Century, when the invention of the musket bayonet blended the roles of pikemen and musketeer. And even the advent of the bayonet did not end the value of the pike as the natural weapon for 'instant' armies. In 1940 the British citizen Local Defence Volunteers or Home Guard, raised to challenge any invasion by Hitler's **Wehrmacht**, relied predominantly on home-made pikes until rifles could be found for the volunteers. Five years later the Japanese, faced with an imminent American invasion of their home islands, prepared to raise a citizen militia 28 million strong which would have been armed with bamboo pikes. Fortunately the Japanese surrender, prompted by the use of the first atomic bombs, precluded the inevitable slaughter which must have ensued had the American invasion gone ahead.

Changes in the cavalry

Nor could Pavia and other demonstrations of the infantry's new fire-power eliminate the need for armoured protection for mounted troops. In the better-off military establishments, heavy cavalry continued to be provided with fully enclosed or 'close' helmets, breast and/or backplates and segmented limb armour until the middle 17th Century. Cheaper alternatives were the open helmet or **burgonet** and the plate-reinforced jerkin or **brigandine (right)**. Even the use of chain mail survived into the 17th Century, to be carried to the New World by European colonists. (Close helmets, plate trunk armour and chain mail remnants apparently used as limb armour have been unearthed at Martin's Hundred, Virginia, by excavations in the later 1970s.) The only real change in cavalry armour by the late 16th Century were in favour of lighter, more flexible suits; 100 per cent protection, as vainly pursued by the development of full plate armour, had been abandoned as impractical.

The biggest change in cavalry was therefore not in protection or even in edged and pointed weaponry. It was the provision of fire-power with the development of the long 'horse pistol' which, by the early 17th Century, had given a new twist to the employment of cavalry formations in combat.

Dreux, 1562: specimen battle from the wars of Religion

The Battle of Dreux was fought on 19 December 1562 in the French Wars of Religion (Protestant Huguenots versus Catholics). In many ways it provides a perfect 'test tube sample' of warfare in the later 16th Century. The encounter is notable for the high proportion of hired foreign professionals which fought on each side, and the outcome of the battle speaks volumes for their respective strengths and weaknesses.

The Catholic army

Commanded by the Duc de Guise, the Catholic army was the stronger of the two. By spinning out token negotiations with the Huguenots, Guise had won time to bring in considerable reinforcements to his army, which on the day of the battle numbered around 19,000 men.

The bulk of the cavalry in Guise's army seems to have been heavily-armoured **gendarmes** (this famous French word really means 'man-at-arms') lancers, protected with close helmet, breastplate and limb armour for arms and thigh. So far as it is possible to estimate numbers, Guise would have had about 3,000 **gendarmes**, with perhaps 500 light horse effective only in scouting or pursuit.

The Catholic infantry probably numbered about 15,000 strong and represented all major infantry types to emerge in the previous half-century; pikemen, halberdiers, arquebusiers, and **landknechte** with their pike-slicing heavy swords. There were probably about 6,500 French infantry, 3,200 Swiss and 3,200 Spanish and about 1,500 **landsknechte**. The Catholic infantry were backed by about 10-12 field guns which seem to have been of heavier metal, and certainly better served, than those on the Huguenot side.

Guise knew that the Huguenots, out-numbered as they were and operating in country virtually bare of supplies, were desperate for a decisive action. He deployed his forces to 'lie on the ropes' and soak up the Huguenot attack before unleashing his own counterstroke. The light horse and powerful **gendarme** concentration were stationed on the Catholic left flank; the Swiss pikemen held the centre, flanked by French infantry on the left and **landsknechte** on the right, with a powerful infantry/cavalry reserve including the Spanish foot behind the right flank.

The Huguenot army

Under the Prince de Condé, the Huguenot army numbered perhaps 12,00 strong, of which about 4,000 were cavalry. To make up his deficiency in heavy cavalry **gendarmes**, Condé had hired about 2,000 German mercenary **ritterrs** who proved to be a decided liability on the day of action: the **ritters** had to have their orders translated. Significantly, Condé also had to rely on about twice as many light horsemen as were serving in the Catholic army: probably over 1,000.

The Huguenot infantry consisted of about 5,500 French and 2,500 **landsknechte**, the latter massed in the centre with French infantry on each flank.

The battle lines were drawn by about noon on a December day, leaving only four hours of reasonable daylight. Condé, who was trying to march through Normandy to join an allied English expeditionary force holding Havre-de-Grace on the coast, was hoping for at least a partial victory which would drive Guise's army out of play until the Huguenots had crossed the Eure and Seine rivers. This he planned to accomplish with his cavalry. **Gendarmes** and light horse formed the Huguenot front line, the **ritters** formed the second line, and the infantry the third.

The Huguenot defeat

Condé opened the battle with a powerful gendarme charge against the Swiss in the centre, and another, commanded by his sub-commander Coligny, against the Catholic left-wing cavalry. Condé's first charge forced the Swiss to give ground, losing six guns; but a follow-up charge by the **ritters** was easily held by the Swiss, who proceeded to advance against the 'old enemy', the Huguenot **landsknechte**.

Huguenot prospects were not helped by Coligny's horsemen, who scattered the Catholic left-wind cavalry but made the familiar error of pressing too far in pursuit. This left the Huguenot infantry centre open to attack in overwhelming strength. Condé's **landsknechte** surrendered **en masse**, leaving the Huguenot French infantry to be crushed by the Catholic French and Spaniards, Condé himself being captured.

Most of the captured mercenaries were disarmed and sent home, with a hard core - professionals that they were - promptly joining the victorious army.

Armoured Cavalry in decline, c. 1618-1648

By the outbreak of the Thirty Years War (1618-1648) between the Protestant and Catholic states of imperial Germany, cavalry theory had been well on the way to becoming as rigid as it had been 300 years before, in the heyday of the armoured knight. But three murderous decades of intensive campaigning experience - not only during the German wars but in their parallel tailpiece across the Channel, the English Civil War of 1642-48 - broke the mould again.

As late as the 1630s it was still possible for the military theoretician to publish a handbook like John Cruso's **Militarie Instruction for the Cavallrie** (1632), in which the main types discussed were the armoured lancer and cuirassier. The ideal equipment for both, in Cruso's book, was the full close-helmet and 'three-quarter' armour, enclosing back, breast, arms, and the front of the leg to the knee. The cuirassier's weapons, however, were not lance and sword but the long 'pistolls' carried in holsters on each side of the saddle front.

Cumbersome drill for mass fire

Cruso's drillbook reveals that the pistol-carrying cuirassiers were expected to manoeuvre in square formations eight troopers across and eight deep, trotting sedately into pistol-shot range to 'give fire' before retiring to reload. Cruso gives an incredible total of 13 separate drill movements to accomplish the loading sequence between the initial 'Uncapp your Pistoll' to 'Present and give Fire'

and 'Returne your Pistoll'. The chief objections to this cumbersome equipment were fatigue to the wearer and a woeful loss of speed in return for only a modest weight of mobile firepower on the battlefield.

Hard experience taught practical sense. In 1639 the Knight Marshal of England was writing that 'it will kill a man to serve in a whole Curass. I am resolved to use nothing but back, brest and gauntlet **(steel guard for the left or bridle-hand)**; if I had a Pott for the Head that were Pistoll proofe it maye bee I would use it if it were light'. And those words of supreme practicality were written **before** the decade of hard experience provided by the English Civil War.

The Swedish system

In the Thirty Years War Gustavus Adolphus of Sweden, intervening as champion of the Protestant princes of Germany, demonstrated a new system vastly superior to the lumbering rigmarole advocated by Cruso. This involved a long-overdue return to the essential interdependence of cavalry and infantry.

To confound the imperial army at Breitenfeld (18 September 1630) Gustavus deployed his cavalry squares in an initially defensive pattern. Between each cavalry square was a musketeer company five files deep, the front-rank men kneeling so that the foremost two ranks could fire as one. They would then move to the back of the formation to reload while the rear ranks fired, resulting in a rate of fire three times greater than that of the imperial musketeers. The real advantage, however, was the tremendous flexibility which this 'checker-board' deployment gave the Swedes, enabling them to face instantly in any direction as a danger threatened. Gustavus declined to squander his cavalry in useless attacks but held it back for a decisive charge which split the imperial infantry from its supporting cavalry. The imperial army was routed with the loss of all 20 of its guns.

Results like this were not achieved by relying on attacks consisting of repeated measured doses of pistol fire.

Training-ground for the English

When the English Civil War broke out in 1642 the German wars, which still had six years to run, had served as a training-ground for volunteers from Britain for some two decades. At the outset of the war the Royalists had absorbed the lessons first, personified by Prince Rupert of the Rhine, nephew of King Charles and commander of the Royalist cavalry.

On the eve of the first battle between the Royalist and Parliamentatian armies, at Edgehill (23 October 1642) Rupert personally issued orders to the Royalist horse which were in startling contrast to the precepts of Cruso and his ilk - 'giving positive Orders to the Horse, to march as close as was possible, keeping their Ranks with Sword in Hand, to receive the Enemy's Shot without firing either Carbin or Pistol, till we broke in amongst the Enemy, and then to make use of our Fire-Arms as need should require; which order was punctually observed'. Hand-in-hand with the abandonment of the old pistol-volley technique came a new cavalry deployment reducing the depth of cavalry formations from six ranks or more to three. This broadened the front of the attack and enabled all the troopers to make full play with the sword after a charge at the gallop, it being easier to train cavalry recruits in basic swordplay than in the tricky art of handling a lance.

There was, as ever, a trade-off in results between the old system and the new. Slower, more deliberate cavalry attacks could rarely achieve the rapid results of a charge at the gallop. On the other hand, they were less likely to advance too far and leave the infantry exposed, a besetting sin of 'gung-ho' cavalry commanders.

OPPOSITE: *Lancer of c.1620 in heavy 'three-quarter' armour - stifling fully-enclosed or 'close' helmet, plate pauldrons and vambraces for the arms, backplate and breastplate, segmented plate tassets for the thighs. By the 1640s experienced campaigners were opting for an open 'pot' helmet (usually with face-protecting bars), back and breast, and maybe an extended steel gauntlet to protect the left or bridle arm, vital to be sure of controlling the horse in action.*

ABOVE: *The new-look - Swedish cavalry trooper of the later Thirty Years War, with the accent now on practicality rather than all-round protection regardless of fatigue.*

Out of the armoured chrysallis:cavalry

BELOW: Vignette of the heroic Royalist counterattack during the Battle of Lansdown Hill (5 July 1643) in the English Civil War. In this battle all the honours went to the Cornish pikemen who, regardless of losses from Parliamentarian artillery, musketry and repeated cavalry charges, stormed Lansdown Hill and held it until relieved. This achievement wiped out the early advantage won by the ponderous charge of Sir Arthur Haslerig's 'Lobsters', the only regiment of old-style mounted cuirassiers raised, by Parliament, during the Civil War. Having forced their way on to the hilltop the Cornishmen beat off three charges by the 'Lobsters' before they were reinforced by the rest of the Royalist army.

The trooper at centre is a dragoon: a type destined to be classified, by the late 18th Century, as a heavy cavalryman. In the mid-17th Century, however, the dragoon was still employed mainly as a 'musketeer on horseback'. He did not form part of the established shock cavalry but normally dismounted to fight, his principal weapons being the pistol and the short musket or carbine.

In what proved to be the decisive Royalist defeat of the war at Naseby (14 June 1645), a regiment of dismounted Parliamentarian dragoons provided covering fire from behind a line of hedges before remounting to join in the final sequence of charges against the hemmed-in Royalist infantry.

and infantry in the mid-17th Century

BELOW: A man-to-man infantry/cavalry encounter, this time from the Battle of the Dunes (4 June 1658). The battle was fought three months before the death of Oliver Cromwell, from 1653 the **de facto** dictator or 'Lord Protector' of the English Republic; it was an incident in Cromwell's highly effective foreign policy against Catholic Spain.

Cromwell had sent an expeditionary force to help France secure her frontier with the Spanish Netherlands by taking Dunkirk; the price for this assistance was the cession of Dunkirk, once taken, to England. The Battle of the Dunes was fought to repel a Spanish army advancing to the relief of Dunkirk, under siege by the Anglo-French army under Marshal Turenne. The resultant Spanish defeat ensured the capture of Dunkirk and its brief-lived spell under English rule. (Charles II sold Dunkirk to France for £400,000 in 1662).

In a sense the campaign was a miniature extension of the Civil War, for exiled Royalists were fighting on the Spanish side. Richard Scollins has depicted an encounter during the battle between an English Royalist officer and a musketeer. The latter's bandolier of cartridges can be seen but he has been caught out in the open with an unloaded musket. Fortunately for the musketeer his mounted opponent lacks a loaded pistol with which to shoot him down where he stands.

What is interesting is the stand-off nature of the confrontation, in which the natural advantage of a horseman over a dismounted opponent is largely cancelled. Though temporarily useless as a firearm, the reversed musket makes a formidable bludgeon, easily capable of beating down the officer's sword and leaving him helpless with a broken arm or leg. This is still some 20-odd years before the adoption of the muzzle bayonet, which effectively ended the dual role of the musket as firearm and club. Faced with a single infantryman armed with musket and fixed bayonet, the officer would find the odds much more in his favour.

Pikemen and gunner, 1650

By the middle 17th Century, the basic infantry building-block was still the square of pikemen, for the best employment of whose principal weapon an intricate arms drill was required. The pikeman at **left** is advancing in the charge, necessarily conducted at a steady pace to avoid breaking formation - 'very stately' was the phrase used to describe the advance of the English Royalist pikemen at Naseby in 1645.

Once the pike squares collided, the issue was decided 'at push of pike', the deciding factors being momentum, stamina and morale. Though enemy cavalry were usually received immobile, enemy pikemen were best met head-on to avoid being pushed off balance - the same principle as with a scrummage at rugby football. Only the adoption of the bayonet in the latter deciades of the 17th Century, merging the roles of musketeer and pikeman, brought the long history of pike infantry to its close.

RIGHT: *A gun team of c.1650, Artillery pieces were still mounted on heavy carriages and flying horse artillery, suitable for being whisked about the battlefield, still lay far in the future. This, plus an extremely low rate of fire, tended to restrict the value of artillery to the opening stages of battle, before the decisive infantry collision took place at close quarters.*

Soldiering on the eve of the

BELOW: *English cuirassier of 1658, of the time of the Dunkirk campaign. Body armour has now shrunk, like the shrinking tail of a metamorphosing frog, to a back-and-breast worn over a slash-proof tunic of buff leather.*

The three decades which followed the close of the Thirty Years War and the English Civil War (c. 1650-1680) were of profound importance to the history of the soldier. This period may be thought of as the 'military renaissance': a return to the state-funded, standing army of professional soldiers which had been unknown in Europe since the collapse of the Western Roman Empire twelve hundred years before.

Many inter-related historical trends helped bring about this military renaissance, but the most obvious was the new emergence of powerful monarchies, with the centuries-old dominance of the feudal nobility broken from above. This particular trend has been given the historians' label of the 'Age of Absolutism': the period 1660-1789, cut short by the French Revolution. The strengthening of absolute monarchies was a phenomenon which applied to every one of the leading powers which had fought across the religious divide in the Thirty Years War, Catholic and Protestant alike. It marked a formal acceptance of the need for military professionalism established by every major armed conflict since the latter half of the 15th Century.

In these years, England was the exception proving the rule. After a ten-year exile the monarchy was restored in 1660 with the powers of Parliament, not of the Crown, in the ascendant. Indeed, England's recent experience of military dictatorship expressly forbade the establishment of a standing army by the Restoration settlement. But even in England a standing instrument of armed force was retained as an essential item of state expenditure - not a royal army, but the Royal Navy.

Features of the military renaissance

Perhaps the most striking feature of the 17th Century military renaissance is the near-total eclipse of mercenary soldiering, an indispensable element of warfare in the 16th Century. The reason for this eclipse is that the mercenary 'soldier of fortune' no longer enjoyed a monopoly of the most effective blend of modern weaponry and technique. Since ancient times, mercenary troops have always thrived when such a blend is in high demand but limited supply. There are two reasons why, in military history, mercenary heydays have always tended to be brief. The first is the natural urge of mercenaries to 'retire on their earnings', which in the process of time limits both their effectiveness and their attractiveness to potential hirers - as witness the performance of the **landsknechte** on the losing side at **(**Dreux **pp.92-93)**. The second is the inevitable result of market forces: mercenaries have always been put out of business as soon as their particular weaponries and techniques are imitated on a wide scale.

As early as the middle years of the Thirty Years War, it was clear that the alternative to the hiring of mercenaries had already become established. This was the remodelling of national armies to include crack troops such as the Spanish pikemen, Swedish cavalry, musketeers and artillery, and, in England, the no less successful'New Model Army' raised by Parliament in the latter years of the Civil War. Nor, by the middle 17th Century, were infantry firearms and cannon in short supply, effective only in the hands of expensive specialists. Having increased dramatically both in quantity and quality, firearms could be purchased in sufficient quantities for national armies to be trained in their use. The mercenaries' monopoly was already part of history: demand no longer outstripped supply.

Drill-books and military systems

Another revealing symptom of the military renaissance was a growing tendency to treat warfare as an abstract phenomenon deserving of detailed study. This had not been the case during the Middle Ages, when warfare had been accepted as a fact of life by the largely illiterate laity and as a necessary evil visited on sinful man by the churchmen who held the monopoly of literacy and learning. But the new power of the printing-

'military renaissance', c.1650-1680

press festered the quickening interest in the human condition and natural phenomena (usually lumped together, in popular reference, as **'the Renaissance'**) from the late 15th Century, and by the early 17th Century the waging of war was coming under a deepening scrutiny.

Early proof that this new scientific approach to war was under way was furnished by the printed drillbooks, with which the early 17th Century abounded. Reference has already been made to one of them: John Cruso's **Militarie Instruction for the Cavall'rie (pp.94-95).** A superficial label for the period might well be the 'Age of the Military Drillbooks'; there had been nothing like them since the **De Re Militari** of the Roman Vegetius in the 4th Century AD. And they were accompanied by military treatises which brought all the new resources of mathematics and science to bear on the successful waging of war. All of them were based on the detailed application of geometry to the battlefield, starting from the premise that as guns fire in straight lines it was essential to use those lines to the best effect. This applied not only to field warfare but to siege tactics, yielding a rich crop of designs for geometrical fortress defences and of tactics for their reduction. Of all these military theoreticians the 'high priest' was the Frenchman Vauban (1633-1706), whose boast was that no fortress of his design was ever taken, and that no fortress which he attacked remained untaken.

New weaponry, new equipment

In terms of military 'hardware' the way to the military renaissance was paved by the grudging acceptance that there was no practicable antidote to the bullet and cannon-ball, other than the speedy capture or disablement of the enemy musketeers. Armour was not the answer; even with light or so-called 'pistol-proof' armour, the price in sacrificed mobility and rapid fatigue was too high. In the 1620s this had been the experience of the first colonists in America, with their armour and firearms yielding no decisive advantage over the naked Indians of Virginia. 'The savages are so light and swift, though we see them (being so loaded with armour) they have much advantage of us', lamented the redoutable Captain John Smith (of Pocahontas fame).

__BELOW:__ Officer of the Duke of York's Guard, Dunkirk 1658 – again with the accent on mobility rather than on rigid protection.

By 1660, therefore the days of the infantry pikemen were as numbered as those of the armoured lancer had been 30-odd years before. The search was on for an improved firearm suitable for general issue to the infantry, and no longer to specialized companies of musketeers. The pikeman was a species doomed by musketry and artillery, and the tactical thinkers were beginning to realise that the only answer to enemy musketry was musketry employed not necessarily in superior numbers, but in more effective concentrations at the key point.

The Franco-Dutch Wars,

In the late 16th and 17th Centuries the Dutch Republic, battling to break free from Spanish rule, restated the lesson taught by the Scots and Swiss 200 years before: that a small nation bent on national self-preservation can take on and beat a 'superpower' if it gets its military priorities right.

Apart from sea power, which remained more than a match for that of England until the 1670s, the Dutch relied on disciplined and soundly-armed infantry which could be mobilized at great speed. They also used natural defences, in emergency never shrinking from opening the sluice-gates and flooding their own farmland to stop the invader. With no manpower to waste on redundant, 'cannon-fodder' pike formations, which lingered on in other leading European armies, the Dutch followed the Swedish lead and went all-out for infantry and artillery fire-power.

Louis XIV and the new French army
In 1660 the young King Louis XIV of France assumed personal control of the French state, his immediate foreign policy consisting of conquering the Spanish-held provinces threatening the French northern and eastern frontiers. His biggest asset was that he was supremely well served by administrators steeped in the latest military developments. Foremost among these were his first two war secretaries, Michel le Tellier and the Marquis de Louvois (father and son), who rebuilt the French army on a sound regimental basis (instead of the traditional, quasi-feudal company system) and gave the service a proper administrative structure. Another leading light was Vauban, whose talents were by no means limited to siege warfare and the intricacies of military engineering. It was Vauban who urged Louvois (1669) to scrap obsolete pike formations and adopt the efficient new flintlock musket, and shortly after the revolutionary device of the ring or sleeve bayonet. Fortunately for the Dutch, who became adept in raising anti-French alliances, few of these French army reforms had taken full effect when Louis invaded the Netherlands in 1672.

c.1660-1680

OPPOSITE: French cavalry man, c.1680.
LEFT: Dutch infantry, c.1672.

Britain and France, c.1660-1690

BELOW: *British Royalist infantry, Sedgemoor campaign, 1685. The far more efficient flintlock musket was still not in general use; at Sedgemoor, during the rebel night attack, the glowing points of Royalist matches caused heavy casualties among Dumbarton's Scots. Note the clumsy 'plug' bayonet, which gave the musketeer a pike-weapon when charging or repelling cavalry, but which had to be removed when firing.*

Of all the new standing armies formed by the European powers in the late 17th Century, the most reluctantly created was that of Britain. In the Restoration Settlement which brought King Charles II home from exile in 1660, Parliament was determined to prevent a replay of the Civil War on the one hand, or the recent dictatorship of Cromwell's Republican army on the other. The restored King was therefore denied the right to maintain a standing army apart from a handful of guards regiments: the 1st Foot Guards, the Coldstream Guards, and two regiments of horse guards. These were to form the hard core of any British army which Parliament might deem necessary to raise for service abroad. The Guards regiments thus grudgingly conceded to Charles II were therefore the first regiments in the history of the standing British Army.

Had the Royal Navy failed to prevent an invasion of England (and it came perilously close in the 1690s) the ultimate defence force was the national militia. Fortunately never put to the test, in view of the military professionalism of Britain's leading enemies, the militia could on paper yield over 70,000 foot and about 6,000 horse; but as the militia was given little or no training or modern equipment its combat value on European battlefields was nil.

The standing army grows

But the hopes of the Restoration Parliament for a 'demilitarized' British monarchy were dashed by the all-too-military ambitions of Louis XIV and the need to take action against them. This inevitably took the form of sending troops to assist the blood enemy of Louis XIV: William of Orange, Stadholder or hereditary chief magistrate of the Dutch Republic. With Ireland's natural role as the ideal target for a flank attack against England, garrison troops had to be found to serve there. By the time that James II replaced Charles II in 1685, the strength of the standing British Army had already crept up to 19,000.

to a strength of some 35,000 and sought to make it his main guarantee of power by staffing it with Catholic officers. His reign began promisingly with the defeat of rebel forces supporting the Protestant Duke of Monmouth (Charles II's illegitimate son) at Sedgemoor in July 1685. But the pro-Catholic policies of James ended in disaster three years later when the 'Protestant wind' delivered the invading army of William of Orange to Torbay (5 November 1688). The mis-placed trust of James in his army was revealed by its support of William - most notably on the part of James's trusted general, John Churchill, the future Duke of Marlborough.

The exiled James attempted a comeback by landing in Ireland with French support, but William defeated him in the Battle of the Boyne (1 July 1690). Having made good his claim to the British throne, as the husband of James II's Protestant daughter Mary, William set about the expansion of the British Army to join the Dutch in opposing the French in the Netherlands.

The wars of William III

Given that it was 30 years since British troops had come up against first-rate Continental opposition, they acquitted themselves well during the weary campaigning in the Low Countries (1692-95), though forced to recover from costly defeats such as Steenkerk (August 1692) and Neerwinden (July 1693). The worst setback was at Landen in July 1693, which cost the Allies nearly 20,000 men. The biggest problem was not the quantity of British troops, whose numbers rose to a peak of over 90,000 in 1694 (less than half in the Low Countries): it was the precarious nature of British national finance to pay for it all. This was tackled (1693-94) by the creation of the National Debt and the founding of the Bank of England, which funded the momentous British achievements in the wars of Marlborough which followed William's death in 1702.

The army of James II

Aware of his acute unpopularity as a Catholic, James II expanded the army

ABOVE: *French infantryman of the time of the Battle of Steenkerk (August 1692). Distinctive uniform coat, flintlock musket with sleeve bayonet - the blueprint for standard infantry costume and equipment for the next 100 years.*

c.1700

THE 18th CENTURY

-1793

Neither change nor growth is always continuous. Sooner or later a temporary saturation-point is reached, and the upward line of growth levels off onto a plateau. After the prodigious changes undergone by warfare in the 16th and 17th Centuries, such a plateau was reached in the 18th Century. A conflict between an army of 1600 and 1690 is almost unimaginable, but an army of 1700 would have differed from an army of 1790 in few essentials. With regard to the latter contrast, the main differences would have been in details of costume.

From 1700 to the 1790s, the waging of war followed a clearly recognizable pattern notable for its limitations – on the size of armies, on their range of operations, on the duration and scope of campaigns. A direct legacy of the 17th Century was an obsession with sieges of strategic fortresses, limiting freedom of movement. But these limitations on warfare were not imposed, as is often suggested, by the influence of the contemporary 'Age of Reason' in philosophy. They stemmed rather from the high cost of maintaining standing armies and the badness of Europe's roads.

These considerations tended to tie the hands of even the greatest commanders. The Duke of Marlborough, for instance, was an unchallenged master of the 'set-piece' battle; but in ten major campaigns in the War of the Spanish Succession (1702-1715) he conducted only four major field actions compared with 30 sieges. Moreover, the comparative uniformity of 18th Century armies rendered battles extremely costly to both sides, and hence uncertain in outcome; at Zorndorf in 1758, during the Seven Years War (1756-1763) Russian casualties totalled 50 per cent while the Prussians lost 38 per cent. The uncertain issue of battle' was the classic phrase of the period.

If there was a pointer to the shape of things to come, it was the discomfiture of the British by the American colonist (1776-1783), the latter nevertheless being assisted to outright victory by the professional skills of their French allies.

Battle in the early 18th Century

BELOW: *British cavalry, French infantry at Blenheim (13 August 1704). This, the most famous of Marlborough's four great victories was clinched by a massed cavalry charge, some 6,000 strong, against the French centre. Constant British pressure against the village of Blenheim on the French right flank had drawn vital infantry support away from the French centre, where Marlborough chose to deliver his decisive blow. As he deployed his army Marlborough had blunted the French cavalry attacks by keeping line infantry, with its bayonet-hedge and blasting musketry, in close support of his own cavalry. The French cavalry, which committed the error of receiving the charging British at the halt, broke and fled at the first shock. This collapse left some 10,000 French infantry to be surrounded in the blazing ruins of Blenheim village with no option but surrender to avoid total annihilation.*

The 18th Century opened with Europe racked by two prolonged and exhausting conflicts whose combined spread extended from the Ukraine to Gibraltar, with 'brushfire' extensions fought by rival colonial outposts overseas. Both of these wars ended in

Blenheim (1704) and Poltava (1709)

victory for alliances formed to prevent the achievement of outright military supremacy by a single 'superpower'.

The **Great Northern War** of 1700-21 was no less hard-fought. In 1700 the young King Charles XII of Sweden was confronted by the Russia of Peter the Great, Saxony/Poland, and Denmark. Eliminating the Danish threat by August 1700. Charles invaded Saxony and brought its ruler Augustus, King of Poland, to terms in the Treaty of Altranstadt (1706). After subsequent victories in Poland Charles invaded Russia, reached Smolensk, but then suffered a crushing defeat at Poltava in the Ukraine (8 July 1709). Returning to Sweden in 1714 Charles battled on with his former enemies augmented by Prussia and Hanover. His death at Frederikshald in 1718 removed the last obstacle to peace.

BELOW: *Poltava, 1709 - Russian grenadier, Swedish Drabant or life guards cavalry (right).*

War of the Spanish Succession (1702-1715)

The Spanish Succession war was prompted by the attempt of Louis XIV to gain control of the global Spanish empire on the death of Charles II, the last Hapsburg King of Spain (1665-1700). This was challenged by the 'Grand Alliance' of the Hapsburg Empire, the Dutch Republic and Britain. The war spread to Italy and Spain (Britain's tenure of Gibraltar dates from 1704) but the main war theatre lay in the Low Countries and along the Rhine.

Though the war in the Low Countries mainly featured sieges and associated manoeuvre by the main field armies, the one major distraction was the Blenheim campaign of 1704. This featured Marlborough's daring invasion of southern Germany, ignoring the protests of his Dutch allies, to break France's ally Bavaria. Blenheim was no more an all-British victory than it was an all-French defeat. It should be seen as an Anglo-Imperial victory over a Franco-Bavarian army. The greatly superior teamwork on the Anglo-Imperial side was gained by the natural partnership of Marlborough and his 'great lieutenant', Prince Eugene of Savoy. A gifted general in his own right, Eugene commanded the allied right wing at Blenheim.

Marlborough's other great victories were Ramillies (23 May 1706), Oudenarde (11 July 1708) and Malplaquet (11 September 1709). The latter was the bloodiest 'Pyrrhic victory' of the war; the French withdrew in good order, having cost the allies some 25,000 killed and wounded, losing only two-thirds as many.

Frederick the Great and Prussia

BELOW: Austrian light infantryman, Loudon, 1759. Breaking ramrods were a problem from which the Prussians had been spared by adopting the iron ramrod.

One of the most momentous creations of the 18th Century was that of the Kingdom of Prussia, proclaimed on 18 January 1701 by consent of the Hapsburg Emperor Leopold I. The former Electorate of Brandenburg, ruled over by the Hohernzollern family which now became the royal dynasty of Prussia, was financially poor, geographically scattered and almost entirely devoid of natural resources. Converting this unpromising legacy into one of the most formidable military powers in the world was a superb achievement on the part of the first three Prussian Kings: Frederick I (1701-1713), Frederick William I (1713-1740) and Frederick II 'The Great' (1740-1786).

Prussia in the 18th Century was the nearest equivalent to an all-military state - the ancient Spartan ideal - since the Duchy of Normandy some 500 years before. Everything was subordinated to the needs of the Purssian Army whose development was naturally hindered by the modern Prussian population of little more than 2.5 million. The Prussian response to this fundamental population problem was to recruit from all over Europe, by force if need be. In the reign of Frederick William I over 40,000 foreigners were recruited or impressed into the Prussian Army, which by 1740 had been raised to an impressive strength of 89,000.

Frederick William's single-mindedness towards the expansion of his army was not without its bizarre side. This took the form of a royal mania for giant soldiers - 6 ft tall without shoes was the bare minimum height requirement - who formed the Potsdam 'Giant Grenadiers'. Foreign powers desirous of pleasing the Prussian King sent him presents of giant recruits, but no really tall man in Europe could count himself safe from the King's agents; it was said that a tall Italian priest was coshed in the middle of celebrating Mass and dragged off to be impressed into the Giants.

This manic obsession could well have been fatal for the Prussian Army as a whole - the upkeep of the Potsdam Giants was said to be eight times that of an ordinary infantry regiment - but this has to be kept in proportion. Crazy though he was when it came to outsize soldiers, Frederick William had a limitless eye for detail and practicality. It was on his orders that the Prussian Army was issued, from the 1720s, with iron ramrods instead of wooden ones. This apparently obvious, it may seem even trivial, improvement was in fact a vital reform. It was in every sense a life-saver, sparing the soldier from being left with a useless firearm when his ramrod broke on loading. This consideration apart, the adoption of iron ramrods boosted the rate of fire to over three rounds per minute. During their first defeat by the Prussians at Mollwitz in 1740 the Austrians (still gingerly using beechwood ramrods) reckoned that the Prussians were firing five rounds per minute to their two. Other considerations apart, an iron ramrod served as a useful fireproof spit on which the soldier could cook his dinner in the field.

Frederick the Great took the ramrod revolution even further by introducing the double-headed ramrod: one that did not have to be reversed for use after being withdrawn from its housing below the musket barrel.

LEFT: Prussian cavalryman of the Seven Years War (1786-63). Ably assisted by his cavalry commanders Seydlitz and Ziethen, Frederick trained his cavalry to press home their attacks at a full gallop, regrouping for as many charges as might be necessary.

The wars of Frederick The Great

In May 1740, Frederick II of Prussia inherited an army consisting of the best-drilled infantry in Europe, adequate in artillery but weak in cavalry. Though the Prussian Army had never been put to the test of a real war, Frederick had no hesitation in using it at once to snatch at a unique opportunity: the death of the Emperor Charles VI, who left no male heir. Eventually Maria Theresa succeeded as Emperess but Frederick exploited the period of disputed succession to seize the Austrian province of Silesia. He wanted Silesia for eminently practical reasons: for its minerals, for its industries and for its population of a million - vital recruiting material. As events were to prove, he had chosen an objective which the Prussian Army was just able to take and hold.

Frederick later admitted that no general ever made so many mistakes as he did in his first campaigns. The first battle of the Silesian wars, Mollwitz (10 April 1741), was won by the soundness of the infantry, Frederick and the indifferent Prussian cavalry having been chased from the field. But Frederick was a commander who rarely made the same error twice, and Silesia remained Prussian after the ensuing War of the Austrian Succession (1740-1748).

Well aware that the recovery of Silesia would be the primary Austrian objective in any future war with Prussia, Frederick used the precarious peace agreed in 1748 to build up the Prussian cavalry arm. In working out the type of cavalry he wanted, Frederick came to perfect an entirely new pattern of making war. Prussia lacked the resources for leisurely campaigning, in which the avoidance of battle became almost a virtue of generalship. Nor could the Prussian homeland be secured by a strict defensive; the scatter of Prussian territories lacked interior lines and a cohesive frontier for such a luxury. Frederick's new strategy was aimed at carrying the war into enemy territory (which could then be used to support the Prussian Army) and forcing a decisive battle against the most dangerous enemy of the moment.

Crisis and triumph, 1756-63

Frederick was granted an eight-year respite before, in 1756, he was confronted by an intensely dangerous alliance between Austria and Russia. In the ensuing Seven Years War (1756-63) Prussia received only token aid from her main ally against Austria, Russia and France: Britain. Small wonder that Frederick's epic defence of Prussia against all comers is still held in such unique regard in German history. In those seven years Frederick experienced all the extremes of triumph and utter despair which it is possible for a general to know. He won repeated victories over enemies who, he bitterly knew, would never rest until he and his kingdom were destroyed; he suffered repeated defeats; he had to suffer the humiliation of paying the invader to evacuate the burning ruins of the Prussian capital, Berlin. But he never gave up until the 'miracle of the House of Brandenburg', the death of the Russian Tsarina Elizabeth in January 1762, caused the enemy coalition to fall apart.

Frederick's two classic victories were won over the French at Rossbach (5 November 1757) and over the Austrians at Leuthen (5 December 1757). Both vindicated his refusal to follow the conventional pattern of 18th Century combat (a gory frontal collision in line-abreast with the infantry in the centre and the cavalry on the flanks) and heralded a new era in tactics.

'Fifteen' and 'Forty-Five':

In Britain, the years 1715 and 1745 saw the defeat of two challenges to the Hanoverian dynasty which had succeeded Queen Anne in 1714. These challenges were mounted by the Jacobites, supporters of the family of the exiled King James II, who based their hopes on the exploitation of Scottish resentment at English rule.

In fighting off the Jacobite threat the English were considerably helped by the mediocre talents of the 'Old Pretender' Prince James Edward (in the 'Fifteen') and the 'Young Pretender' Prince Charles Edward (in the 'Forty-Five'). Both were left to their own devices as their French patrons could spare neither ships nor troops to assist Jacobite rebellions in Britain. Though both were supported by the majority of the Scottish Highland clans, neither managed to win large-scale backing in the Lowlands.

The resultant contest between the Jacobites and the British Government forces therefore came down to clashes between drilled troops and motley arrays of Highland clansmen; but until the British opened up the Highlands by the building of military roads their task was one of considerable difficulty. Regular troops were, in the main, tied to the few roads for their supplies; the Highlanders thrived on ambushes and hit-and-run attacks, pressed home with the claymore or 'great sword'. At the outset of each rising the numbers of Government troops facing the Jacobites were small, but this was more than offset by clan disunity and resistance to discipline.

defeat of the Scottish clansmen

The only stand-up fight in the 'Fifteen' was at Sherriffmuir (13 September 1715) when 3,300 Government troops fought 10,000 Jacobites to a standstill and prevented the insurgents from breaking south into the Lowlands. On the same day, at Preston in Lancashire, 4,000 Highlanders and Bordermen, after an abortive invasion on north-west England, surrendered after being surrounded by Government forces. There was no Government follow-up after Sherriffmuir; the Jacobite forces melted away after their lacklustre Prince returned to France.

The attempt of Prince Charles Edward in the 'Forty-Five' was altogether more serious and opened with a resounding Jacobite victory. This was the 'battle' of Prestonpans, when a force of ill-trained Government troops under General Sir John Cope was cut to pieces in under ten minutes by a Highland charge out of the mists. After the ill-judged invasion of England turned back from Derby however, the Jacobite host was pulverised by Government musketry at Culloden (16 April 1746).

OPPOSITE: *Vignette of the action at Sherriffmuir in 1715.*

BELOW LEFT: *Clansman of the 'Forty-Five', with claymore and target (shield).*

BELOW RIGHT: *Government officer, Culloden.*

America's fight

ABOVE: *Private of 64th Regiment, biting open a cartridge during reloading.*

RIGHT: *Grenadier of 5th Foot Regiment.*

OPPOSITE: *The great British hope which never materialised in sufficient numbers - an American 'Tory' or Loyalist infantryman, enlisted for service against the rebel 'Patriots'.*

for freedom, 1775-1783

When resistance to the force of British arms began in the American 'Thirteen Colonies' in the spring of 1775, only a handful of American activists really believed that total independence was their true goal. Indeed, most 'Americans' in 1775 were proud to be British and only took action against the mother country because they felt their rights **as** Britons were being infringed by unfair, remote-control taxation. It was only 12 years since Britain had emerged from the Seven Years War - a true world war in which France and her allies had been confounded in land and sea battles from Canada to Bengal. As British subjects, the American colonists had played their part in that victory (on land against the French and their surrogate Indian 'troops' in Canada, and at sea as privateers preying on French trade) and were proud of it. What they objected to was the heavy postwar taxation levied by the British Government to pay for the war which the colonists had helped to win; and the garrisonning of regular troops on American soil (also to be paid for by the colonists) to enforce British authority.

The 'shots heard round the world'

By the autumn of 1774 the American colonists were so far from obtaining satisfaction for their objections to the new taxation that they summoned a 'First Continental Congress' at Philadelphia. Main item on the agenda were the recent 'Coercive Acts' passed by the British to levy compensation on Boston, Massachusetts, for dumping tea into Boston Harbour in protest. Congress advised the Massachusetts delegates to form its own government and raise its own citizen militia to resist all attempts at further coercion.

The enthusiastic response to the forming of the Massachusetts militia was an obvious direct challenge to the 4,000 British troops in Boston under General Gage, the Military Governor. Gage did what he could to lessen the threat by seizing all arsenals and ammunition depots likely to fall into the hands of the colonists. One of these attempts sent 800 British troops from Boston to Concord in April 1775.

On 19 April the 'shots heard round the world' were fired against 70 American militiamen at Lexington. The British marched on to Concord after a heartening skirmish which had cost them one man hit in the leg, eight militiamen dead and ten wounded. But the day ended with a miserable and costly British fighting retreat back to Boston, sniped at all the way by militiamen who inflicted heavy losses: 73 killed, 174 wounded and 26 missing. By the end of the month, Gage's men in Boston were hemmed in by some 15,000 militiamen from all over New England. Up on the Canadian border, militiamen under Benedict Arnold and Ethan Allen captured the forts of Ticonderoga and Crown Point.

Bunker Hill: Heavy British Losses

Emboldened by these successes, a second Congress authorised the formation of a 'Continental Army' based on the militiamen round Boston. Three days later, however, Gage (who had been reinforced and ordered to scatter the rebels) launched a disastrous attempt to push the militiamen off the heights round Boston. The result was the Battle of Bunker Hill (17 June 1775), which the British only took at bayonet point after the American defenders had run out of ammunition. British casualties were appalling: 1,054 out of 2,200 with at least 226 killed.

After Bunker Hill Gage resumed the defensive in Boston, pleading for reinforcements that never came.

Throughout the autumn and winter of 1775-76 the Virginian George Washington strove to lick the Continental Army into a semblance of regular order. On 4 March 1776 he moved, occupying Dorchester Heights and emplacing guns dragged south from Ticonderoga to menace Boston and its harbour. Thus surprised, the British evacuated Boston on 17 March and shipped their garrison to Halifax, Nova Scotia before despatching an expeditionary army for the reconquest of the rebel colonies.

The turning point: Saratoga, 1777

The success of the Continental Army in forcing the British to evacuate Boston was fleeting, for the Royal Navy was still supreme at sea; and in July 1776, even as the leaders of the American Congress in Philadelphia were drafting their 'Declaration of Independence', British troop transports were pouring into New York to begin the build-up for the reconquest of the rebel colonies.

Did the British ever have a hope of winning? The answer has to be yes, if 'winning' is taken to mean destroying the Continental Army. Whether or not such a victory (measured in conventional terms) would have won the war is an entirely different matter. It is certain that Britain lacked the manpower to hold down 2.5 million colonists over an area of a quarter of a million square miles - as she would have had to do, given the mood of the colonists by 1776 and the utter refusal of the British Government to accede to their demands.

At its maximum paper strength the entire British Army was understrength by European standards, yet because of Britain's ever-increasing need to provide colonial overseal garrisons no other European army every found it so hard to concentrate its available forces on a single vital objective. The timing of the American war could also hardly have been worse from the British point of view. In 1775 the British Army had just enjoyed 12 years of peace, which had had the inevitable result of shrinking actual complements still further.

The hated Hessians

The British therefore followed a completely typical ploy (typical, that is, by European standards) and hired surrogate troops for service in America. The German principalities were combed for the hiring of troops, most notably from the Hesse, Brunswick, Waldeck and Anspach, to flesh out the understrength British forces available for service across the Atlantic. This the Americans took as a personal insult in what they regarded as a purely domestic quarrel. Though the British could not have done without them, the employment of these German troops has to be considered an adverse factor when the chances of a successful outcome for Britain are weighed in the balance. The actual combat value of these German troops, generically referred to as 'Hessians', was uncertain and they were naturally prone to desertion, but they were certainly not as useless as has been claimed. Indeed, the sharp-shooting **jägers** from Anspach were among the best troops serving on either side.

Indifferent British leadership

What let the British down was not the combat value of the troops they used in America, but mediocrity in command. There was nothing like enough energy or imagination to tackle this war without precedent, in which the destruction of Washington's Continental Army as a fighting force was nevertheless an obvious first priority. The best efforts of the troops were squandered by the British attempt to direct the war from across the Atlantic, instead of entrusting operations to a commanderinchief 'on the spot'. Indeed, no such commander-in-chief was ever appointed and the campaign which cost Britain the war was bungled by misunderstandings between the generals involved, compounded by errors at home.

Autumn 1776: the New York campaign

New York was chosen as the base from which the reconquest of the American colonies would proceed. Thanks to the good offices of the Royal Navy, by September 1776 the Continental Army was confronted by some 45,000 British and German troops, 10,000 of them in Canada and the rest concentrated in New York under General Sir William Howe. The second phase of the war began in October/November 1776, with Washington's army successively pushed out of Long Island, away from New York and across New Jersey into Pennsylvania. If Howe had pressed an energetic windter campaign it might

BELOW: *From rebel militia to regular infantry - private of the Delaware Company, Continental Army.*

RIGHT: *Anspach* ***jäger*** *in British service. These marksmen were by far the most effective of the 'Hessian' troops from the German states which the British hired for service in the American War of Independence.*

have been a very different story, but he allowed Washington to strike back across the ice-laden Delaware River (25 December), surprising the Hessians at Trenton (26 December/ and capturing 1,000 of them. He then bypassed 6,000 British troops under Lord Cornwallis, and at Princeton (3 January 1777) surprised and defeated three British regiments moving up to support Cornwallis. These victories, earned by a daring completely lacking on the British side, induced Howe to go into winter quarters before settling accounts with Washington in the following year.

The British master-plan for 1777 was coined in London and bungled from London. The idea was for Howe to march north from New York and join with a second army advancing south from Canada under Generaly Burgoyne. This was to be the prelude to the isolation and reconquest of New England, regarded in London as the hotbed of the American rebellion. But the outcome was a disastrous failure to achieve proper collaboration between the two British armies. Having failed to destroy Washington, Howe switched his objective to the capture of the rebel 'capital', Philadelphia, shifting his forces from New York to the head of Chesapeake Bay by sea. This left Burgoyne, all unknowing, completely isolated as he began the southward march from Canada.

Burgoyne's advance through difficult country, burdened by an excessively powerful artillery train of over 40 guns, was slowed by American militiamen who constantly ambushed outposts of the labouring column and felled trees in its path. By the end of July he had reached the headwaters of the Hudson but his rate of advance was down to a mile a day, while American militiamen continued to reinforce the opposing General, Horatio Gates. On 16 August a column of 700 Hessians and Loyalists, sent by Burgoyne into the Green Mountain country to forage for horses, food and wagons, was cut to pieces by 2,000 Americans at Bennington; a relief force of 650 was also driven back after being badly mauled.

Burgoyne nevertheless pushed on to the hoped-for rendezvous with Howe (whose foces never even landed in the Chesapeake until 25 August) but was halted at Saratoga by some 7,000 Americans, dug in to block Burgoyne's roiad south to Albany. After failing to break through on 19 September he waited for three weeks, hoping for Gates to attack - but Gates sat it out, gaining reinforcements daily while Burgoyne's men went on half rations and their morale slumped. On 13 October Burgoyne accepted the inevitable and sued for terms.

The war transformed

Howe's subsequent capture of Philadelphia was a trivial exchange for the Saratoga fiasco, which transformed the war. This outright American victory brought first France, then Spain and Holland into the war on the American side. The most important direct result of Saratoga was the signing of treaties of commerce and alliance (6 February 1778) between France and the newly-styled 'United States of America'; Saratoga had earned the Americans the right to be taken seriously by Britain's most bitter enemies. The British would hold New York; they would even win some impressive victories in the southern colonies; but after Saratoga their last chance of victory had gone.

23

Battle in the South, 1778-1781

The British disaster at Saratoga in October 1777 more than outweighed the limited successes won by Howe on the Delaware. Howe had begun his march on Philadelphia in early September, beating Washington on the Brandywine River (11 September) and entering Philadelphia on the 26th. While Howe's army of nearly 20,000 went into comfortable winter quarters, Washington's men passed a winter of acute discomfort 20 miles away, at Valley Forge. For the second winter of the war, Howe's refusal to depart from the set pattern of 18th Century warfare and wage an agressive winter campaign saved Washington and his army from disaster.

Howe had, in fact, accepted that there was no chance of foreseeable victory in America and asked for permission to resign his command. This was granted in February 1778, Howe's successor being the former commander in New York, General Sir Henry Clinton. The new British commander lacked neither energy nor the wit to see that the original British plan for reconquering the American colonies had been ruined by the events of 1777. Clinton's strategy was to cut his losses in the north and, while retaining New York, set about the conquest of the southern colonies. He therefore evacuated Philadelphia on 18 June 1778 but his southern strategy had to be shelved for a year by the entry into the war of a new factor: the battle fleet of France, which arrived off the Delaware Capesd on 8 July.

This transformed the whole situation, for with French support from the sea Washington had every chance of taking New York: the only British base in the colonies. Clinton thereupon set off on a rapid overland march across New Jersey, battering Washington's reinforced army out of the way at Monmouth Court House, and making sure of New York with the excellent co-operation of Admiral Lord Howe's naval force. Thwarted at New York, the French fleet under d'Estsaing sailed for the West Indies; but its undefeated presence in American waters meant that Britain's formerly undisputed control of the sea was in jeopardy.

PREVIOUS PAGES. The rival armies at the Battle of Guilford Court House (15 March 1781), a hard fought victory for the army of Cornwallis on its ill-fated march to surrender at Yorktown.

The war shifts south

By December 1778 the immediate threat to New York had passed, and Clinton wasted no time in resuming his strategy for the conquest of the Douthern colonies. His first objective was Georgia, where American opposition was weakest, using troops shipped south from New York as well as the small British gfarrison in Florida. On 23 December 1778, 3,500 troops were landed near Savannah, capturing the town six days later while 2,000 more came marching up from St. Augustine in Florida. Marching inland, the combined British forces took Augusta on 29 January 1779.

Despite this promising start, the British still needed a secure base to supply their forces in the south and the new campaign spread inexorably northward. Though delayed by another ineffective foray by d'Estaing's fleet, Charleston in South Carolina was captured in May 1780. This solid British success was largely made possible by the prowess of the famous 'British Legion', a force of Loyalist volunteers raised by Lieutenant-Colonel Sir Banastre Tarleton. The Legion, trained to fight either as cavalry or as infantry, severed American communications between Charleston and the North and was instrumental in the isolation of Charleston from the landward.

From Charleston to Yorktown

Charleston was, however, the last major American setback of the war. In July 1780 the Comte de Rochambeau landed at Newport with an expeditionary force of over 5,000 regular French troops to operate with Washington's army. When he advanced from Charleston into Virginia, Cornwallis was trapped on the

RIGHT: *The cavalry of Banastre Tarleton charges to defeat in the Battle of the Cowpens (17 January 1781) during the North Carolina campaign.*

Yorktown peninsula and forced to surrender (19 October 1781) with 7,000 men.

Guilford Court House, 1781:

The Battle of Guilford Court House was fought on 15 March 1781 between the British army under Lord Cornwallis and the southern American army under General Nathanael Greene. Cornwallis had been seeking a decisive action with Greene to clinch the British conquest of North Carolina, but by the middle of March 1781 the vicissitudes of the campaign had reduced his army to 2,000 effectives. The bulk of Greene's army - 4,000 out of 4,500 - consisted of militia, but these were armed with rifles (the most effective American weapon of the war) and had performed well against Banastre Tarleton's men at the Cowpens in January.

The balance of forces on the morning of 15 March therefore featured greatly superior American numbners against veteran British regulars; and American rifle-fire, with its greater accuracy, against the smoothmore musket volleys of the British and Hessian infantry.

Greene deployed his militiamen in two forward lines, with his Continentals in the rear and the light horse on the flanks, to meet the British and Hessian attack. The advancing ranks suffered heavy losses from the American rifle fire, but held together

harbinger of American victory

with great bravery to drive back the militiamen and close with the Continentals.

Faced with the choice of gambling everything on an all-out battle of attrition, Greene chose to withdraw. Cornwallis could claim his victory - but he had lost 100 dead and over 400 wounded, while American losses were lower. Not only was Cornwallis unable to follow up the retreating Americans and make certain of victory, but after the battle he was no longer able to maintain himself in North Carolina. Cornwallis accordingly headed east, via Wilmington, to Virginia - and eventual surrender at Yorktown.

A puny skirmish by European standards, Guilford Court House may therefore be considered one of the decisive actions in the last phase of the War of Independence - a conflict which the British had undertaken in the fatal belief that mere colonials would never stand up to the fire-power of regular troops. It was Greene, and not Cornwallis, who resumed the offensive after Guilford Court House, pinning down the British in South Carolina and Georgia.

1792

THE REVOLUTIONARY AND NAPOLEONIC WARS

-1815

The wars of 1792-1815 shattered the 18th Century concept of warfare conducted by small professional armies. In the wars of Frederick the Great, a period (1740-62) almost identical to the Revolutionary and Napoleonic Wars, only 12 battles had been fought engaging more than 100,000 men on both sides. Between 1792 and 1815 there were 49 such battles. The age of mass armies had arrived, and with it the temptation to rely on voracious draughts of manpower to recoup the mistakes of generals which played so large a part in Napoleon's eventual downfall.

Before their eventual defeat by the Allied coalitions of 1813-1815, the huge conscript armies of Revolutionary and Napoleonic France had marched into every capital of Europe save London. But these spectacular French victories were not solely due to the energy released by the French Revolution or the genius of Napoleon in exploiting it. For over half a century before the Revolution, military thinkers had been advocating the concept of the CITIZEN SOLDIER, fighting to defend his homeland from motives of patriotism and duty.

Moreover, the pre-Revolutionary French army had undergone several important reforms, most notably in the improvement of artillery. This latter factor was vital, for revolutionary zeal proved no substitute for military professionalism. After a shattering series of defeats, the French Republican victory at Valmy in September 1792 – won by regular army units stiffening the revolutionary levies – was the prelude to the great years of Republican and Imperial conquest.

Republican triumph: the legend of

The outbreak of the Revolutionary War in April 1792 was the work of comparatively moderate revolutionaries in Paris, who saw a 'people's war' against hostile neighbouring monarchies as the ideal way of getting King Louis XVI to declare either for the Revolution or against it. The green Republican volunteers were assured that the will to conquer and revolutionary fervour would guarantee victory - but most Revolutionary recruits had barely learned how to load muskets, fix bayonets and form square when charged by cavalry. The first encounters with Austrian regular troops were disastrous, with units breaking and fleeing amid shouts of betrayal, often murdering their officers.

After three months of unbroken French defeats on the frontiers, the extremists in Paris launched a second revolution, jailing the King, proclaiming not only a National Convention but a crusade of terror against all internal enemies of the Republic. Luckily for them Austria, Prussia and Russia were all concentrating on the final division of defenceless Poland. Had this not been the case the armies of the anti-Revolutionary 'First Coalition' could probably have marched right into Paris by the high summer of 1792. It was not until 19 August that the Duke of Brunswick led a coalition army of Prussians and Austrians into France. Whereupon the weather broke, weeks of rain reducing the countryside to a bog and slowing the Allies to a muddy crawl. Their strength of 75,000 began to shrink as dysentery took its toll in the ranks and the supply columns strung out further and further to the rear. By 8 September, however, Brunswick's leading troops were across the Meuse River and pushing into the forests and defiles of the Argonne.

Waiting for them on the other side, blocking the road to Paris, were the combined French 'Army of the Centre', some 40,000 strong. This army was not like the ramshacksle forces which had been so badly beaten since the outbreak of the war. Every one of the French Generals was a pre-Revolutionary veteran; the French C-in-C, Charles François Dumouriez, 53 years old, had first seen action in the Seven Years War (1759-62) and his artillery commander, the Comte d'Abovile, had first fought the British at Fontenoy in 1745. The French Republican units were soundly underpinned by regular forces, particularly with regard to the artillery. The latter was to prove the decisive factor in the coming engagement: the Battle of Valmy on 20 September.

The 'cannonade of Valmy'

Confident though he was of victory, Dumouriez failed to keep all the passes from the Argonne properly covered and allowed the painfully advancing Allied columns to wheel south, cutting off the French from Paris and trapping them with their backs to the Argonne. Despite this

Valmy, 20 September 1792

apparently hopeless position, the French held firm as the Prussians advanced to attack on 20 September, encouraged by the steadiness of the regular army units whose guns were sited along a low ridge covering a muddy valley.

Brunswick had planned an artillery bombardment of the French line, followed by a frontal attack; but the effect of the Prussian bombardment was lessened by the mud (which prevented shot from ricochetting through the French ranks) and the spirit with which the French gunners returned fire. The evident difficulties encountered by the Prussian infantry, struggling forward through the mud, prompted Brunswick to call off the attack. Further Prussian fire again failed to dislodge the French and Brunswick finally decided to decline further action. The troops of Revolutionary France had emerged with credit from their first baptism of fire, against the most feared soldiers in Europe: the military machine bequeathed by Frederick the Great.

OPPOSITE: *Prussian infantry of the time of Valmy - a defeat of inept Prussian leadership rather than of the Prussian soldier.*

BELOW: *French troops at Valmy, after which a Prussian officer shrewdly wrote "You will see how these little cocks will raise themselves on their spurs ... We have lost more than a battle. The 20th September has changed the course of history".*

ABOVE: British infantry of the time of the Helder campaign (August-November 1799). The troops were quite unable to mount a rapid advance south from the beach-head, largely because the War Office had landed them without adequate stores or wheeled transports. The culprit was, as usual, political ignorance. Confident expectations in Whitehall that the Dutch farmers would flock to hand over their horses and wagons to their liberators were dashed, and the French had removed all boats and barges from the canals.

The momentous run of French Republican victories after Valmy was greatly assisted by the inability of France's enemies - Britain, Austria, Prussia and briefly Spain - to agree on a joint strategy and pool their efforst against the Republican armies. This enabled the French to tackle their enemies piecemeal and in the space of four years achieve what the armies of Louis XIV had failed to do in 50 years: conquer the entire Left Bank of the Rhine and replace Austria as the dominant power in northern Italy.

After Valmy and the retreat of the undefeated but over-stretched Prussian army, Dumouriez advanced into the Austrian Netherlands, won a second victory at Jemappes on (6 November 1792) and took Brussels; but in the spring of 1793 the Allied First Coalition (now including Britain, Holland and Spain) hit back. After being beaten at Neerwinden (18 March 1793) Dumouriez deserted to the Allies and the Austrians retook Brussels. Under the organising genius of Lazare Carnot, however, the Republic mobilized the entire male population capable of bearing arms and put 14 hastily-organized armies into the fdield. This was a burst of energy (sustained by the terror of the guillotine radiated by the Committee of Public Safety back in Paris) completely unmatched on the Allied side, which paid the price in 1793-95.

Belgium, Holland and Italy

The full fury of the Republican offensive broke in May-June 1794, when the Austro-British cordon defending Belgium was shattered by three rapid French victories at Turcoing, Charleroi and Fleurus. Belgium had been overrun by Autumn 1794, but the river barriers of Holland granted the Allies no respites. An unusually cold winter froze the River Waal, offering General Pichegru an ice-bridge across the river which he avidly took. On 20 January 1795 the French entered Amsterdam and proclaimed a puppet 'Batavian Republic'.

The French conquest of the Low Countries prompted the break-up of the First Coalition, with Prussia concluding a separate peace with France in March 1795. Though repeatedly defeated and forced to retire beyond the Rhine, Austria fought on in Italy; but in March 1796 a further run of Allied disaster began with the first Italian campaign of the French 'Army of Italy' under General Bonaparte.

Bonaparte in Italy 1796-97

When the young Napoleon took over the Army of Italy in late March 1796, he was only 27. His first army command did not consist of veterans from the conquest of the Low Countries. Morale in the Army of Italy was near rock-bottom due to arrears of pay, uninspired leadership, and gross neglect in supply and equipment; "one battalion has mutinied on the grounds that it had neither boots nor pay", he reported. Bonaparte therefore had tod start by restoring discipline and fighting spirit, promising not only victory and fame but ample supplies and cash from the spoils of Italy.

Bonaparte's first victories were mountain battles in the Maritime Alps (Montenotte, Millesimo, Dego, San Michele, Ceva, Mondovi) in April 1796. These actions, all contrived to yield French attacks in superior local strength, split the Austrians from their Piedmontese allies and forced the Piedmontese to sue for a separate peace. He then pursued the Austrian army east, beating the Austrian rearguard in a hard-fought river crossing at Lodi on 10 May, and entered Milan on the 14th. By the end of the month he had given his men half their pay in silver which, added to the experience of unbroken victory, reinforced their confidence in their young commander - and encouraged him to make further demands on their endurance.

ABOVE: Russian infantry, 1799. The experiences of the Italian/Swiss campaign showed that given the right leadership there was little to distinguish the Russian soldier from the French in courage and endurance. Flexibility, the need to react positively to the unexpected setback, was the Russians' weakest point; the Russian troops serving with the British in North Holland were severely demoralized by the news of the setbacks suffered by their countrymen in Switzerland.

Due to the failure of the French offensive north of the Alps across the upper Rhine, the Army of Italy was exposed to repeated and weighty Austrian attempts to raise the siege of Mantua (blocking the French advance into Austrain Venetia.) There were four such attempts, yielding the French victories of Castliglione (August 1796), Bassano (September 1796), Arcola (November 1796) and Rivoli (January 1797), after which Mantua capitulated. Reinforced by two fresh divisions, Bonaparte invaded the Austrian Tyrol in March 1797 and pushed to within 100 miles of Vienna before the Austrians accepted his offer of an armistice. The ensuing peace treaty of Campo Formio took Austria out of the war, leaving Britain to battle on alone. Nearly 18 months passed before a second anti-French coalition took shape, this time consisting of Britain, Austria and Russia.

The Russians in Italy

The most spectacular intervention of the ensuing 'War of the 2nd Coalition' (1798-1800) was that of the Russian expeditionary force sent through the Mediterranean to help the Austrians eject the French from northern Italy and Switzerland. It was commanded by the famed General Suvorov, whose victories on the Trebbia and at Novi virtually destroyed the French Army of Italy and recovered all provinces lost to Bonaparte in 1796-97. When Suvorov led his Russians over the St. Gotthard Pass into Switzerland, however, he found that General Massena had routed the combined Austro-Russian force under Korsakov in Zurich; there was nothing for it but a costly retreat.

The other Russian intervention during the War of the 2nd Coalition was in collaboration with the British: the ill-fated Helder campaign of August-November 1799. This ambitious venture was intended to be integrated with the Allied moves against the French forces on the upper Rhine, in Switzerland and in northern Italy, driving south to liberate Holland and Belgium. Though the British expeditionary force landed and took Den Helder on 28 August 1799, the liaison between the Allied forces was wretched and the Russians did not arrive until the British in their beach-head had beaten off a series of French attacks. Inept and ill co-ordinated Allied pushes in September and October were beaten off with ease; the only real chance had been a headlong advance after the first landings. Conversely, the French failed to liquidate the Allied beach-head and a stalemate resulted, resolved by an armistice on 18 October This provided for an unmolested Allied evacuation to be completed by the end of November.

Though 1799 ended in ignominy for the Allies, it was nevertheless remarkable for having provided the first (and so far the only) operations of Russian troops in Holland and Italy. The Helder campaign was also a timely reminder that amphibious operations have little chance of success without meticulous preparation and training. For the British, however, it did provide invaluable experience for the expedition sent to eject the French from Egypt (FOLLOWING PAGES), during which the problems created by inter-allied friction were absent.

The French and British in Egypt,

BELOW: *French cavalry in action with the heavy cavalry of the Mameluke army during the Battle of the Pyramids (21 July 1798). Bonaparte's victory outside Cairo destroyed the Mamelukes as a fighting force and gave control of Lower Egypt to the French.*

After his Italian triumphs of 1796-97, Bonaparte was entrusted with the most ambitious offensive venture ever mounted by the French against Britain: the conquest of Egypt and the Middle East to cut off the British from the source of their wealth in India. The 'Army of the Orient', 36,000 strong, sailed from Toulon on 19 May 1798, protected by the battle fleet of 13 ships of the line under Admiral Brueys. Most of Bonaparte's troops were veterans from the Army of Italy - at least a partial explanation for the French collapse in Italy in the following year. The fleet of transports numbered some 300 ships.

The expedition's first success was against Malta, captured from the Knights of St John after only token resistance on 12 June. Leaving 3,000

July 1798-November 1801

troops to garrison Malta, the fleet sailed on to disembark the army and capture Alexandria on 2 July. Bonaparte then left 6,000 men to hold Alexandria, leading the remaining 25,000 on a strenuous desert march towards Cairo. The Mamelukes, warrior overlords of Egypt, then played into the hands of the French by offering battle with their only field army.

Battle of the Pyramids

The destruction of the Mamelukes at the Pyramids (21 July 1798) anticipated the destruction of the Dervish army at Omdurman (pp.174-175) a century later. It was certainly the same story: the savaging of fanatical attacks by modern European fire-power, most notably artillery firing grapeshot and musketry volleys from infantry deployed in square formation. French losses at the Pyramids were only 30. Bonaparte entered Cairo in triumph on 24 July, but on 1 August the French battle fleet in Aboukir Bay was annihiliated by Admiral Nelson's superbly-handled fleet. This left the Army of the Orient virtually marooned in Egypt.

The news of Aboukir Bay - the Battle of the Nile - prompted an immediate declaration of war on France by Turkey. It was as much to prevent his troops becoming demoralized by inaction, as to block a Turkish invasion from the north, that Bonaparte marched into Syria with 13,000 men in February 1799. He took Jaffa on 7 March (disgracing the French Army by having 3,000 prisoners shot) but, without siege artillery, was halted at Acre. After a costly two-month siege, with his troops reduced by the onset of plague, Bonaparte retreated to Eqypt.

After this failure, with all the other demoralizing factors such as disease, isolation, and the hostility of the people, nothing offered so much proof of the quality of the French troops in Egypt as their defeat of an invading Turkish army at Aboukir Bay: barely 10,000 French routing 20,000 Turks. But this last victory in Egypt was the immediate prelude to Bonaparte's secret return to France (24 August 1799) through the British blockade, impelled by news of the Allied successes earlier in the year.

After Bonaparte's assumption of supreme power as First Consul in the coup d'etat of November 1799, he crossed the Alps to knock Austria out of the 2nd Coalition at Marengo in June 1800. This left Britain, isolated again, with French Egypt as the only theatre in which the war could be successfully prosecuted.

The English expedition, 1801

Even though many of the lessons of the Helder campaign had been taken to heart, the British expedition to Egypt was a tremendous gamble. The numbers of effective French troops in Egypt were under-estimated by at least 10,000 and the help expected from the Turks never materialized. If the French commander, General Menou, had called in all his outposts and concentrated his forces in the Nile Delta, the result would probably have been a disaster for the British. In the event the French force of 2,200 covering Aboukir Bay - the only section of the Egyptian coast about which the British had any information - was crushed by the British assault force on 8 March 1801. Two heavy defeats, inflicted by the superior fire-power of the British line infantry, left Alexandria besieged, the French commanders clinging tamely to the defensive, and the British road to Cairo open. Refusing any further set-piece battles, Menou in Alexandria finally sued for armistice terms in the last week of August 1801, the surrendered troops being repatriated.

BELOW: *British infantry, Alexandria, 1801. It was in this campaign that the formidable superiority of British volley fire first impressed itself on the French veterans of Italy -* ***'l'infanterie anglaise en duel, c'est le diable!'*** *was the general verdict.*

Troops of the Austrian Empire:

Over the 300 years before the Revolutionary and Napoleonic Wars, the hereditary lands of the House of Hapsburg had formed the dominant power within the shell of the Holy Roman Empire. The Hapsburg heartland of Austria/Bohemia/Hungary remained the strongest power in central Europe, unchallenged until the rise of Prussia in the 18th Century: an empire within an Empire. This Austrian Empire had always opposed French expansionism, and in the Revolutionary Wars and their Napoleonic sequel remained second only to Britain as the most persistent challenger of France's bid for mastery in Europe.

Apart from its two major peoples of German Austria and Hungary, the Austrian Empire embraced Czechs, Slovaks, Italians, Croats, and, since the partition of Poland in the later 18th Century, Poles. The fighting value of this multi-national complex was nevertheless high and was destined to remain so until its dissolution at the end of the First World War. Enlisting the support of the Austrian Empire remained a major objective of British strategy against militant France between 1792 and 1815. Austria fought France in the First Coalition (1793-1797); the Second Coalition (1799-1801); the Third Coalition (1805), the Fourth Coalition or 'War of 1809'; and the so-called 'Wars of Liberation' of 1813-1814. Even the marriage of Napoleon to the Austrian Archduchess Marie-Louise in 1810 failed to detach Austria permanently from the muster of France's enemies, and in 1814 Austrian forces took part in the invasion of France which brought about Napoleon's abdication.

Austria's combat record

Napoleon himself never under-estimated the military potential of the Austrian Empire. It had handed him his first clear-cut defeat in the field: at Caldiero near Verona (12 November 1796) during his first Italian campaign. Though the 'bridge of Arcola' remained one of the brightest items in the Napoleonic legend (Napoleon was forced to rally his troops from the front, raising the French flag to encourage his men to resume the attack) the tough resistance of the Croat troops blocking the Adige crossing brought him within an ace of a second defeat.

In the War of the Second Coalition, with Napoleon absent in Egypt, Austrian victories at Stockach (on the upper Rhine front) and Magnano, Cassano, and Novi in Italy, placed France in danger of outright invasion for the first time since 1794. Austria fought on with Britain after Russia dropped out of the Second Coalition (October 1799) and Napoleon's first campaign as First Consul was against the Austrians in Italy.

Crisis at Marengo, 14 June 1800

For Napoleon, the Marengo campaign of May-June 1800 was a strategic masterpiece all but lost on the battlefield of Marengo near Alessandria. Having crossed the St Bernard Pass in May, Napoleon brought his hastily-formed 'Reserve Army' against the Northern flank of the Austrian forces blockading Massena in Genoa, only to be surprised by the speed and competence with which the Austrian General Melas regrouped against him. While Napoleon dispersed his divisions for a converging attack on the army of Melas, the latter kept his army concentrated and attacked across bridges which Napoleon had believed to be destroyed. The result was that Napoleon, with 22,000 and 15 guns, was driven back by 30,000 Austrians with 92 guns. Disaster was only averted by the arrival of General Desaix's division, from which a perfectly-timed counter-attack was improvised, Desaix dying as he led his men into action. Cynics have never ceased to argue that the timely demise of Desaix, on whose initiative Marengo was won, was not the least of many contributions of the Napoleonic legend. Certainly to the end of his life Napoleon always remembered Marengo as 'his' battle.

Aspern and Wagram, 1809

A similar pattern recurred in the war of 1809 when Austria, encouraged by the unexpected resistance of Spain to French invasion, renewed the struggle against Napoleon. Once again - as in the Ulm-Austerlitz campaign of 1805 - the campaign opened with a brilliant series of manoeuvres and minor actions down the Danube valley which led to the capture of Vienna in less than a month. Though this time Austria was fighting without the support of the Russians (as in 1805) Napoleon was anxious for a quick end to the war to discourage Prussia from seeking revenge for her shattering defeat in the Jena campaign of 1806. He therefore wasted no time in moving out to attack the last Austrian field army - 100,000 men under the Archduke Charles, the best of all the Austrian generals - on the north bank of the Danube east of Vienna.

Napoleon's plan was to cross to the left bank of the Danube from the island of Lobau and develop a decisive attack. He had, however, under-estimated the Austrian strength, and after seizing the villages of Aspern and Essling found himself penned in a narrow bridgehead under heavy attack at odds of nearly three to one. A major disaster threatened when the Austrians broke the only bridge across which French supplies were being fed, and Napoleon had to authorise a costly retreat on to Lobau. There he regrouped for a second attack after a month and a half of superb improvisation, calling in reinforcements to raise his strength on Lobau to 180,000. The result was the two-day Battle of Wagram (5-6 July 1809), a brutal killing-match with both sides losing more than 20,000 men. Though the Austrians conceded defeat they did so in good order, withdrawing with 80,000 still in the field; but the French were in no condition to withdraw. It was not Wagram but the refusal of Prussia and Russia to enter the war which prompted Austria to accept the humiliating 'Peace of Schönbrunn' in October 1809.

Caldiero in 1796; Marengo in 1800;

a patchwork of nationalities

Aspern-Essling and Wagram in 1809 - these were the three biggest object-lessons which Austria gave Napoleon on the battlefield. His failure to appease Austria in 1813 was fatal.

BELOW: *Infantry and cavalry of the Austrian Empire - grenadier and* ***uhlan*** *(lancer). When in late 1809 one of Napoleon's ministers spoke sneeringly of the Austrians, the Emperor retorted 'It is obvious that you were not at Wagram!'*

Instrument of Empire: the Grande

The destruction of the Second Coalition at Marengo and Hohenlinden left a war-weary Britain wholly isolated and enabled Napoleon to negotiate the time-buying Peace of Amiens (signed March 1802). He was already working flat-out on tshe remodelling of the Republican French Army to create one of the most potent elements of the Napoleonic legend: the **Grande Armée.**

Heyday of the Grande Armée, 1802-12

The heyday of the **Grande Armée** lasted little more than ten years, from the Amiens breathing space of 1802-3 to the Russian campaign of 1812. As as instrument of conquest, nothing quite like the **Grande Armée** had been seen since the Caesarean armies of the Roman Civil Wars, in the 1st Century BC. The only remotest parellel since has been naval, not military: the American Pacific Carrier Task Force of 1943-45, which never returned lto base as long as hostilities lasted. From its first campaign in 1805 until its destruction of Russia, the men of the **Grande Armée** rarely if ever saw France. They represented the raw force on which was based Napoleon's Grand Empire: the reconstruction of Europe into a pattern of allied and client states, under the total domination of the French Empire. And wherever the **Grande Armée** marched, there the strength of the Grand Empire was greatest.

The corps system

The pattern into which Napoleon moulded the **Grande Armée** was derived from the overall experience of the French Revolutionary Wars, not just Napoleon's own experience in his early campaigns. This confirmed that armies enlarged by conscription were best handled in **divisions,** with divisional commanders working as a trusted team under the general's eye. Apart from improving the army's performance in battle, the divisional system had the advantage of easing the supply burden. Under the famous principle of 'disperse to march, concentrate to fight', each division could be assigned its own line of march, avoiding not only congestion along a single route but the rapid exhaustion of supplies.

By 1802 Napoleon has seen three of his most crucial battles - Rivoli and Castiglione in the first Italian campaign of 1796-7, and Marengo in 1800 - saved and won by the versatility of the divisional system. For the expanded French Army with which he planned to conquer England and dominate Europe, Napoleon not only retained the divisional system but scaled it up into **army corps.**

A Napoleonic corps was nothing less than a minature army, each with its own complement of infantry, cavalry, artillery, and engineer troops. A corps could, and often did, take on a whole enemy army until other French corps converged on the scente of action to concentrate the **Grande Armée** in full strength. This gave the **Grande Armée** a wonderful flexibility. In their original development (1803-5) the seven original corps of the **Grande Armée** were strung out in a great arc from Bamberg in Germany to Brest, most of them concentrated along the Channel coast for the invasion of England which never sailed, but all poised for a converging march in the opposite direction towards the Danube - the road to Ulm and Austerlitz.

Napoleon's Marshals

Napoleon's creation of the Marshalate came before his proclamation of the French Empire and his coronation. The new Marshals (18 of them in the first creation of 1804) were the professional commanders of the Army, and their promotion to this exalted rank had a two-fold significance. First, it was the nation's reward for outstanding services in the previous wars of the Republic; second, it was a symbol of how far the profession of arms in France had advanced since the Revolution. The eminence of the Marshalate was not a closed caste: it was open to any soldier regardless of birth or social status.

A breakdown of the original 18 Marshals shows Napoleon's shrewdness in bestowing this supreme promotion. Seven were great names from the Revolutionary Wars in the Low Countries (Jourdan, Kellermann, Moncey, Pérignon, Serurier, Lefebvre and Brune); eight were generals who had served under Napoleon in Italy and Egypt (Berthier, Murat, Masséna, Lannes, Bessières, Augereau, Davout and Bernadotte).

There was, of course, much bitterness among generals equally (if not more) distinguished, who were not made Marshals in the first creation. One of these was Marmont, described as 'the Emperor's oldest friend': a fellow-gunner who was nevertheless only 30 in 1804. Marmont was nevertheless given a corps command in 1804 and received his Marshal's baton five years later.

The great campaigns, 1805-7

The commanders of the **Grande Armée** at the outset of its first camfpaign in 1805 were Bernadotte - I Corps; Marmont - II Corps; Davout - III Corps; Soult - IV Corps; Lannes - V Corps; Ney - VI Corps; Augereau - VII Corps. The breakup of the invasion camps along the Channel coast was promted by Napoleon's decision to knock out Britain's Third-Coalition allies, Austria and Russia, in one gigantic campaign east of the Rhine. The first trick was won with the encirclement, by the converging French Corps, of the main Austrian army under Mack at Ulm. This was followed by the pursuit of Kutuzov's Russian army down the Danube valley and its destruction at Austerlitz (2 December 1805). In this as in all major camfpaigns of the **Grande Armée,** the vanguard cavalry was commanded by Murat and the Imperial Guard by Bessières.

After Austerlitz came the rout of Prussia at Jena-Auerstädt (14 Octodber 1806) and the final destruction of the Third Coalition in Poland, with Russian defeats at Eylau (7 February 1807) and Friedland (14 June 1807).

Armée, 1802-1812

At Leylau, however, VII Corps was so mauled that it had to be disbanded: the first proof that the **Grande Armée** was not invincible.

BELOW: *Trooper of the Elite Company, 1st Hussars - Eylau/Friedland campaign, 1807.*

ABOVE: *When weeks of hard marching had long taken off the parade-ground splendour - Fusilier of the 8th Line Regiment, 1812-13.*

The fighting men of Spain, 1808-1813

Napoleon never made a bigger mistake - not even in his invasion of Russia - than when he ejected the Spanish monarchy and set about converting Spain into a puppet kingdom in 1808. In this venture he was certainly encouraged by the supine reaction of Bourbon Naples to the imposition of French rule in Italy; but the national temper of Spain was entirely different to that of the Neopolitans. 'Dress them in red coats or green coats, they'll run away just the same' was how King Ferdinand of Naples had described his own soldiers. But the Spaniards were willing and eager to fight.

The main problem with the Spanish resistance movement was that it lacked central direction, with the insurgent **junta** of each province usually at loggerheads with its neighbour. This did not, however, prevent the Spaniards from taking early advantage of French over-confidence, and inflicting a humiliating defeat on Napoleon's army at what seemed to be the height of its power.

French capitulation at Baylen

This came about in July 1808 when the French General Dupont, acting on Napoleon's orders, was ordered to march south through Andalusia and capture Cadiz. For this task Dupont was given a single division, with support promised from the French army lodged in Portugal since the previous year. But Dupont never reached his goal. He was encircled and trapped at Baylen by a motley force of 30,000 Spanish regular troops and peasant freedom-fighters or **guerrilleros** before he had even crossed the Guadalquivir River, and forced to surrender on 20 July 1808. The **junta** of Seville then repudiated the convention made by the Spanish General Castanos that Dupont's force should be repatriated, and 17,000 French troops went into captivity.

The Spanish triumph at Baylen was the beacon-light which fired national resistance to the French throughout the war in the Spanish Peninsula. It followed, moreover, on other French setbacks, all of them resulting from the attempt to capture the main cities of the north and east without adequate forces or siege artillery. In June 1808 Marshal Moncey had been repulsed from Valencia, General Duhesme from Gerona and General Verdier from Saragossa. And the astonishing news of Baylen more than redressed the defeat of the two Spanish field armies in Old Castile, north of Madrid, at Almanza and Medina del Rio Seco (3 and 14 July).

The Spanish army

It was true that the regular Spanish army was no match for the French in all-round combat capacity. Under the Bourbon regime, some foreign estimates had put its real strength at no more than 50,000 out of a theoretical strength of 130,000 men. Though the army's manpower was sustained by conscription, this could be avoided, and there were widespread regional exemptions. The best arm of the service was the artillery, but infantry and cavalry tactics were far gone in obsolescence.

Few of these weaknesses, however, mattered in the war against the French. The national hatred of the alien armies created an entirely new mood reflected most clearly in the performance of the local **guerrillero** bands - resistance groups held together by the personality and ruthlessness of their leaders. The targets of the **guerrilleros** were French supply convoys, despatch riders, parties of foragers - any force small enough to be surprised and liquidated. Though small beer in comparison with the movements and collisions of great armies during the Napoleonic Wars, this form of warfare was immensely draining for the French, both in manpower and morale. It has been calculated that between 1808 and 1813 the French in the Spanish Peninsula suffered an overall daily average loss of 300 men.

Napoleon in Spain, 1808-9

Napoleon's Spanish campaign of 1808-9 was waged to avenge Baylen

ABOVE: *Spanish infantry, 1808 - repeatedly beaten by the professionals of the French Army, yet always capable of coming back for more and disrupting the already precarious French plans for the military rule of Spain as a French puppet state.*

BELOW: *Spanish irregular or* **guerrillero**. *Though capable of operating with regular Spanish army units, the guerrillero's best targets were French outposts, billets and lines of communication in the war of terror against the invader.*

and the other French humiliations of the summer, and to re-establish his brother Joseph Bonaparte as King of Spain. Judged on purely military terms the campaign was successful, with the Spanish armies beaten at Durango, Espinosa, Gamonal and Tudela, the Somosierra Pass stormed north of Madrid, and the Spanish capital reoccupied in early December. But the need to concentrate and strike at the British army under Sir John Moore, threatening in the French rear, prevented any systematic exploitation of these successes. Nor were the British trapped and destroyed in the north, turning to inflict a sobering defeat on Marshal Soult's forces before re-embarking at Corunna (16 January 1809).

When Corunna was fought Napoleon was preparing to quit Spain, leaving the mopping-up after the recent campaign to his Marshals. If the Marshals in the Peninsula had had the will to pool their resources, Spanish resistance could probably have been broken in 1809-10. Personal rivalries between the Marshals were of the greatest benefit to the Spaniards and their British allies, who returned in 1809 to operate in support from Portugal. On the other hand, the failure of the Spaniards to co-operate with the movements of the British remained an enduring problem for the British commander, Wellington.

In early 1809 Corunna was followed by the agonising end of the eight-week siege of Saragossa, which fell to the French on 24 February. It cost them around 4,000 men to take this one objective against the fanatical resistance of Saragossa's defenders, of whom (troops and civilians combined) about 54,000 died in the siege. The heroism of Saragossa was another focus of inspiration for the Spanish resistance. The most notable characteristic of the ensuing months was the speed with which loose-knit Spanish patriot armies were formed in the provinces and loosely hung on the sagging backbone of the regular army units available. Until the Russian campaign of 1812, this resilience made Spain the only country to suffer the full weight of a Napoleonic invasion and fight on instead of accepting a dictated peace.

Working with the British

It should not be forgotten that the failure of the French marshals to collaborate with each other was not the only reason why the Peninsular War dragged on until 1813. The British army, operating from its Portuguese base under Lord Wellington's command, was repeatedly frustrated by the failure of the Spanish commanders to concert a joint strategy and stick to it. Spanish dilatoriness ruined the Talavera campaign of 1809 and made it touch and go as to whether the British could withddraw safely to Portugal. Whereas the Portuguese army was raised to a high standard of efficiency under British training, Spanish obduracy prevented any such improvement in the Spanish army, which continued to go its own way.

This was the nadir of Anglo-Spanish military collaboration, all the more regrettable because in the actual Battle of Talavera (28 July 1809) General Cuesta's 30,000 Spaniards had performed far better than had been expected, holding the right of the Allied line. In the spring of 1810, when the French overran Andalusia, the threadbare, 18,000-strong Spanish army under the Duke of Albuquerque was instrumental in holding the vital prize of Cadiz until 9,000 British and Portuguese could come to their aid. And the finest hour for the Spanish army came at Albuera on 16 May 1811, when four Spanish battalions holding the extreme right of the Allied line stood up heroically to the fire of two French divisions, winning vital time for the British to redeploy against Marshal Soult's brilliant flanking manoeuvre.,

If unpredictability in action was certainly the keynote of the Spanish forces (Wellington never relied on Spanish co-operation after the Talavera campaign) that very unpredictability, coupled with an undying hatred of the invader, was nevertheless a potent factor in denying the French the easy victory which they had expected in 1808.

Portugal to the Pyrenees:

ABOVE: British light infantryman, 1808. Even for the Rifles, full kit was a crushing burden, according to Rifleman Harris. 'Besides my well-filled kit, there was the greatcoat rolled on top, my blanket and camp kettle, my haversack ... ship-biscuit and beef for three days ... my canteen filled with water, my hatchet and rifle, and eighty rounds of ball cartridge in my pouch; this last, except the beef and biscuit, being the best thing I owned, and which I always gave the enemy the benefit of, when opportunity offered'.

The defeats suffered by Britain during the land campaigns of the 1st and 2nd Coalitions had, by the outbreak of the Peninsular War in 1808, brought about several important reforms in the British Army. Added to the already formidable musketry fire-power of British infantry, these reforms created the troops which handed Napoleon's Marshals an unprecedented string of defeats in the Spanish Peninsula: Soult at Corunna and Victor at Talavera (1809), Massena and Ney at Bussaco (1810), Marmont at Salamanca (1812), Jourdan at Vittoria (1813). All these victories cracked the myth of French invincibility and proved that the first British success over the French in the Peninsula - the defeat of General Junot's army of Portugal at Vimiero in August 1808 - had been no lucky fluke.

The need for light infantry

The great victories of the French Revolutionary armies in the 1790s had been won by assaulting columns of infantry. These columns were preceded by swarms of skirmishers and sharpshooters, the **voltigueurs** and **tirailleurs**. The role of these light infantry forces was a classic one: to soften up the enemy line before the decisive attack. Such tactics proved highly effective against the rigid infantry formations favoured in 18th Century warfare. They created a paramount need to fight fire with fire: to screen the main infantry force with light infantry protection of its own.

The need for light infantry had first impressed itself upon the British during the War in America, when it had been partially met by the employpment of German **jägers** **(pp.116-117)**. It was, however, the rough handling experienced from the French in the Wars of the 1st and 2nd Coalitions which inspired the creation of the first British light infantry units. These were to be armed not with the smoothbore musket but with the far more accurate rifle (also first experienced by the British in America). The man who ordered the formation of an Experimental Rifle Corps was the much-maligned Duke of York, British C-in-C during the abortive campaigns in the Low Countries in the 1790s. The first experiments with this Rifle Corps, made in the aftermath of the 1799 Helder campaign, resulted in the creation of the first British rifle regiment in the spring of 1801.

This was the 95th Foot, a corps d'elite trained on entirely new principles. The men of the 95th did not wear the familiar scarlet, white and gold of other infantry regiments but a dark green uniform with black buttons and braid facings. They were trained not in traditional musketry by volleys but to make every shot count with the new Baker rifle, using terrain and firing from behind cover whenever possible. The long bayonet, served also as a useful short sword - which is why the British Rifle Brigade 'fixes swords' where other infantry regiments 'fix bayonets'.

Sir John Moore's Light Brigade

In October 1802, with the likelihood of a French invasion of Britain looming, the new 95th Foot with the 52nd and 43rd Regiments were sent to Shorncliffe Camp for training as a light infantry brigade. Their commander was General Sir John Moore, one of the most respected and admired commanders in the British army, and the first to teach the principle of the 'thinking fighting man'. Moore's forte was a new form of discipline which did not rely on brutal discipline but on encouraging the priate soldier to take pride in his appearance and his craft. Standards were recognised by merit badges and cockades for marksmanship; the light infantryman was taught to move fast, at the most economical pace, living off the country when he had to. This was an unheard of form of training beginning from such basics as 'To bring down the feet easily without shaking the upper part of the body is the grand principle of marching'. The objective was the provision of a sensitive infantry screen which would prevent the army from surprise whether in advance or retreat.

Proved in combat

The value of the new British light infantry companies was proved beyond doubt in the British Army's first two Peninsular campaigns: the Vimiero campaign of 1808 and the Corunna campaign of 1809, the latter under the personal command of Sir John Moore., This value was twofold. Light infantry operations compensated for the Peninsular Army's lack of cavalry, and was particularly well suited to the hills and mountains of Portugal and Spain where conventional cavalry operations were in any case severely curtailed. (Of the seven 'set-piece' battles won by the Peninsular Army between Vimiero in 1808 and Vittoria in 1813, only Salamanca in July 1812 could be described as a 'cavalry' battle. Even at Salamanca, the main weight of Wellington's shattering flank attack on Marmont's army was carried by the infantry.)

British cavalry in action

Though the crowning honours of the Peninsular War necessarily went to the British infantry, this did not mean that the cavalry regiments serving with Wellington's army failed to distinguish themselves. One such famous action took place at Benavente during the retreat to Corunna at the end of December 1808, when the Chasseurs of the French Imperial Guard tried to trap the British rearguard. They were counterattacked by the British 10th Hussars and 3rd Hussars (German Legion) and driven back across the Esla River with the loss of nearly 200 out of 600, the French General Lefebvre-Desnouettes being casptured in the action. Lefebvre, however, not only survived the rigours of the retreat to Corunna as a prisoner but escaped from England to resume his Guards cavalry command.

BELOW: *French dragoon, 1809. Though the cavalry ranked among the best arms of Napoleon's* **Grande Armée** *at peak strength, it had little chance to shine in its encounters with the British Peninsular Army.*

The Grande Armeé in Russia, 1812:

From the sheer size of the troop numbers involved, Napoleon's invasion of Russia in June 1812 remains one of the most awe-inspiring ventures in all military history. The Russian venture involved every territorial unit in the top-heavy reorganisation of Europe imposed by Napoleon since 1805: the French Empire itself, with its Belgian, Dutch, and Italian provinces; the northern Kingdom of Italy and southern Kingdom of Naples; the so-called 'Illyrian Provinces' along the Adriatic coast, ripped from the Austrian Empire after the 1809 Wagram campaign; the puppet states of the West German 'Confederation of the Rhine'; the reconstituted Polish 'Grand Duchy of Warsaw'. Napoleon's forces even included quisling troops from Spain and Portugal, and contingents provided by his unwilling allies Prussia and Russia.

No such concerted, multi-national military effort had been made since the Persian invasions of Greece in the early 5th Century BC. An alphabetical list of the states supplying regiments or cavalry squadrons to serve in Russia includes Anhalt, Austria, Baden, Bavaria, Berg, Croatia, Dalmatia, Denmark, France, Hesse-Darmstadt, Holland, Illyria, Itraly, Lippe, Mecklenburg, Poland, Portugal, Prussia, Saxony, Spain, Switzerland, Westphalia and Württemberg. Nor, as in the case of the imperial Persian armies, is it possible to give a precise figure for the mass of humanity which surged across the Niemen into Russia on 24 June 1812. Estimates vary between 430,000 to 610,000, the likeliest figure being in the region of 530,000 troops of all French and allied powers. The artillery park included over 1,000 guns, plus 30,000 wagon transports and over 150,000 horses.

Army of futility

This stupendous array of armed force certainly reveals the immense military resources available to Napoleon at the height of his power, but it should also be taken as a perfect example of the brutal wastefulness of Napoleonic warfare. There was no way on earth that an army of such size could be supplied and fed, but under the Napoleonic system this was never intended. The army must, in time-honoured French style, live off the country - 'war must sustain war'. At the cost of looting his allies bare, Napoleon amassed barely enough supplies to sustain 400,000 men for at most 25 days; but **two months** passed before Napoleon got the chance of fighting the knockout battle on which all his campaigns depended. By that time the effective strength of the **Grande Armée** had been more than halved.

The culmination of the 1812 campaign, the retreat from Moscow, has always remained a byword for tragedy and suffering - the death of an army. Far less well known is the grim fact that the **Grande Armée** began to die from the moment it crossed the Niemen. Within the first 50 miles of the march heat and poor forage had killed off no less than 10,000 horses, setting in motion a deadly chain reaction. Scores of guns had to be abandoned, the wagon trains labouring over the roadless Russian terrain lagged further and further behind the front-line troops, who found themselves advancing deeper and deeper into a country devoid of supplies. Though the main body of the **Grande Armée** was flanked by two separate corps totalling some 70,000 men, it still was unable to muster no more than 124,000 effectives for the Battle of Borodino outside Moscor on 7 September. By then the Russian strategy of constant retreat, using the enormous distances of their country as an ally, had already inflicted losses on the **Grande Armée** equivalent to three major defeats. Two-thirds of those

RIGHT: *Polish Lancer, 1812*

BELOW: *Bavarian infantry, 1812*

a polyglot host

losses had been inflicted by the deadly wastage of the advance, with another 47,000 (killed, wounded and captured) lost in 13 engagements from the clash at Eckau on 19 July to the French capture of the Schevardino Reboubt on the eve of Borodino.

Borodino, Moscow, retreat

On 7 September 1812 the Russian armies, safely united after their long retreat, at last offered Napoleon the battle he had been seeking since the beginning of the campaign. By the day of Borodino Russian tenacity and Napoleon's own gross miscalculations had already wiped out the enormous French superiority enjoyed at the outset of the campaign. The Russians at Borodino opposed Napoleon with 122,000 against 124,000. In the crucial sphere of artillery the Russians were actually the stronger, with 637 guns against 507. Borodino was one of the worst 'slaughterhouse' battles of the Napoleonic Wars, costing the French 28,000 casualties (22.6%) and the Russians 52,000 (42.6%).

It has been well argued that the decisive battle of the campaign was not Borodino but Maloyaroslavets, fought south-west of Moscow on 24 October. After this second clash the Russians withdrew, but the engagement induced Napoleon to order what was left of his army to retreat along the devastated line of its advance. Burdened with Russian loot, collaborators and stragglers, the army had shrunk to about 55,000 effectives and 12,000 fit horses by the time of the first heavy snowstorm on 6 November.

The **Grande Armée's** last battle was fought on 26-28 November 1812, breaking through the cordon of Russian armies seeking to prevent the French retreat across the Beresina. Only 20,000 of the main body recrossed the Niemen, with another 65,000 escaping from the two flanking corps. They escaped merely because conditions had been scarcely less rough on their pursuers; the chase from Tarutino to Vilna had cost Kutuzov's army 70,000 out of 97,000.

The battle for Germany: Leipzig, 1813

Given the enormity of the French disasters in 1812 it seems little short of miraculous that Napoleon, thanks to the voracious efficiency of French conscription, raised a new army of 150,000 ready for the defence of Germany by April 1813. The bulk of this new army was cannon-fodder pure and simple: raw conscripts in their late teens and early twenties, plus units of the French National Guard released from metropolitan duties for foreign service, moulded thickly on a framework of regular troops withdrawn from Spain and Italy. On paper, indeed, Napoleon could have raised replacements for the entire half-million he had let to disaster in Russia the previous year. What he could not replace was the quality of his lost battalions, and this was particularly serious with regard to the cavalry arm; all the best surviving French cavalry in 1813 was tied down in Spain.

With this material, however, Napoleon in 1813 confidently prepared to repeat his classic campaign of 1805 and defeat an enemy coalition of two hostile powers: not Russia and Austria this time, but Russia and Prussia. Until too late, he believed that his father-in-law, the Austrian Emperor Francis, would remain neutral. To this misconception Napoleon added the error of failing to judge the far-reaching improvements made to the Prussian Army since its humiliation in the 1806 Jena campaign. These included cracking the traditional officer caste to draw more talent from the middle classes, increasing the light infantry element with an increased emphasis on markmanship, and finally (from 1813) adopting a French-style conscription programme by calling up the **Landwehr** or national militia. Thanks to these reforms - all of them prompted, like those in the British Army, by the proficiency of the French military machine down to 1812 - the performance of the Prussian Army in 1813-1815 was far sharper than it had been in the wars of the 1st and 3rd Coalitions.

In 1813, however, Napoleon's grasp of military reality was as weak as it had been in the previous year. His objective was to keep Germany under French domination, and he had only one chance of doing this: to demonstrate, by a quick and economical campaign, that the armed forces of France were still formidable, then negotiate a settlement with Austria as a friendly neutral, mediating on his behalf. This, however, he could not accept. In 1813 Napoleon behaved as though his troops were the tough veterans who had won him the peace he wanted by their deeds at Ulm, Austerlitz and Jena, not raw conscripts who would need time to learn their trade. As a result Napoleon's stiff-necked demands for 'all or nothing' drove Austria into the Allied camp, landing the French Army with a task beyond its strength or skill.

The conscripts of 1813

Napoleon's political miscalculations in 1813 were all the more tragic because no troops could have given more than the French conscript armies of 1813. At Lützen (2 May 1813) the untried boys of Ney's 3rd Corps manfully withstood the attack of the Prussian Army under Blücher, responding to the personal example of Ney and the appeal of Napoleon himself - 'Young men, I counted on you to save the Empire. Are you going to desert me?' Ney himself, known in the French Army, variously, as 'The Bravest of the Brave' and 'Old Red-Head', was fulsome in his praise. 'I doubt if I could have done the same thing with the old grenadiers of the Guard. The docility and perhaps inexperience of those brave boys served me better than the trained courage of veterans. The French infantry can never be too young'.

This, of course, was going too far. The conscripts earned every word of the praise heaped on them, but they **were** too young for the job they were asked to do. They were simply not up to the forced marching, in thrusts at the Allied flank and rear, which would have converted the partial success of Lützen into a decisive victory. The same applied to the second engagement of the campaign, at Bautzen on 20-21 May, Ney's conscripts took far too long to complete the deep 'left hook' into the Allied rear which Napoleon ordered, and the result was only another partial victory. At both Lützen and Bautzen, not even partial success would have been won without the committal of the Imperial Guard - a significant pointer to how much had changed since the great days, when the intervention of this famous corps of veterans had seldom been necessary.

For all that, Lützen and Bautzen won Napoleon an armistice with Russia and Prussia to accompany a Peace Congress at Prague - but he had no intention of negotiating a secure peace as reward for his young soldiers' efforts. He used the armistice to buy time in which to raise the French Army in Germany, by continued conscription and cross-postings from other theatres, to over 400,000; but 100,000 of these never joined the army in the field, being assigned to static duty in the main garrison towns. Worst of all, Napoleon's obvious temporaising in the peace talks finally caused Austria to join the Allies, giving them over half a million men, ample reserves and a decisive superiority over the French. They entered the Leipzig campaign of August-October 1813 determined to concentrate all efforts against the detached French corps commands and only accept battle with Napoleon when in overwhelming strength.

Leipzig, 16-19 October 1813

After a final victory over the Austrians at Dresden on 26-7 August, the French Army came under a series of piecemeal attacks against the corps of Vandamme, Oudinot, MacDonald and Ney. These reduced the main army's effectives to 160,000 by mid-October, nothing like enough to defeat the converging Austrian, Russian and Prussian total of 300,000 plus. In the three-day 'battle of the nations' at

Leipzig the French lost 73,000 killed, wounded, and captured, and over 320 guns; the combined Allied loss was 54,000. After Leipzig Napoleon had no choice but to fall back to the Rhine, losing another 40,000 men in the process as well as the German fortress garrisons. Leipzig, completing the ruin of Napoleon's continental empire, must be counted the most protracted as well as the greatest battle of the Napoleonic Wars.

BELOW LEFT: *Russian grenadier in marching order, 1813.*

BELOW RIGHT: *Cossack trooper - the tough and dreaded irregular cavalry of the Russian Empire.*

Arbiter of the battlefield: the artillery

It was during the Napoleonic Wars that artillery emerged as a 'third arm' in its own right, with its performance vital to the success or failure of the cavalry and infantry. This was not due solely to the fact that Napoleon was a gunner himself; trends at work long before the French Revolution had been pointing the way to an enhanced status for the artillery. The most important of these trends was the greatly improved science of casting durable and accurate field-gun barrels thanks to the first stirrings of the Industrial Revolution of which England (contrary to one of the more enduring myths of the period) did not enjoy a monopoly. By 1789 France was producing twice as much pig-iron as England and had opened the first coke-blast smelting works on the Continent, at Le Creusot. The French therefore had the wherewithal to implement the theories of Gribeauval and du Teil, who suggested that a systematised artillery arm could transform the waging of war.

The artillery reforms undergone by the Frency Army before the Revolution meant that no other arm of the service suffered less during the Revolution. By 1793, the year of Valby **(pp.126.127)** some 55% of the French artillery had enlisted **before** 1789. (The figure for the French Army as a whole was 5%). Throughout the Revolutionary Wars and the early campaigns of Napoleon, however, the artillery continued to serve mainly as a 'service department' for the infantry and cavalry. From Valmy in 1793 to Friedland in 1807 nearly every French victory was won by manoeuvre and shock. It was not until 1809, the year of Wagram, that a new and dominant role began to emerge for the artillery.

Napoleon's 'grand batteries'

At Wagram Napoleon first improvised a 'grand battery' of 84 guns whose concentrated fire was used as a meat-grinder, weakening the ranks of the Austrian centre before the decisive attack. From Wagram until Waterloo, six years later, systematised artillery attrition of the enemy ranks played an increasing part in Napoleon's tactical thinking.

Taking the historical overview, there was nothing surprising in this. Since medieval, even ancient times the classic counter to steady enemy infantry had been to threaten a charge, make the enemy adopt its favourite defensive posture, then use missile fire-power to destroy the enemy where he stood. But there were other pressures at work in Napoleon's later battles, and the most important was the mushrooming size of armies. Controlling a battle purely by manoeuvre and shock was frankly impossible with an army 100,000 strong, even for a commander with Napoleon's gifts; reaching for the artillery sledge-hammers became an increasingly tempting alternative.

French artillery team on the move, 1815

Waterloo, 1815: supreme ordeal

Having abdicated in April 1814 after failing to repel the Allied invasion of France, Napoleon returned to France in March 1815 to be hailed again as Emperor. Though he vowed that his second reign would feature 'no more war, no more conquests', he nevertheless planned to break the Allied coalition immediately formed against him by quick victory over the British, Dutch and Prussian forces masking the French frontier in Belgium.

The field army raised by Napoleon for his 1815 campaign was the best he had had since Russia in 1812. For a start, it consisted predominantly of experienced troops including all prisoners of war who had been returned to France since his abdication. Without conscription (belatedly introduced in June 1815) Napoleon was able to raise an army of over 280,000 men, but over 100,000 of these had to be stationed to cover the Alps, Pyrenees and the Rhine frontier. This left him with a striking force of 124,000.

Belgium was defended by over 200,000 Allied troops, but these were strung out from the Rhine to the sea. Though the likeliest line of a French invasion of Belgium was the direct route to Brussels, there could be no certainty of this and both Wellingtron and Blücher were forced to station sizeable troop detachments to the east and west. Napoleon's first mistake of the campaign, and the most enduring, was to believe that once the two Allied armies had been driven apart by a concentrated blow at their point of junction, they would fall back to the east and west on their respective lines of communication. He therefore planned to destroy the main Prussian concentration at the outset before marching on Brussels, sweeping the British and Dutch aside as he advanced.

Prelude: Quatre Bras and Ligny

Napoleon's strategy for the campaign was to operate with two wings and a central reserve. At Ligny on 16 June he planned a frontal attack on the Prussians with his right wing while the left wing, under Ney, came in from the west. Ney's enveloping attack was however frustrated by the resistance of the British at Quatre Bras while the central reserve corps (d'Erlon) made a futile countermarch between the two actions without engaging in either. At Ligny Napoleon drove back the Prussians with a loss of over 11,000 French against 16,000 Prussians, ordering Marhsal Grouchy to pursue with 33,000 while he advanced to destroy the British with the main French army. His assumption that the Prussians had been too badly battered to re-enter the fray proved fatal.

Retreating on Brussels from Quatre Bras, Wellington only stood and fought at Waterloo for two reasons. He knew the terrain and the best defence line; and he had been promised the intervention of at least two Prussian corps by messenger from Blücher. This intervention was delayed by swampy terrain created by torrential rain on 17-18 June; but the mud also delayed the deployment of the French artillery, preventing the assault on Wellington's line until after noon.

Fruitless French attacks

Speed and precision were essential for the French, particularly after the approach of the Prussians was detected shortly before 1 pm; but the keynote of the French attacks on the afternoon of 18 June was piecemeal commitment, a growing desperation and lack of logical thought. The French cavalry was expended in repeated mass charges which forced the Allied line infantry to form square but failed to break it; Wellington saved his line from destruction under the French bombardment by posting units on the rear side of the Mont St Jean ridge. Though terribly battered the squares held, while Napoleon's infantry reserve was depleted by the need to deploy against the approaching Prussians. By 7 pm Napoleon had no choice but to gamble all on a frontal assault by the 12,000 veterans of the Imperial Guard, advancing against weakened but unbroken line infantry supported by guns which the French cavalry had failed to capture or disable.

of the line infantry

Waterloo, 1815: the Allies

Though Napoleon in June 1815 had experience in dealing with groups of enemy armies dating back to the Austerlitz campaign of 1805, the Waterloo campaign of 1815 was a novely for Wellington, and a desperately worrying one at that. In Spain (with the exception of the 1809 Talavera campaign) he had had to fight with seasoned British regiments whose capacity he knew to the inch, without being dependent on the performance of less able allied forces. In the Waterloo campaign, however, Wellington was not only forced to rely on the closest possible co-operation from Blücher's Prussians; British troops formed the minority of the army under Wellington's direct command. Expressed in percentages of the infantry force with which Wellington blocked Napoleon's march on Brussels, the balance was roughly 27% British, 30% Dutch, and 43% German.

Given the multi-national composition of the motley army blocking his path, the inordinate confidence displayed by Napoleon on the morning of Waterloo becomes much easier to understand. Even after the leading Prussian troops were spotted approaching from the East, Napoleon believed that he had blocked the main Prussian army sufficiently far out of play to be able to finish off Wellington's army in short order.

BELOW: *Prussian lancer (Uhlan), Waterloo, 1815. The Prussian onset against the French right flank not only ensured the Allied victory at Waterloo, but provided the cavalry for the all-important night pursuit of Napoleon's beaten army. The resultant inability of the French to rally after Waterloo prevented Napoleon from carrying on the war and brought forward his second abdication on 22 June.*

Wellington's deployment

Apart from the dubious qualities of the bulk of his army, Wellington had to weigh other factors in deciding on his best deployment at Waterloo. At every turn he envisaged the 'worst possible case' that might befall, and planned accordingly. He never dreamed that Napoleon would adopt the bull-headed tactics of the French Marshals in the Peninsula, and content himself with a simple frontal assault. To prevent any wide encircling sweep enveloping the Allied right flank, Wellington stationed 18,000 Netherlanders, Hanoverians and British some 10 miles out, at Hal. These would serve as a rallying point for the Allied right wing if the French should achieve a breakthrough in the centre.

The keynote of Wellington's

in the field

deployment was the Prussian guarantee of intervention from the east. With this guarantee, Wellington could afford to leave his left flank to look after itself and reinforce his right centre. The Forest of Soignes, behind the centre of the Allied position, offered security against a French central break-through — 'I could have got into the wood and I would have defied the Devil to drive me out', Wellington claimed.

It was therefore on the centre and right that Wellington stacked his most reliable troops to provide defence in the greatest possible depth. Out on the far right of the line, at Braine l'Alleud, he put the Dutch and Belgium battalions of Chassé's 3rd (Netherlands) Division, 6,000 strong. To their left, the defences increased dramatically in depth. Out in front of the main Allied position, acting as a breakwater in the path of the French left-wing corps, was the walled manor house of Hougoumont held by four British Guards companies plus 700 Nassauers and Hanoverians. The Hougoumont garrison was supported to the west by Mitchell's 4th (British) Brigade, and backed by four Guards battalions along the ridge. Behind the Guards lay the 2nd Anglo-Hanoverian Division, and behind them again the Hanoverians and Brunswickers covering the village of Merbe Braine. Wellington's right flank was therefore a four-echelon stack, some 22,000 men strong.

The Allied centre, straddling the Charleroi-Brussels road, was also defended in depth. Out in front the farm of La Haye Sainte was held by a brigade of the King's German Legion, supported by two British rifle companfies of the 95th. Behind La Haye Sainte the main position, linking with the Guards behind Hougoumont, was held by Kielmansegge's Hanoverians, a King's German Legion brigade and four British battalions, backed by two brigades of heavy cavalry. An invaluable bonus, reinforcing the Allied centre, was the arrival of General Lambert's three fresh battalions of Peninsular troops, who arrived on the morning of the battle.

The left centre was fronted by Bijlandt's Netherlands brigade of Belgian line infantry and Dutch chasseurs, with three militia battalions. These had fought bravely at Quatre Bras on the 16th but, like the eight fine battalions of Picton's Peninsular division at their backs, had taken heavy losses.

The lightest section of the Allied line was the far left, extended by two Hanoverian infantry brigades to end with the two British light cavalry brigades of Vandaleur and Vivian. Four farms on the valley floor - Papelotte, La Haye, Smohain and Frischermont - were garrisonned by the Nassau troops of the 2nd (Netherlands) Division who had taken the first shock of the French attack at Quatre Bras.

Apart from its concern for the centre and right, Wellington's deployment was admirably suited for a multi-national army which had never fought an action in full strength and was about to be attacked in superior strength. With no central reserve, his 'stacked' deployment nevertheless permitted small reinforcements to be drawn from the less threatened sectors and fed to the latest point of crisis. These proved just enough - 'the nearest run thing you ever saw in your life', as Wellington put it.

The other admirable characteristic of Wellington's deployment was the encouragement given to the weaker Allied units by the parcelling-out of the British infantry to provide maximum moral support. This only failed once: during the charge of d'Erlon's corps against the Allied centre. This caused Bijlandt's Netherlands brigade, which had never had the heartening experience of halting a French column with musketry volleys, to break and run, but the crisis was averted by Picton's division in the Netherlanders' rear and the charge of the British heavy cavalry. Wellington's only real mistakes were in underestimating the time it would take the Prussians to enter the fray, and overestimating the subtlety of tactics with which Napoleon would try to destroy him.

BELOW: *Dutch infantryman at Waterloo. Though Wellington posted the bulk of the Netherlands units on the flanks, the 1st Brigade of Chassé's division, withdrawn from the right ring, took part in the desperate fire-fight which routed the charge of the Imperial Guard with musketry and grape-shot.*

Waterloo, 1815: defeat of the Imperial Guard

The great climacteric of the Battle of Waterloo was the charge of the French Imperial Guard, Napoleon's last desperate bid to break Wellington's battered line before Blucher's Pusssians could intervene. After their repulse of the French Army's line infantry and cavalry, the battle-weary, depleted formations of the Allied line were faced with a mass assault by the most famous troops in the world, a corps unbeaten in action since its formation 11 years before.

The aura of the Guard

As one of the most celebrated corps d'elite in all military history, the French Imperial Guard naturally bears comparison with the Praetorian Guard of Imperial Rome **(pp.36-37)**. Its ranks contained the cream of the professional Army and appointment to the Guard was, apart from the cross of the **Légion d'honneur** from the Emperor's own hands, the highest honour to which a French soldier could aspire. But there the comparison stops. None of the politicians and soldiers who dreamed of toppling Napoleon between 1799 and 1815 ever had a hope of buying the support of the Imperial Guard, which from start to finish of its brief career remained fanatically loyal to Napoleon.

But the Imperial Guard was far more than just an elite, ultra-loyal bodyguard. It was the crack corps of the French Army: the supreme reserve and, when sent into action, the ultimate guarantee of victory. Though French Line regiments frequently grumbled that the Emperor favoured the Guard and spared it from the burden and heat of the day on campaign, they also knew why. As long as the Guard was present, poised for action, defeat was unimaginable. Though the Guard's popularity with the rest of the Army repeatedly diminished on campaign, its fighting prestige never did.

An army within an army

Though the original Consular Guard of 1799-1800 had been little more than a bodyguard with a strength of 2,000, it had always retained the framework of a regular army corps and as such was a self-contained army in miniature, with its own complements of infantry, cavalry, and artillery. There was even a battalion of Marines of the Guard recruited from the Navy (always a valuable source of trained gunners), of which a company was present at Waterloo. For the elite of elites, the Old Guard, ten years' service was the minimum for rankers, and 12 years for officers and NCOs.

The Imperial Guard numbered some 20,750 men at Waterloo, with eight battalions of grenadiers and chasseurs in the Old Guard, seven in the Middle Guard and eight of tirailleurs and voltigueurs in the Young Guard. The Guards Cavalry numbered 4,100, with the light cavalry consisting of two lancer and one horse chasseur regiments and the heavy cavalry of the Horse Grenadiers, the Empress Dragoons and the Gendarmerie d'Elite.

The Guards Artillery (13 foot and three horse batteries) had 122 guns - as against 46 guns in 1st Corps, 46 in 2nd Corps and 38 in 3rd Corps. It was supplemented by one company of Engineers and one of Marines.

The last act

Napoleon's supreme error at Waterloo was not to commit the Guard after Ney had captured La Haye Sainte and left Wellington's battered centre wide open. Napoleon did not release the Guard until 7 pm, by which time Wellington had stripped the Allied right wing to shore up his centre. When the Old Guard staggered and recoiled from their deadly fire, the unimaginable had at last happened - **'La Garde recule!'**

1815

THE 19th CENTURY

-1914

The hundred years between the defeat of Napoleon in 1815 and the outbreak of the First World War introduced profound changes to the waging of war, the most profound of these changes occurring in weaponry. In 1815, for instance, the infantryman still wielded a smoothbore, muzzle-loading musket yielding an average of two shots per minute. By 1914 he had a breech-loading magazine rifle capable of 15 shots per minute, with each shot capable of killing at a range far greater than that of any weapon since the medieval long-bow. By 1914, too, the 'hosepipe' fire of the machine-gun offered still more deadly infantry fire-power, while muzzle-loading artillery and solid shot had been replaced by rifled breech-loaders firing explosive shell.

The gradual advent of this new lethality in weaponry made the 19th Century the last heyday of military splendour, with ornate uniforms to sustain regimental pride and impress the enemy on the battlefield. By 1914, colour and glitter in uniform had been banished to the peacetime parade-ground: it made far too good a target in action.

With no continental conflicts on the scale of the Napoleonic Wars apart from the American Civil War, armies tended to revert to 18th Century size. Supply remained a major problem conspiring to keep armies small. On the other hand, a plethora of minor wars of colonial conquest helped prevent any such stagnation of military practice as had settled on the armies of Europe by 1789. The major problem thrown up by the Napoleonic Wars – how to maintain and manoeuvre mass armies – was to remain unsolved until the unprecedented demands of the First World War.

When the Bourbon dynasty returned to Paris in 1815 'in the baggage-train of the Allies', it had one priceless asset: the military legacy of Napoleon, both in reputation and available talent. Though the restored Bourbon monarchy could not begin to call itself secure until the death of Napoleon in 1821, it nevertheless had the wherewithal to distract attention from domestic problems by conducting successful adventures abroad.

One of the most extraordinary reversals of fate was the French military intervention in the Spanish civil war of 1823, on behalf of the endangered Spanish Bourbon monarchy. This was conducted by Marshal Moncey, one of the least effective French commanders in Spain during the Peninsular War, barely ten years after Wellington's expulsion of the French from Spanish soil. The French march on Madrid was conducted with speed and economy, the recently loathed troops of France being welcomed as liberators by the royalist bulk of the Spanish population.

The other major French adventure of the 1820s was the despatch of a naval contingent to join the British and Russians in shattering the Egyptian fleet in Navarino Bay (October 1827); but the first instance of renewed French imperialism took place in July 1830: the invasion of Algeria.

The Algerian expedition of 1830 was, incidentally, the first major French operation in Africa since Bonaparte's invasion of Egypt 32 years before. In 1830 the objective was the liquidation of the problem posed by the Corsairs of Algiers. Preying on the shipping of all nations, the Corsairs had been an international pest for centuries and even the most successful naval expeditions sent against them (the last being an Anglo-Dutch bombarding fleet in 1816) had only won temporary respites from Algerine attacks. In 1830, having obtained no redress for repeated outrages on the part of Algiers, the government of King Charles X determined on amphibious operations to capture and occupy Algiers.

The officer chosen to command the Algiers expeditionl was the War Minister: the Comte de Bourmont, who in 1815 had deserted Napoleon on the eve of Waterloo. Despite his chequered reputation in the eyes of French Army veterans, Bourmont planned and executed the operation with complete success, storming Algiers from its less defended landward side three weeks after landing on 5 July 1830. But though the conquest of Algiers put an end to the menace so long posed by the Corsairs, it was only the beginning of a long guerrilla war waged against the French by the Algerian Dey, Abd el-Kader. For over a decade the fast-riding Arab raiders outpaced and eluded the clumsy lunges made by the French garrisons based on the coast.

In 1840 Marshal Thomas Bugeaud took command as governor-general and C-in-C of the precarious French foothold in Algeria. Another Napoleonic veteran whose rise to the Marshalate had begun with promotion to corporal on the field of Austerlitz, Bugeaud had also served in Spain and realised that not only different tactics but different troops were required to combat guerrillas.

Bugeaud started from the assumption that warfare in Europe and warfare in Africa were, by nature of the terrain as of the enemy, clean different things. In Europe, the ultimate objective was the enemy army; in Algeria, the objective had to be the population. As the enemy forte in Algeria was mobility, there was nothing to be gained by marching conventional 'all-arms' detachments to and fro, or by studding the hinterland with garrisons which would require a major effort to keep supplied.

To fight the Algerians, Bugeaud developed a system of highly mobile columns whose supplies were carried

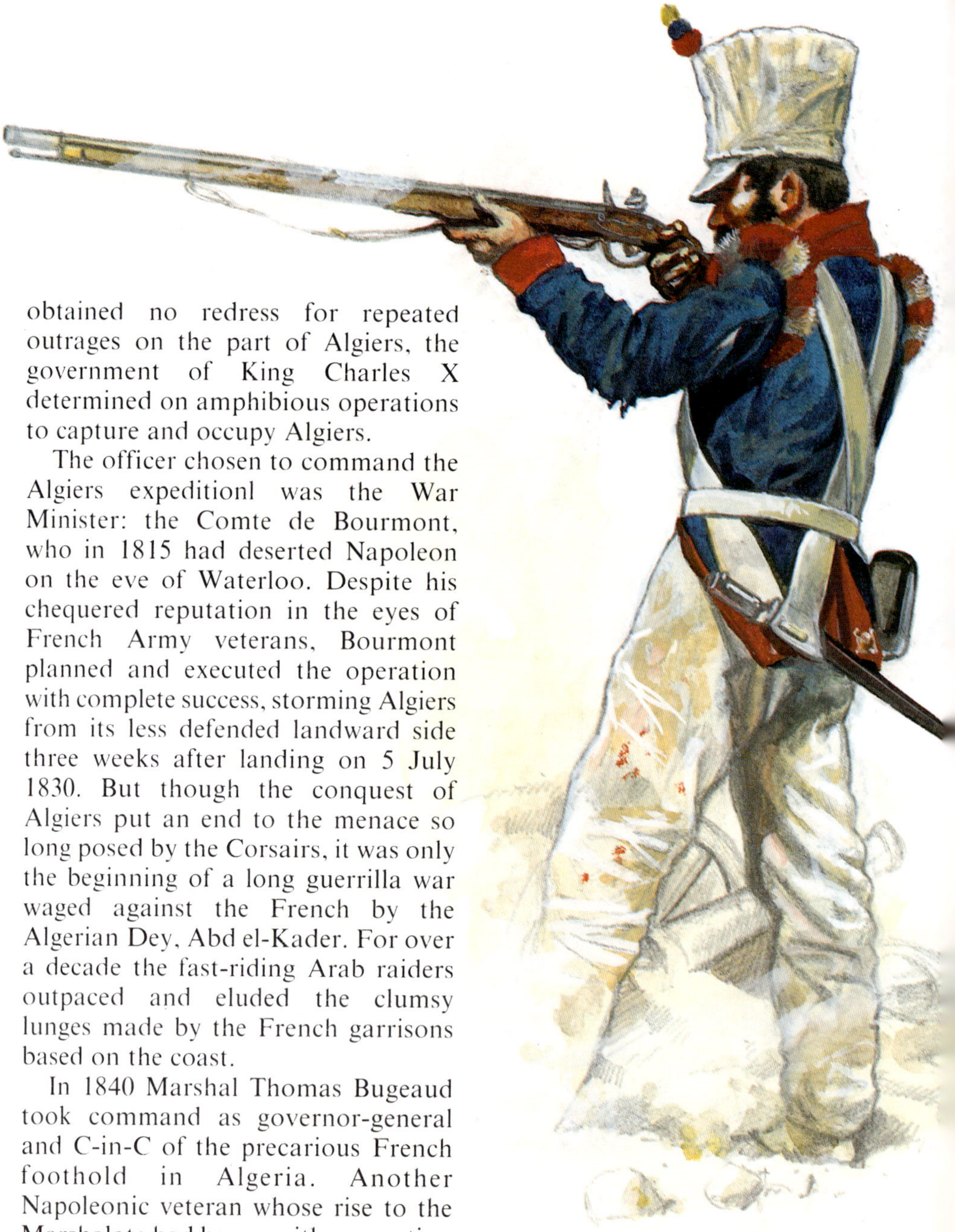

ABOVE: *French Royal Infantry of the time of the capture of Algiers in 1830. The troops of the expeditionary force were more than adequate for the capture of this initial objective but their training and equipment were unsuited to prolonged campaigning in the North African theatre.*

Birth of the French African Empire: Algeria, 1830-1848

BELOW: *The stamp of Bugeaud - French colonial infantry in Algeria, c.1850, with uniform and equipment modified to meet the harsh demands of the country.*

by horse or camel, not in lumbering wagon trains. The force he favoured was a light column of about 6,000 troops and 1,200 horses, able to carry out rapid strikes over short distances, and catch the enemy forces before they could disperse into the wastes of the interior. Mountain fighting was tackled by mutually-supporting groups of such columns, striking from different directions and keeping the enemy in a constant state of uncertainty until too late.

This by no means meant that Bugeaud relied solely on hit-and-run tactics in retaliation. His policy in Algeria had stability through pacification as its ultimate objective. As the area under French control expanded with each new tribe accepting defeat, so roads were pushed forward protected by blockhouses serving as depots and bases for future advances. Nor was Bugeaud's thinking directed solely to the problem of bringing an elusive enemy to action, particularly in difficult mountain country. He argued that as enemy resistance could only be sustained by popular co-operation, the people's will to resist must be broken by calculated ferocity. Attacking commanders had to familiarise themselves with the basics of local economics and the most telling way of disrupting them. And a grasp of local politics was as essential as a grasp of local economics, exploiting rivalries and further weakening the enemy by playing off one group against the other. All this seems obvious enough, but in the 1840s as it was seen as as challenge to the accepted interpretation of Napoleonic technique: that forcing a single bloody encounter on the enemy was all that was needed. In fact. Bugeaud's technique used the essence of Bonaparte's technique of concentrating separate columns at speed to strike where the enemy least expected it.

Where it was impossible to achieve superiority in strength, Bugeaud showed that decisive results could still be obtained by the adoption of a defensive 'hedgehog' formation, encouraging the enemy to attack and have his superior numbers whittled away. In the case of the North African theatre, the French deliberately referred to ancient Roman military history and adopted the tactics used by Roman armies against the North African tribesmen, whose fighting technique had changed little by the 19th Century.

Bugeaud's rapid successes against Abd el-Kader, who surrendered in 1847, secured Algeria as France's first North African province and established Bugeaud as the great pioneer of French colonial military theory. 'The object' he wrote, 'is not the present war; victory will be sterile without colonisation. I will therefore be a fervent coloniser, for I attach less importance, less glory to victory in battle that to the establishment of something valuable and useful to France'. Though Bugeaud's attempts to plant colonies of soldier-settlers in Algeria (the old Roman model again) were less successful, the colonial forces raised and trained in North Africa - most notably the irregular cavalry known as the **Chasseurs d'Afrique** - soon proved to be the most 'valuable and useful' additions to the French Army.

South Africa, 1815-1850: Kaffir

BELOW: *Shaka, king of the Zulus (1828-28) in his distinctive costume: lory tailfeather headband plume, civet fur collar and kilt, leather elbow and knee bands ornamented with fringes of white cowtail.*

When British sovereignty over the Dutch Cape Colony was confirmed in 1814, the long-delayed battle for mastery of South Africa between European settlers and the southernmost Bantu tribes was fast approaching. At the time of the Dutch landings at the Cape in 1652 the nearest Bantu tribesmen, spreading slowly east and south through the Continent, had been 500 miles away. By the time that the Bantu finally made contact with the Afrikaners or Boers in the 1770s, the latter were a fully-established and expanding race, determined to push north into the African hinterland.

The battle for supremacy in South Africa was then complicated by phenomena transforming the situation on each side of the racial divide. The first was the overlay of British authority on the traditional Afrikaner way of life, prompting the urge to migrate inland away from British rule; the second was the sudden rise of the Zulu nation among the Bantu, causing pressure waves of Bantu refugees to surge south and west. It was never a simple story of white against black, but of Afrikaner against British, Zulu against all comers.

The British used the same name for the Bantu as the Afrikaners: Kaffirs, an Arab word signifying 'infidel'. All they asked was grazing land for the herds of cattle on which their society, divided into a myriad tribal clans, depended. Warfare, such as the Bantu understood the term, was waged sporadically between rival clans or larger tribal confederations. 'Army' was perhaps too grandiose a term for the Bantu **impi**: basically a muster of all men of fighting age. Bantu weapons consisted of the club or **knobkerrie** and a sheaf of light throwing **assegais,** the last of the sheaf being retained for hand-to-hand combat. Bantu warriors also carried long oval shields with a tough hide covering on a wooden frame-work, these shields doubled as useful weapons in close combat. Though no match for European fire-power in a stand-up fight, the Bantu nevertheless had the advantage of superior numbers, fieldcraft, and cross-country speed They were always prone to carry ou damaging raids on the farmsteads o the white colonists, their direct rivals for grazing land.

The Bantu migration into south-east Africa had carried them past the Portuguese settlement at Delagoa Bay and down the coastal stripo between the Drakensberg Mountains and the Sea; the foremost tribal group, the first to make contact with the Afrikaners on the Great Fish River was the Xhosa. The Xhosa bore the brunt of British and Afrikaner expansion across the Great Fish River into modern-day Transkei which set in after 1815. The result was the long series of 'Kaffir Wars', interspersed with official attempts at pacification and co-existence. The latter, though sincerely enough intended, never stood a chance because of the fundamental rivalry of black and white cattle-grazing peoples for the same commodity: free land and no interference.

Rise of the Zulus

By the middle of the 1820s the disputed lands across the Great Fish River, already known as 'British Kaffraria', were no longer the only source of hostilities between European and Bantu. When a group of British merchants, probing north-east along the coast, landed in 1824 to proclaim the base of a new colony at Port Natal (afterwards Durban) they immediately made contact with a wholly unforseen phenomenon: a Bantu warrior nation of great power, united under the rule of a powerful king. These were the Zulu ('people of heaven'), who had thriven mightily under the eight-year rule of their chieftain Shaka, the greatest warrior-king in modern African history.

Shaka's conversion of the Zulu from a minor clan into the mightiest power in black Africa began as a favoured lieutenant of the Mtetwa king Dingiswayo, who built a short-lived 'empire' between about 1810 and 1818. Though Dingiswayo used war only as as means to bludgeon

tragedy, Zulu triumph

recalcitrant neighbouring clans into quick submission, Shaka used war to accelerate political growth. It was from Dingiswayo that Shaka inherited the keystone of what was to become the Zulus' military supremacy: the training of Bantu warriors into drilled regiments. It was as the bravest and most ferovious warrior in Dingiswayo's **iziCwe** regiment that Shaka first made his name, in about 1810. In these years Shaka's family clan, the Zulu, accepted Mtetwa supremacy. When Shaka's estranged father died in 1816, Dingiswayo released Shaka from service in command of the **iziCwe** to become chieftain of the Zulu.

It was during Shaka's time with the **iziCwe** that he introduced a deadly combination of new weaponry and new tactics. Shaka abandoned the light throwing assegai, replacing it with a broad-bladed thrusting spear - the **iKlwa** - for underhand thrusting and stabbing. This innovation has been compared with the adoption of the short stabbing sword by the Roman legions. Shaka taught his men to claw the opponent's shield aside with his own shield, thus exposing the opponent's left side to a deadly thrust with the **iKlwa.**

For maximum speed over the roughest terrain, Shaka insisted that his men abandon their rawhide sandals and toughen their bare feet. Fast and silent approaches, and pursuits of ruthless duration until the enemy's liquidation was certain, were other innovations. Shaka also transformed the Zulus' battle formation, introducing a pinning attack by a central 'chest' while from either flank an encircling 'horn' trapped the enemy force. By 1818, when Dingiswayo was killed by treachery, Shaka had built the Zulu army up tod a strength of 2,000 trained warriors and quadrupled the Zulu lands.

This was the starting-point from which Shaka, over the ensuing six years, waged war after war against the encircling Bantu clans. Shaka's conquests extended the Zulu power from the Drakensberg to the sea, and from Swazi frontier on the Pongola River deep into Natal. By the year of his assassination, 1828, Shaka, had effectively destroyed all organised Bantu society south of Zululand and created a vacuum in South-East Africa.

It was into that vacuum north and east of the Orange River that the Afrikaners came swarming on the 'Great Trek' of 1835-37, outflanking Zululand to the west and founding what would in time become the first Boer Republic: the Orange Free State. Meanwhile, to the south, the British continued to struggle with the Bantu on the Cape frontier, winning a seventh 'Kaffir War' in 1846.

BELOW: Cape Colony, 1846: Government soldiers at the time of the 'Seventh Kaffir War'

Risorgimento: soldiers of the new Italy, 1848-1860

After the final defeat of Napoleon in 1814-15 it was natural that the leading European powers of the last anti-French coalition tried to turn back the clock and re-draw the map of Europe on traditional lines. Though Revolutionary and Napoleonic France had ruthlessly exploited the new client states created in the wake of the French armies, the idea of national self-determination which France claimed to champion outlived memories of how bad that exploitation had been. And nowhere in Europe was this new sense of nationalism more frustrated, in the years after Waterloo, than in Italy. The biggest spur to Italian nationalism after 1815 was the restoration of Lombardy and Venetia to direct Austrian rule.

From this power base on Italian soil, Austria could offer speedy assistance to her main allies in the peninsula: the Papal States in central Italy, and the restored Bourbon Kingdom of Naples in the south. She could at the same time discourage any attempt to champion the hopes of Italian liberals and nationalists on the part of the kingdom of Sardinia, which included Genoa and Piedmont in the north, with Turin as its capital. Would-be Italian freedom-fighters might dream of a united kingdom of Italy, a Roman Republic, or a confederation under the headship of the Papacy, but none of those dreams had a hope of becoming reality without a war producing a decisive Austrian defeat.

Even after the ousting of the French Bourbon monarchy in the revolution of 1830 the new French King, Louis Philippe, remained a dutiful client of Austrian Chancellor Metternich. This seemed to rule out hopes of France intervening in an Italian war of liberation against Austria, and by the mid-1840s Metternich's Italian set-up seemed likely to endure indefinately. In 1846, however, Italian hopes were stoked to white heat by the election of a new Pope, Pius IX, who announced a programme of liberal reforms. Not for the first time, the new Pope's liberalism fell hopelessly short of expectations; he had no intention of proclaiming an Italian crusade against Catholic Austria. The resulting sense of frustration found its outlet in 1848, the extraordinary 'Year of Revolutions' in Sicily, France, Prussia and Austria. The news that Vienna was in revolt and Metternich had fallen immediately promted risings in Venice and Milan. This wholly unforseen combination of circumstances prompted King Charles Albert of Sardinia to launch the first of the Italian wars of liberation.

False dawn: the wars of 1848-49

Unfortunately for the Italians the Austrian commander in Italy, Radetzky, was a tenacious professional who had fought at Wagram and had served as Austrian chief-of-staff at Leipzig. He had no intention of squandering troops in trying to hold Lombardy but fell back on the 'Quadrilateral' fortresses (of Mantua, Peschiera, Legnano, Verona) to await reinforcements. Charles Albert's Piedmontese advanced into Lombardy in good heart, believing that Papal troops would be coming to their aid, and Italian morale went sky high when the Piedmontese army caught one of Radetzky's detachments and beat it at Pàstrengo (30 April 1848). The Piedmontese besieged Peschiera and took it after beating off an Austrian relief attempt at Goito (30 May); but from then on the balance swung back. With no help from the Papal States, Naples or 'liberated' Lombardy, the Piedmontese were left to fight the Austrians alone. Beaten at Custozza on 24 July, Charles Albert retreated on Milan, his army's morale hard hit, and reluctantly agreed to abandon Lombardy in the armistice of Salasco (9 August).

The Roman Republic

Meanwhile, in Rome, the Pope's attempt to introduce a liberal tinge to his government had stoked further frustration in Rome. This resulted (November 1848) in the murder of Prime Minister Rossi, the Pope's flight from Rome and (February 1849) the proclamation of a Roman Republic. The new republic was hailed by all the foremost names in the Italian revolutionary cause including Giuseppe Garibaldi, whose band of exiled freedom-fighters returned from 12 years of supporting revolutionary movements in South America. Hopes rose high when the Piedmontese reopened the struggle with Austria on 12 March, but on the 23rd they were decisively beaten at Novara by Radetzky, with King Charles Albert abdicating in favour of his son Victor Emmanuel. This left the Roman Republic isolated against the Neapolitan Army and an expeditionary force sent by the new French Republic, seeking legitimacy under its President Louis Napoleon, Napoleon I's nephew. Rome fell on 3 July 1849 but only after a spirited resistance which established Garibaldi and his irregular 'Redshirts' as the heroic champions of the Italian **Risorgimento.**

LEFT: *Piedmontese regular infantry of the Novara campaign, March 1849.*

BELOW: **Garibaldino** *'Redshirt' of the siege of Rome, April-July 1849.*

The war of 1859

After the dashed hopes of 1848-49 the burden of Italian reunification rested on the Kingdom of Sardinia, the only Italian state to have fought the Austrians with any show of success. To the Piedmontese statesman Cavour (premier after 1852) it was evident that his country could only resume the struggle with foreign aid if she were to have a hope of success. Invaluable French and British goodwill was bought by the despatch of a Sardinian expeditionary force to fight with the Allies in the Crimea (1855); but three years passed before Cavour struck a deal with Napoleon III for French assistance in the new war against Austria.

This however, turned out to be no war of liberation. Daunted by the casualties suffered at Magenta (4 June 1859) and Solferino (24 July) Napoleon concluded an early armistice with Austria without consulting his Italian allies, who gained only Lombardy.

In May 1860 Garibaldi invaded Sicily with his 'Thousand' picked volunteers to overturn the Bourbon regime with local support. Against any other troops but demoralised Neapolitans he would never have stood a chance but by the end of July, after two hard-fought actions at Calatafimi and Milazzo, he was master of the island. After receiving reinforcements from the north Garibaldi crossed the straits and took Naples (7 September), while Piedmontese forces pushed south to join him on 10 October. After this remarkable campaign the kingdom of Italy was proclaimed in March 1861.

India: the Sikh Wars,

BELOW: British infantry (31st Foot) of the Sikh Wars.

Few colonial wars fought by the British in the 19th Century gave them tougher fighting than that demanded by the Sikh Wars of the 1840s. The Sikhs of the Punjab were no loose tribal confederation, poorly armed, weak in discipline or prone to internal rivalry; they were the most formidable enemy faced by the British in India until the Mutiny of their own native regiments in 1857. The British were indeed lucky that the Sikh kingdom had, after the death in 1839 of its great ruler Ranjit Singh, been deprived of the leadership which its superb warriors so richly deserved.

Throughout his 30-year reign Ranjit Singh had maintained good relations with the British East India Company centred on the Ganges valley, but he had not done so out of weakness or fear. His policy, while avoiding direct confrontation, had been to command British respect by virtue of strength. No other Indian ruler had gone to such lengths in adopting the latest European military techniques and equipment. Tshe Sikh army, with its hightly-disciplined regimental breakdown, European-style uniforms and weaponry and even system of pay, had the further advantage of its martial religion over the regular British and native Indian regiments, for which the Sikhs considered themselves more than a match.

Origins of the conflict

The first Sikh war had a double trigger: distrust of the latest programme of expansion by the British East India Company coupled with the disastrous British retreat from Afghanistan in 1842, shattering the myth of British invincibility. The year after the Afghan debacle, 1843, the British conquered Sind. As this was territory formerly claimed by Ranjit Singh, the Sikhs were naturally incensed, and further encouraged by the spectacle of Company native troops mutinying rather than serve as garrison troops in Sind. The most that can be said is that the British Governor-General Hardinge, was not caught napping when the Sikh army crossed the Sutle River on 11 December 1845; he had moved substantial forces westward to concentrate against the Sikhs should the need arise.

1st Sikh War, December 1845-March 1846

Mudki, the first clash, was fought on 18 December: a head-on encounter between General Gough's 11,000 and part of the advancing Sikh army, which at full strength numbered 75,000. The excellent Sikh artillery, modelled on that of Napoleonic France, had heavier guns than the British but the Sikh commander Lal Singh had insufficient infantry to protect them after the Sikh cavalry was driven back. Mudki cost the Sikh army 17 guns, but on the British side the Bengal native troops showed a worrying reluctance to close with their formidable opponents.

The second battle, Ferozeshah (21-22 December 1845) featured a combined attack on the main Sikh encampment by the British main army under Gough and the corps of General Littler, who had eluded the superior Sikh force under Tej Singh to take part in this 'blow at the heart'. Gough's attack, launched an hour before sunset, was immediately subjected to heavy punishment by the massed Sikh batteries. A desperate cavalry charge by Sir Harry Smith, of Peninsular War fame, overran the Sikh camp but he was heavily counter-attacked during the night and forced to withdraw. Yet another British attack just before daybreak overran the Sikh position and captured 70 guns - but the approach of Tej Singh's 10,000 threatened disaster, for the British artillery was out of ammunition. A crushing defeat for the main field army of British India was only averted by the unexpected retreat of the Sikh army, which has been explained as Tej Singh's refusal to complete a triumph for Lal Singh (hated as the lover of the boy Maharajah's mother, the Rani Jindan).

None of these sobering lessons prevented Gough from squaring up for another head-on butt at the Sikh army in its new position at Sobraon; but while he was waiting for a convoy of heavy artillery and replacement ammunition, a Sikh corps under Ranjur Singh threatened the British lines of communication. This new menace was averted by Sir Harry Smith who, with 11,000, caught Ranjur Singh at Aliwal (January 1846) and routed him, taking 76 guns. Thus encouraged and with the artillery reinforcements safely arrived, Gough attacked the Sikhs at Sobraon on 10 February. After two hours' bombardment, however, the Sikh Artillery had not been silenced and British artillery ammunition was running low. Gough's reaction to this information was 'Thank God! Then I'll be at them with the bayonet!'. It cost him 2,200 casualties before the Sikhs, furiously pressed from all sides, fell back on their single bridge of boats across the Sutlej. When this was broken the retreat became a slaughter, with perhaps 8,000 Sikhs killed. When the British crossed the river on the following day the Sikhs could offer no effective resistance, and the 1st Sikh War ended with Hardinge dictating peace terms in Lahore (8 March 1846)

The Lahore peace settlement of 1846 sought to weaken the Sikh state rather than annex it outright. This was attempted by reducing the Sikh army and lowering its artillery by another 36 guns, and installing a British nominee to rule Kashmir province. It was, perhaps, inevitable that Sikh pride should take increasing exception to this manipulation, though the spark did not detonate until April 1848. This was the revolt of Multan province in the southern Punjab, whose Divan Mulraj could not accept the new **status quo**. The British put Multan under siege (Gough having vetoed any large-scale operations during the Indian hot season), and hoped that Multan's surrender would restore order. But the siege of Multan, undertaken not only with the approval of the Sikh Regency Council but with the token aid of 5,000 Sikh troops, had to be temporarily abandoned in mid-September. On the 14th, the Sikh commander Sher Singh went over to the besieged Multanis with his whole force; and the entire Sikh nation rose in revolt as the news spread.

The 2nd Sikh War

When Gough advanced against Sher Singh in November 1848 his clumsy manoeuvres were roughly handled; his leading forces were repulsed by the Sikh rearguard and he failed to cross the Chenab river. Though this siege of Multan was reimposed, the Sikh leader Rajah Chattar Singh secured the aid of an Afghan expeditionary force, sent by Amir Dost Mohammed to help the Sikhs crush the British. Gough therefore attempted to deal with Sher Singh before this new force came down on him; and the result (13 January 1849) was the Battle of Chillianwallah.

Though Gough came up to the main Sikh position in the later afternoon and issued orders to bivouac until the following day, he allowed himself to be provoked into attacking before he had a clear idea of the Sikh deployment; the main Sikh position was screened by a belt of jungle, through which the British artillery ineffectively fired. Gough's subsequent infantry attack was repulsed, the main victims being the 24th Foot, which suffered 50% casualties (most killed). But worse was to follow. The British cavalry brigade on the right flank panicked and broke before an inferior force of Sikh cavalry, with three regiments losing their colours. The day was only saved by renewed heroic assaults by the savaged infantry and left-flank cavalry, causing the Sikhs to withdraw; but Gough was in no condition to pursue.

Gough now declined further action until Multan fell (22 January) and the besieging force joined him, by which time the Sikh army had to move south in search of supplies. On 21 February 1849 Gough encountered the Sikhs in open country at Gujrat. This time there were no mistakes. The British artillery silenced the Sikh guns; flanking cavalry dealt with the Afghan and Sikh horse, while the infantry broke clean through in the centre. On March 14 what was left of the Sikh army surrendered at Rawalpindi.

RIGHT: *Gunner of Sikh artillery.*

The Crimean War, 1854-55

The Crimean War was the first major conflict between the European grreat powers - Russia versus Britain and France, the latter in alliance with Turkey - since the defeat of Napoleon in 1815. Strategically, it was an unusually pointless conflict. By the time that the British and French expeditionary forces landed in the Balkans the Turkish forces on the lower Danube had beaten the Russians unaided. An amphibious expedition to the Crimea to capture the Russian Black Sea base of Sevastopol was then launched to gain the allies a bargaining counter at the peace conference-table; but ever if Sevastopol had fallen it would hardly have brought the Russian Empire to its knees.

The capture of Sevastopol was certainly possible, and was nearly achieved. Onced ashore in the Crimea (14 September 1854) the Allied march on Sevastopol, 25 miles from the landing beaches,d was opposed on the River Alma (20 September). A clumsy frontal assault forced the inferior Russian army from its position, but failure to pursue allowed the beaten Russians to reach Sevastopol and establish a defence perimeter.

Balaclava and Inkerman

Besieging Sevastopol from the east and south, the Allies were hamstrung by their lack of heavy siege artillery and by the wholly inadequate unloading facilities in the small harbour of Balaclava, on which they were now entirely dependent for seaborne supply. The first Russian attempt to cut the Allies off from their base and raise the siege brought on the Battle of Balaclava (25 October 1854). Clumsy drives by the Russian cavalry at the Allies' frail land link with Balaclava port were repelled by the 93rd (Highland) Regiment's superb musketry and a spirited counter-charge by the British heavy cavalry; but a disastrous communications breakdown, during an attempt to recover emplaced guns taken by the Russians, sent the British Light Cavalry Brigade charging to destruction against the wrong guns.

On 5 November 1854 the Russians

made their second bid to break the siege with a surprise infantry attack, launched in a dawn mist. This 'soldier's battle' in which generalship played little part saw intense hand-to-hand fighting and musketry at close range, the Russian columns suffering severely from the Allied rifles firing expanding Minié bullets. Inkerman preserved the Allied siege lines but condemned the besieging troops to an appalling winter, starved of fuel, shelter, winter clothing, and all supplies required for surviving a Russian winter. At least the troops' sufferings, accurately reported, prompted timely relief work and the base hospital reforms organized by Florence Nightingale.

The spring of 1855 brought the Allies the welcome aid of the Sardinian expeditionary force **(pp.158-159)** and plans were laid for the first frontal assaults on the Russian siege lines. The French army had been reinforced to 90,000 strong, outnumbering the British, and carried the weight of the attacks in June. These took the outermdost defence positions but even the fire-power of over 500 guns failed to silence the batteries and fixed defences protecting the keypoint of the Malakov Redoubt, and the British also failed to take their objective, the Redan. After a final attempt to breach the Allied lines along the Tchernaya River (16 August), the Russian Sevastopol garrison was left to its own devices.

In their preparations for the second attempt on the Malakov, the French pushed their trenches to within 25 yards of the objective to accelerate the speed of the assault. This study of the new art of trench warfare paid handsome dividends and the French took the Malakov with ease on 8 September. The British, using their old tactics, were bloodily repulsed from the Redan. Having lost the Malakov, however, the Russians evacuated Sevastopol (8-9 Septemsber 1855) before the Allies could renew the attack. With Russia unable to recapture Sevastopol and the Allies unable to exploit it, the war ended in stalemate.

OPPOSITE: **Russian infantryman (far left)** *and Guardsman, winter 1854-55.* ***BELOW:*** *British grenadier officer of the 95th (Derbyshire) Regiment of Foot. Apart from the traditional sword, he carries a new multi-shot sidearm: the 1851 model Adams revolver.*

India's 'Black Year': the Mutiny,

In the entire history of soldiering and the profession of arms, it is hard - if not impossible - to find a more tragic chapter than that of the Indian Mutiny of 1857. 'Mutiny', indeed, is a barely adequate word, normally referring, as it does, to a refusal to serve until intolerable grievances have been fairly considered and redressed. There was no such reasoned bargaining behind the Indian Mutiny, only a frantic, agonising renunciation of every tie of loyalty which makes a soldier what he is - loyalty to the regiment, pride in **being** a soldier and respect for the officers who command him. And all this genuine trauma was expended in the blood of a hideous race purge: a bid to rid all India of the **gora-log**, the British - respected patrons no more, but hated tyrants to be exterminated without pity.

For the British in India the horror, hatred and blood-lust were, if anything, even greater than for the men who rose against them. The subtle pressure of numbers had made complete trust in the loyalty of Indian native troops an article of faith. Out of an Indian population of about 150 million, the Company's Army numbered 300,000 - of which, by 1857, only about 37,000 were British or Company's European troops. The entire history of the East India was inextricably linked with the recruitment and training of loyal native troops. That the native infantry **(sepoys)** and cavalry **(sowars)** should ever renounce their loyalty was unthinkable - until the unthinkable came to pass in May 1857.

Causes of the Mutiny

The root cause of the Mutiny was fear: of what the British called progress and order, but of what seemed to most Indians to be a calculated assault on their spiritual and material welfare. Well-meaning but crass British missionaries and excessively Christian officers, pledged to impose one faith on a people representing a kaleidoscope of religions, were one source of this fear. British legislation outlawing widow-burning and the sect of **thuggee** (the latter committing ritual murders in the service of the goddess Kali) was another. A host of administrative reforms ignored Indian sensitivities towards caste and the dangers of personal pollution; for instance, the new railways made it all too possible for a high-caste Indian to be polluted by a low-caste travelling companion in the same carriage.

On the more practical level there was resentment over reduction in the pay bonus for serving outside Company territory (as happened in the Sind and Sikh wars of the 1840s), and above all over the new Service Enlistment Act of July 1856, making service overseas compulsory instead of voluntary for future recruits. The decision to enlist the first regiments of Sikhs (scorned as unclean barbarians by Moslem and Hindu alike) helped encourage the idea that all the old values of Company service were under attack by the British.

Mutineer of native infantry

To the Indian rank and file, the horrifying rumours about the cartridges for the new Lee-Enfield rifle came as the last straw. These came in a greased-paper wrapping from which the bullet had to be bitten free when loading; and from January 1857 word spread that this cartridge paper was greased with beef and pork fat. (To get an idea about how Hindus and Moslems recoiled from this rumour, it was as if Europeans had been required to bite cartridges made of Communion Wafers steeped in dog's dung.) The British tried to allay these fears by permitting the cartridges to be torn with the fingers rather than bitten, but it did no good. By the end of February 1857 the first native regiments had begun to refuse the cartridges, heedless of the risk of disgrace and disbandment for mutiny. By April, native troops were even refusing to handle cartridges of familiar type.

The Mutiny breaks

On 9 May 1857 there was a formal punishment parade at Meerut, 40 miles from Delhi, for 85 skirmishers of the 3rd Native Cavalry who had refused cartridges on 14 April. Their public degredation and imprisonment prompted their comrades of the 3rd Cavalry, with the two native infantry regiments at Meerut, to mutiny in support on the following day. The prisoners were freed, the native townsfolk of Meerut broke out in riot and there were widespread massacres of British servicemen and civilians. The cavalry mutineers then rode to Delhi with the news, and similar scenes were repeated there. Lucknow and Agra followed.

Prompt British countermoves to regain the upper hand in the Ganges and Jumna valleys were impossible, because there were only two British regiments between Calcutta and Meerut. Reinforcements had to be called in from the Punjab and shipped in from Burma. Even so, the crushing of the Mutiny in Bengal would have been impossible without the loyalty of the other two native armies of British India: Bombay and Madras.

Delhi, Cawnpore, Lucknow

Delhi was the greatest symbol of the Mutineers' success and the foremost British objective. A partial blockade of the city was in force by mid-June but the siege train was not ready for the decisive bombardment and assault until 11 September. The assault went in on the 14th and after six days of heavy fighting the city was recaptured.

The Mutiny had exploded at Cawnpore on 4 June, with some 300 British troops holding out until 27 June, when they surrendered in return for promises of safe evacuation for the women and children. Mutineers and townsfolk nevertheless butchered their captives with a ferocity which made Cawnpore the key symbol for British revenge; only two days after the massacre (17 July) Cawnpore was recaptured, and immediately became the base for the attempt to relive Lucknow. The first relieving force was however merely a reinforcement (5 September) and the siege of Lucknow was not raised until 17 November; but it took until March 1858 until the city was recovered from a rebel concentration of 120,000. By the late summer of 1858 the loyal Madras Army had scattered the last organised rebel forces in central India.

British infantry, Bengal 1857-58

American Civil War, 1861-65:

When the slave-holding Southern states broke from the Federal Union and formed their own Confederacy in 1860-61, their combined population came to little more than 9 million of which 3.5 million were negro slaves. The North, with a population of some 22 million, not only had well over double the manpower but something like 95% of the mines and factories in the former Union. In manpower as in **materiel**, the Confederacy stood little chance against the North; but the fighting spirit of the South was high and its generalship was, for the first thee years, decidedly superior.

Though the Confederacy was proclaimed in February 1861 the first shots of the conflict, against the small Union garrison of Fort Sumter at Charleston in South Carolina, were not fired until 12 April. Many months passed before the North had raised enough troops to commence hostilities on the three main battle fronts. These were in Tennessee; along the line of the Mississippi River; and in the east, which became the dominant theatre. The Confederate capital of Richmond, Virginia stood less than 100 miles from Washington. Though the ultimate aim of the North had to be the destruction of the Confederacy as a self-sufficient political entity, the lure of taking Richmond dominated Northern strategy from the first month of the war to its last, four years later. By the same token, the foremost armies were those committed to the theatre: the Confederate Army of Northern Virginia and the Federal Army of the Potomac.

Railways, rifles and machine guns

The Civil War has aptly been called the first war of the Industrial Revolution. It was, for instance, the first conflict in which the movement of troops by rail had a decisive effect on campaigns and battles. The first clash between the rival armies at Bull Run (21 July 1861) was a classic example. General McDowell's Northern army had succeeded in outflanking the Confederate army blocking the road to Richmond - only to be flung back, all unexpectedly, by Confederate reserves brought in from the Shenandoah Valley by rail. The Bull Run triumph of 1861 was, however, the exception which proved the rule, for the railway network in the Southern states was nothing like as developed as in the North; such lines as the South possessed had always depended on Northern workshops for their hardware: rails, spikes, locomotives and rolling stock. After Bull Run the Confederacy was only able to achieve one major transfer of troops from east to west by rail, in the Chickamauga campaign of 1863; and even then half the troops never arrived in time, preventing the decisive victory in Tennessee which the South so desperately needed. In railways as in all aspects of military hardware, the North held all the cards.

For the rest, there were few major innovations in weaponry; this was a war of confirmation rather than innovation, the main confirmation being the deadliness of massed rifle fire revealed by the European wars of

the Blue and the Grey

the 1850s. Inflicted on troops deployed and manoeuvred in Napoleonic style - most notably columns of companies massed in close order for decisive shock charges - its natural result was a steady climb in the casualty lists. First Bull Run had resulted in a total of about 5,000 casualties but at Shiloh (6-7 April 1862) there were 20,000; 23,500 at Antietam (17 September 1862); 29,000 at Chancellorsville (2-6 May 1863); 43,000 at Gettysburg (1-3 July 1863). The bulk of these casualties were inflicted by artillery and rifle fire, not the bayonet. The urge to step up fire-power still further had, by the end of the war, introduced the first practicable machine-gun, the Northern Gatling; but as this bulky weapon required wheeled transport it was more of a light artillery piece than an infantry weapon.

Confederate victories, 1861-63

The first two years of the war saw the repeated failure of Union attempts to march on Richmond; but these Confederate successes in the East were paid for by steady Union advances on the Mississippi front. The US Navy's early capture of New Orleans in April 1862 was the prelude to a deadly Union pincer advance along the river from north and south which finally bit the Confederacy in half at Vicksburg (July 1863). This permitted the Union to bring full strength to bear against the Confederate armies in Tennessee and Virginia.

By the spring of 1863, the inspired combination of Generals Robert E. Lee and Thomas 'Stonewall' Jackson had broken or frustrated every Union advance on Richmond. They had beaten McClelland in the 'Seven Days' (June 1862), Pope at Second Bull Run (August 1862), McClelland again at Antietam (September 1862) and Burnside at Fredericksburg (December 1862). Features of these Confederate victories were the dogged defensive on carefully chosen ground; audacious flank marches and attacks from the rear; and well-timed attacks in strength against carelessly exposed sectors of the Union Army. Though he never enjoyed more than three-quarters of his opponent's strength, Lee always convinced the Union generals that he had far more than he actually did. At Chancellorsville (May 1863) Lee daringly divided his dwarfed army (60,000 against 130,000) to launch a devastating flank attack on the Army of the Potomac; but Jackson was mortally wounded in this battle, and he was irreplaceable.

Lee's first big defeat, Gettysburg (1-3 July 1863) was an extraordinary battle, brought on by the eagerness of the two armies to get into action on terrain where neither general had planned to fight. Lee found himself with little choice but costly frontal attacks under deadly artillery fire. He drew off his beaten army intact but the legend of his invincibility had been broken.

1864-65: attrition of the South

After Gettysburg the Union finally succeeded in bringing its full strength to bear, with Ulysses S. Grant given supreme command in the east and Sherman invading Geoprgia from Tennessee. Trench warfare outside Atlanta in Georgia, and before Petersburg in Virginia, slowed but failed to contain the pressure of the Union advance, grinding down the number of Confederate effectives in each action. Once forced out of his position at Petersburg (held from June 1864 to March 1865) Lee's exhausted army dwindled to 8,000 effectives and he surrendered at Appomattox on 9 April, six days after the fall of Richmond.

LEFT: Confederate infantryman and cavalry trooper of 1863.

***RIGHT:** Union cavalryman (above) and infantryman, better equipped throughout the war than their Southern opponents. Despoiling Union dead of their footwear and well-filled haversacks was an inevitable sequel to a Confederate victory on the battlefield.*

Zululand, 1879: Isandhlwana

Fifty years after the death of Shaka in 1828, Zuland was still the most formidable warrior nation in southern Africa, but a question-mark hung over its continuation as an independent country. In April 1877 the British had proclaimed the annexation of the two Boer (Afrikaner) republics - the Orange Free State and the Transvaal - established since the 'Great Trek' of the Boers in 1838. They thus became heirs to long-standing disputes between the Boers of the Transvaal and the Zulus, but had no intention of resolving these to the Zulus' advantage without insisting on reductions to the power of Cetshwayo, king of Zululand since 1873. Cetshwayo, however, refused to play the part of a British vassal. Whjen he ignored the ultimatum ordering him to disband the regiments of the Zulu Army (December 1878), the British prepared to impose their terms by force.

Thanks to the exertions required for the recent 9th Kaffir War (1877-78) the British commander in South Africa, Lord Chelmsford, could muster some 16,000 British, colonial and native troops for the invasion of Zululand. He planned an advance by three columns to converge on Cetshwayo's royal kraal, Ulundi, each column in sufficient strength to look after itself should need arise. He had full confidence in the fire-power of the 1871 Martini-Henry rifle, a single-shot breech-loader for which each man, fully equipped, carried 70 rounds.

It was a sound enough plan, flawed only by the difficulty in communicating between the centre column and its two flankers; and by the slow pace of the advance necessitated by the baggage trains. Where it went hopelessly wrong was in under-estimating the incredible speed with which a Zulu army could move virtually undetected, exploiting the natural cover provided by the terrain.

***LEFT:** Zulu warrior, 1879.*

***RIGHT:** British infantry, Zululand 1879.*

and Rorke's Drift

Isandhlwana and Rorke's Drift
Ten days after crossing the Buffalo River into Zululand on 11 January 1879, the centre column made its second camp at Isandhlwana, still searching in vain for the main Zulu force after clashes with small detachments of Zulus. On the following day Chelmsford made the error of dividing the column into separate probes, hoping to locate the main *impi*. Until the morning of the 21st there was every chance of a battle more or less where Chelmsford had anticipated, but his scouts failed to locate the main *impi*. In a late change of plan it had moved up to the Nqutu plateau north-east of Isandlhwana, bothered by the obvious danger of approaching the British across the open plans to the south. And it was there, on the morning of 22 January, that the resting *impi* was at last discovered - not by Chelmsford's main body, but by a horrified mounted scout from the 1,800-strong garrison of the Isandhlwana camp. The Zulu *impi* amounted to the greatest black -African force ever encountered: 12 regiments in varying strengths, over 22,000 in all. Nine of these regiments fell upon the Isandhlwana garrison; the other three, the Undi corps commanded by Cetshwayo's brother Dabulamanzi, raced on to sever the British line of communications by attacking the small garrison at Rorke's Drift on the Buffalo River.

Colonel Durnford, senior officer in the Isandhlwana camp, had time to form a defence perimeter before the *impi* swept down from the Nqutu plateau. For the first hour all went well, with the Zulu masses immolating themselves against the rifle fire of the 950 European and 850 Natal Kaffir troops. The rate of fire, however, was prodigious against the Zulu numbers in the field, and though there were ample ammunition reserves in the camp the preparations for replenishment, improvised as they were, proved not good enough. The crisis came when the Natal Kaffirs, starved of reloads, broke and fled through the camp. They left a breach 300 years wide through which the Zulus came storming, overwhelming the gallant companies still trying to hold position. Before the 'horns' of the *impi* closed round the doomed garrison, only 55 Europeans and perhaps 300 Natal Kaffirs managed to break out. The other 850 were wiped out, the 2nd Warwickhsire Regiment (24th Foot) losing six full companies who died to a man.

Meanwhile the Undi corps, 4,000 Zulus strong, was fast closing on the diminutive garrison at Rorke's Drift: Lieutenants Chard and Bromhead with 105 fit troops (81 of them formed by 'B' Company of the 2nd/24th) and 35 hospital patients. A flimsy defence perimeter, centered on the stone mission house, had been improvised from wagons, mealie bags and biscuit boxes, but an inner line had to be added when 250 Natal Kaffirs panicked and fled as the Zulus bore down. This time, however, the defence perimeter was so small that the ammunition supply problem which had caused the Isandhlwana disaster could be coped with - just.

The attack of Rorke's Drift began at 4.30 pm on 22 January and raged through the night, dying away at around 4 am. It was a desperate conflict which forced the defenders into their innermost perimeter, but their rifle fire savaged the Zulu ranks and prevented a decisive breakthrough. Before they perished, the defenders of Isandhlwana had killed over 2,000 of their 18,000 attackers, out-numbered though they had been by 10 to 1. At Rorke's Drift, where the odds against the defenders were nearer 40 to 1, the Zulu losses were higher - maybe as high as 25 per cent. It was a high price to pay for postponing the British advance on Ulundi by four months.

There was no mistake about Chelmsford's second invasion, launched at the end of May. At Ulundi on 4 July, the last **impi** of Zululand, 20,000 strong, was shattered by musketry, artillery and Gatling fire in open country, for the loss of only ten dead and 69 wounded.

Prussia's march to empire, 1862-1871

The unification of Italy between 1848 and 1861 **(pp.158-159)** was the immediate prelude to the creation of a second German **Reich** with the kingdom of Prussia as its backbone. Though the creation of the new Germany was not solely brought about by military conquest - there were political and economic factors almost entirely lacking in the Italian **Risorgimento** - it could hardly have been achieved in the space of nine years without resort to war. For Prussia to achieve supremacy in Germany, she had first to demonstrate Austria's inability to do the job; a military showdown between Prussia and Austria, the last act of the struggle opened by Frederick the Great in 1740 **(pp. 110-111)** was inevitable. But where it had taken Frederick the Great 22 years to demonstrate Austria's inability to defend the province of Silesia, Prussia in 1866 took just seven weeks to settle the question of whether Prussia or Austria was to be the master of Germany. And Prussia's defeat of Austria in 1866, confirmed by the even more shattering defeat of the French 'Second Empire' in 1870, would in turn have been impossible without the prodigious reforms achieved in the Prussian Army since the late 1850s.

Prussian Army reforms, 1856-61

The reforms which made the Prussian Army the most formidable military instrument in Europe were prompted by the failure (November 1849) of a premature scheme for German unity under Prussian leadership. This was brought to nothing by vigorous Austrian diplomacy backed by the tacit threat of military intervention in Germany, in the wake of Austria's successes in Italy **(pp.158-159)**. King Friedrich Wilhelm of Prussia backed down when his generals advised him that Austria would probably win any trial of strength. His successor Wilhelm 1 (1858-88), a soldier himself, spared no effort to atone for this setback and was ultimately rewarded by becoming the first Kaiser (Emperor) of modern Germany.

Wilhelm I's prime instruments were War Minister Roon and Army Chief-of-Staff Moltke, who applied themselves to raising the size of the Army and increasing the speed with which it could be deployed in time of war. Roon began by extending the term of service to three years. This was followed by relegating the territorial **Landwehr** to a secondary role: garrison duties and occupation troops in the wake of the regular units. Conscription and reserve service were then expanded to boost the number of trained units available on mobilisation.

When it came to the question of deploying the armies in time of war, Moltke stood revealed as the first true strategist of the railway era. Even before the first German railway had been built, Moltke had seen in railways a method of moving armies six times faster than Napoleon's armies had ever been able to march. Moltke sank his life savings in the Berlin-Hamburg line and, as a director, urged state control of all railway construction to provide a civilian/military role. By 1859, when Germany already had some 10,000 kilometres of track, Moltke was ready to attempt the first large-scale mobilisation of the Prussian Army (prompted by the Franco-Italian war) by rail. Predictably chaotic, it yielded invaluable lessons tackled by the Prussian Army's specialized Railway Department (formed 1861). For instance, it was discovered that rapid train deliveries of troops and supplies only created new problems, and that hopeless snarlups at the railheads could only be avoided by meticulous provision for unloading and distribution.

The other technological innovation to which Moltke addressed himself was the communications breakthrough offered by the electric telegraph. This, used properly, freed commanders from having to ape Napoleon and keep all army corps within reach of the C-in-C's direct orders. During the Austrian campaign of 1866 Moltke became the first general to direct a campaign from his office, by map and telegraph; he only arrived 'on the spot' four days before the decisive battle at Königgrätz.

When it came to weaponry, the Prussian Army was particularly well served. By the late 1850s it had been armed with the first effective breech-loading rifle, the Dreyse 'needle-gun', capable of seven rounds a minute and ranged up to 800 yards. But the Prussian Army's biggest mounting asset was the mushrooming steel production of the Ruhr in the Prussian Rhineland, which by the middle 1860s had already begun to serve the Prussian artillery with steel breech-loaders - the best field guns in Europe.

The Danish War of 1864

The new-look Prussian Army was first put to the test in the war against Denmark (February-June 1864) for the disputed frontier provinces of Schleswig and Holstein. The provinces were quickly overrun but the Danish redoubts at Düppel proved a tough nut to crack, necessitating trench warfare and the careful emplacement of 94 heavy guns. After a six-hour bombardment on 18 April the Danish position was carried by a brilliant and well-planned attack, followed by the triumphant parade of 118 captured Danish guns and 40 standards through Berlin.

Austria defeated, 1866

The Danish war was the first triumph for Otto von Bismarck, Minister-President of Prussia since September 1862. By the summer of 1866, with 492 of the new Krupp breech-loaders in service with the Prussian Army, Bismarck was ready for the showdown with Austria for the mastery of Germany. In his planning for the war with Austria, Moltke was hampered by the demands of politics and diplomacy; it was vital that Austria appear the aggressor, which meant permitting the Austrians to mobilize first. Hardly less important, in drawing up a master-plan for the defeat of Austria, was the need to provide against unexpected
blows at Saxony or Silesia. In the event the crowning Prussian advantage

in 1866 was deployment by rail, using five lines to Austria's one; but though three Prussian armies duly converged on the Austrian army at Königgrätz (3 July 1866) tough Austrian resistance gave Moltke many an anxious moment. The advantage of the Prussian Dreyse rifles was more than offset by the superior siting of the Austrian artillery, the Prussian guns having to be rushed forward to take the weight of fire off the infantry; but the upshot was the decisive victory Prussia needed, Austrian losses being 40,000 to Prussia's 10,000.

The main objective of Prussia in 1866 was not Austrian territory but the unmolested formation of the North German Confederation (1867) of Prussia, Mecklenburg, Hanover and Saxony, with Prussia concluding military alliances 'in the event of French attack' with the south German states of Baden, Wurttemburg and Bavaria. These gains added 6 million Germans to Prussia's population of 18 million, against the 37 million of France.

The Army of the French 2nd Empire was long overdue for reform by the time Bismarck engineered war between Prussia and France in July 1870. The infantry had the **chassepot** breech-loader rifle with double the range of the Prussian Dreyse, but the French artillery consisted mostly of bronze muzzle-loaders. French mobilization was chaotic and fielded less than 250,000 troops; Prussia had 400,000, massed in three armies poised to drive between the two French concentrations at Metz and Strasbourg.

French morale, high at the outset of the war, was dashed by the rapid seizure of the initiative by the Prussian armies. The French fought bravely at Spicheren, but Wörth and Rezonville (4-17 August) and Gravelotte and St. Privat (18 August) but could not prevent encirclement at Sedan (surrendered 2 September) and Metz (surrendered 29 October). Paris, besieged from 20 September resisted superbly under a republican regime until 28 January, 1871.

LEFT: *French infantry, Sedan 1870*

RIGHT: *Prussian infantry, 1870*

Frontier struggle: the 2nd Afghan

After the shattering experience of the Indian Mutiny **(164-65)** the Bengal Army, source of the tragedy of 1857, was radically changed in its reconstruction. It went without saying that many of the new Bengal regiments were formed from native troops which had remained loyal during the Mutiny. The most famous of these was the 1st Bengal Irregular Cavalry, first raised by Captain James Skinner in 1803 - Skinner's Horse, which after the Mutiny became the senior cavalry regiment of the Indian Army. Skinner's Horse headed the eight regiments of Bengal cavalry formed from similarly loyal irregular cavalry regiments in 1861.

Of the pre-Mutiny Bengal Native Infantry regiments, 18 survived to head the line infantry of the new Army. But one of the greatest surprises, in looking back at the Indian Army's reconstruction period, is the number of native Indian cavalry and infantry regiments which had been raised **during** the Mutiny, some 37 in all; and of these by far the most important were the Sikhs and Gurkhas.

The military virtues of the Sikhs had been all too clearly revealed during the two Sikh Wars of the 1840s. **(pp.160-61)** and the recruitment of Sikh battalions in Sepoy regiments had begun before the Mutiny; it had, indeed, been a major source of resentment among the high-caste sepoys of Oudh, who looked down on the Sikhs as hairy barbarians. Brasyer's Sikhs, raised as early as 1846 as the Regiment of Ferozepore, and later known as the Ferozepore Sikhs, had been instrumental in holding Allahabad fort when the Mutiny broke out and had spearheaded Havelock's first relief of Lucknow. Of the post-Mutiny regiments from the 19th to the 45th, nearly all had been raised in the Punjab during the Mutiny. There was also the Punjab Irregular Force which, after the Mutiny, normally came under the orders of the Lieutenant-Governor of the Punjab: five cavalry regiments, nine infantry battalions and four mountain artillery batteries.

To the Gurkhas as to the Sikhs, the British owed an immense debt of gratitude for loyalty during the Mutiny. Four Gurkha battalions had been formed from the Nepalese Army after its defeat in a particularly hard-fought war in 1815, but apart from their hardihood and self-sufficiency they remained a local corps until after the Sikh Wars. The Sirmoor Battalion earned high praise for its courage at Aliwal, and in 1850 the Gurkhas were reformed as a general service corps. On the eve of the Mutiny the Gurkhas refused to accept the ungreased cartridges issued to dispel Hindu and Moslem fears of impurity, asking for the same ammunition as was issued to British troops. Their bravery at the siege of Delhi during the Mutiny was never forgotten by the British, with whose regular units - most notably the Highlanders - the new Gurkha rifle regiments developed an extraordinary affinity. The Gurkhas' hallmark was their deadly **kukri**, a curved chopping-knife used in preference to the bayonet in hand-to-hand combat.

Many metaphors have been coined for the Indian Army as reconstructed after the Mutiny. The process has been compared with the rebuilding of a burned-out cathedral, adding new material to those parts of the fabric which had withstood the fire; or with a surgical graft onto shattered flesh. Either way, the graft took, and many lessons proved to have been learned when British India fought its next major campaign.

The Afghan problem

After the fiasco of the 1st Afghan War (1839-42), the British neurosis about Russian manipulation of Afghanistan had abated under the stabilising reign of Amir Dost Mohammed. By the eve of the Indian Mutiny British had given diplomatic aid to Afghanistan in checking Persian encroachment on Herat, while to the north of Afghanistan the last free khanates of Turkestan, Khokand and Bukhara continued to frustrate Russian attempts at southward expansion. By the late 1860s, however, the buffer provided by the northern khanates had gone with the submission to Russia of

War, 1879-80

Turkestan (1864), Khokand (1865) and Bukhara (1868).

Meanwhile, in Afghanistan, Dost Mohammed had been succeeded by his son Sher Ali (1863). The British were anxious for Sher Ali to receive a mission as a counterpoise to Russian influence, but the Amir refused. From 1873 he accepted increasing amounts of Russian subsidies and finally (July 1878) accepted a Russian mission in Kabul under General Stolyetov. When British demands for a British mission to be established as a counterpoise were rejected, the British resorted to direct action and the 2nd Afghan War began.

Warfare in Afghanistan

The 2nd Afghan War was in total contrast to the contemporary Zulu War in South Africa **(pp.168-69)**. This was mainly due to the appalling terrain which effectively ruled out wheeled transport, forcing the British columns to use pack mules for supply. The numbers of beasts required were prodigious - in one estimate, 70,000 mules to supply 36,000 men for 15 days. With Afghan tribesmen constantly poised to ambush lines of communications it was vital to apportion sufficient troops to defend the supply lines, which meant in practice that there were always more troops engaged on 'convoy escort' duties than were available for front-line service. To take one example, by the end of the 2nd Afghan War 15,000 men were committed to keeping open the line across the Khyber Pass from Peshawar to Kabul. This left only 12,000 for service with the field force.

The Afghan warrior was a formidable enemy, combining fanaticism with cunning, high endurance, and the advantage of knowing his home terrain. Afghan craftsmen turned out highly effective sniping rifles **(jezzails)** and were adept at fitting captured British mechanisms (from flintlock to sliding bolt action)

OPPOSITE: *Afghan warrior with jezzail and Khyber knife, 1879-80.*
RIGHT: *British infantry, 1879-80.*

to their home-made rifled barrels and stocks. The short Afghan chopping sword known as the 'Khyber knife' was a vicious weapon in hand-to-hand combat.

The Afghan War started well for the British, who invaded in three columns: the same technique employed during the invasion of Zululand, but with self-sufficiency for the columns as an invaluable bonus. The Afghans were non-plussed by simultaneous attacks across the Khyber, Kurram and Bolan Passes and were defeated by General Roberts with the centre column at Peiwar Kotal. Sher Ali died while making for Russian Turkestan; his successor Yakub Khan signed a treaty allowing a British Residency and token garrison at Kabul, occupation of the frontier passes and British vetting of Afghan foreign dealings in return for an annual subsidy. On 3 September, however, disaffected Afghan forces in Kabul attacked the Residency. Sir Louis Cavagnari and his civil assistant were killed and, after a superb resistance, the little escort of 52 Guides infantry and 25 Guides cavalry died to a man - having taken 600 Afghans with them.

The situation was retrieved by Roberts, who led another column through the Kurram Pass to defeat the Afghans at Charasiab **en route** to Kabul. The plan was now to leave the Afghans with token sovereignty over Kabul in the north but retain a garrison under General Burrows at Kandahar. In July 1880, however, the Kandahar force was badly beaten by the army of the new Amir, Ayub Khan, at Maiwand. The survivors were cut off in Kandahar. Once more Roberts saved the day with one of the epic marches of modern warfare: Kabul to Kandahar in 23 days. This was a vital demonstration of the British ability to abandon their communications with India and march through Afghanistan at will: 9,987 troops, 7,000 non-combatants and 8,419 transport animals. (The column finally returned to India via the Bolan Pass.) For once, the military successes of the campaign were not wasted by the peace settlement, which wisely declined to insist on the maintenance of vulnerable garrisons inside Afghanistan.

Dervish fury: the Sudan,

When the British occupied Egypt after bombarding Alexandria in July 1882 they inherited an appalling task of reconstruction after years of corrupt administration. Morale of the Egyptian Army could hardly have been lower after the failed rising of its officers which had prompted the British invasion, and nowhere were conditions worse than in Egypt's southern province, the Sudan. By the summer of 1883 the Sudan was imperilled by a revolt of Moslem fanatics, followers of Mohammed Ahmed, the self-proclaimed Mahdi or Messiah, whose initial successes established a reputation for invincibility and took the revolt past its 'take-off' point. Though the British had barely begun the reconstruction of the Egyptian Army they had no choice but to send it into action against the Mahdi's ragged but exalted army.

The British General Hicks - 'Hicks Pasha' in Egyptian service - marched from the Sudanese capital of Khartoum in September 1883. He had 7,000 Egyptian infantry and 500 cavalry, plus another 500 irregular cavalry, four Krupp guns and six Nordenfeldt machine-guns, and ten light mounted guns. The intention was to raise the siege of El Obeid in Kordofan, but this garrison had fallen before Hicks and his army set out. The Mahdi's 40,000 marched to meet the Egyptian force head-on, its earlier successes having yielded several thousand rifles and a few guns. On 3-4 November Hicks's weary force was cut off in open country as it struggled towards El Obeid, and slaughtered with barely 500 Egyptians surviving; Hicks and his officers died fighting to the last. With these and other victories, the Mahdi's Dervish warriors added fire-power to their basic arsenal of long sword, spear, and fury in attack - more than sufficient to panic bad troops fighting a long way from home with little or no motivation. The British Liberal Government had no intention of conquering the Sudan and decided on the evacuation of the last garrisons there, to oversee which task General Gordon was sent to Khartoum in January 1884. His defiance of the

Mahdi's army with a garrison of 7,000 over a city population of 30,000 inspired a belated relief expedition, featuring a dramatic overland march by the newly-formed Egyptian Camel Corps, 1,800 strong. Fighting in square formation, this tiny force beat off attacks by over 10,000 Dervishes at Aby Klea (17 January); but the final dash for Khartoum got under way three days too late to save Gordon, who died when the city fell to the Mahdi's main army on the night of 25-26 January 1885.

Though the Madhi died of smallpox in June 1885 his power passed undiluted to his nominated successor, the Khalifa Abdullah, who for the next 13 years maintained a brutal military dictatorship. British hopes of avenging Gordon meanwhile lay dormant until stability had been restored to the Egyptian state and efficiency to its army. The first encouraging sign that this state was being achieved came in the spring of 1889, when a Dervish force 5,000 strong rashly invaded Egypt. It was slaughtered at Toski by the Egyptian Army, an action in which the cavalry was commanded by the Adjutant-General, Herbert Kitchener. In 1882 Kitchener succeeded Sir Francis Grenfell as **Sirdar** or Commander-in-Chief of the Egyptian Army; but another four years passed before he was ordered to begin the reconquest of the Dervish-held Sudan. By this time the British in Egypt were excellently primed with intelligence on the Dervishes, as they had not been in 1885.

The reconquest begins, 1896

In planning for this 'River War', Kitchener's main problem was the 1,000-odd miles described by the meandering Nile between Cairo and Khartoum, punctuated by the river's five great cataracts impeding easy transport by water. He therefore planned a methodical advance sustained by railway, most of which would have to be built in the wake of the army's advance. From the outset, however, Kitchener was harrassed by demands for economy: this was to be a war on the cheap, and he was not to consider advancing past Dongola, 300 miles short of Khartoum. And all this despite cholera, killing 286 soldiers and 640 labourers; and torrential rains washing away sections of railway track and scores of telegraph poles.

The first stage of the advance (June-September 1896) saw Kitchener's army 'blooded' in a fine success: a surprise attack at dawn on the Dervish advance force at Firket, with 800 enemy dead and 1,100 captured (including the Emir in command), for only 20 killed and 83 wounded. Supported by gunboats built in sections for launching upstream of the cataracts, Kitchener pushed steadily on, and on 19 September routed 5,600 Dervishes at Hafir, 36 miles downstream of Dongola. Shelled by gunboats, Dongola surrendered on 22 September.

Kitchener was satisfied with neither the knighthood nor the promotion which rewarded him for this success. On a flying visit to London he pleaded successfully for a resumption of the advance in 1897 - by a happy coincidence the year of Queen Victoria's Diamond Jubilee, with imperial patriotism rampant. For the next advance Kitchener planned a revolutionary use of the railway in war: cutting off the great bend of the Nile by rebuilding a railway across the desert between Wadi Halfa and Ab Hamed, 230 miles long. Begun on 1 January 1897, the Desert Railway had been pushed to within 100 miles of Ab Hamed by 20 July. A camel-borne flying column of 2,700 troops captured Ab Hamed on 7 August; a week later the British gunboats fought their way through to Abu Hamed from Dongola - whereupon the Dervishes abandoned Berber, occupied by Kitchener's advance forces on 5 September.

For his final advance on Omdurman, the Dervish capital, Kitchener was sent substantial reinforcements. At Nakheila on the Atbara River (7 April) Kitchener shattered a Dervish army of 18,000 with a frontal infantry attack. In the last battle outside Omdurman (2 September 1898) he used overwhelming fire-power to break the Dervish army of 60,000 in less than five hours.

Joint action

In the last year of the 19th Century, the ultra-nationalist rising against European imperialism in China known as the 'Boxer Revolt' prompted that rarest of phenomena: a joint international expeditionary force, sent to defend the interests not only of the leading European powers but of Japan and the United States as well. This joint action by the world powers in China provides an ideal opportunity to sum up the common factors in international soldiering which other colonial wars of the century had established.

The proper name for the Boxers was the 'Society of Righteous and Harmonious Fists'. They were a fiercely nationalistic Chinese sect whose forte was the yoga-like attuning of mind and body as a preparation for combat. The idea was to render the body invulnerable to wounds in combat - proof of which was a popular attraction on days of festival. This state of exaltation was comparable to that prized by the Ghazis ('champions') of Afghanistan; it can be traced right back through military history to Viking beserkers (who fought 'bare-sark', or in nothing more protective than a shirt) and beyond. Against the fire-power enjoyed by every leading modern army of 1900 it stood little chance. But the fury of the Boxers was first unleashed on civilians, and shocked the world by its savagery.

The focal point of Boxer resentment was the extensive grants of Chinese ports and territory for foreign diplomatic and commercial exploitation, and the easiest targets were European Christian missions. The trigger to Boxer resentment was the humiliating defeat of China by Japan in the war of 1894-95. Countermoves against foreigners led by Boxer fanatics broke out in Shantung province in 1898 and were exploited by the ruthless Empress Tz'u-hsi, who overthrew her own son to impose a third regency, pledged to reaction and a purge of foreigners, in September 1898.

European protests at the Boxer outrages were not slow in coming but at first took the form of naval

in China, 1900: the Boxer Rising

squadrons sent to Taku Bay, near Tientsin. By June 1900 a force of 426 marines from these ships had been sent to Peking to protect the European diplomatic corps in the capital, but a relief force 2,000 strong arrived too late to prevent the siege of the legation compound which began on 20 June. Fortunately for the defenders the Boxers and regular Chinese troops sent to their aid lacked modern artillery, and though ammunition was short the rifle fire of the 450-odd defending troops proved just sufficient. The allied relief force took Tientsin on 14 July but waited to build up its strength to around 20,000 before marching on Pekling on 4 August. Ten days later, troops of the Russian contingent broke into Peking; the first troops to reach the legation after 55 days of siege were Indian, with British officers; 2 miles from the legation the Japanese contingent relieved the besieged Catholic cathedral. The cost of the Peking siege had been 66 non-Chinese killed; Chinese casualties were never recorded.

Common factors, 1900

The crushing of the Boxer Revolt in 1900 was the only occasion when British, Indian, German, Austrian, Japanese, Russian, French, Italian and United States troops have ever served together in a joint campaign. Despite natural variations in design and efficiency the standard infantry weapon was the breech-loading rifle, fitted now with a magazine capable of holding up to 10 rounds. The survival of the bayonet for hand-to-hand combat belied the enormous changes made possible by the advent of breech-loading. The most important of these changes was that the soldier no longer had to stand in order to reload, as in the muzzle-loading era, but could maintain a rapid rate of fire lying down or from behind cover.

Other improvements made over the preceding 30-odd years had been to the cartridge and its propellant charge. In the Zulu War of 1879, for instance, the British had been distressed by the tendency of their cartridges, when used in rapid fire, to foul the barrel with black powder deposits, and render the barrel red-hot. The base of the cartridge, in an over-heated rifle, also tended to shear off and leave the rest of the cartridge case to be dug from the barrel with the point of a knife. By 1900, however, nitro-glycerine had replaced black powder, resulting in less smoke and barrel fouling, less heat and greater range. The same advantages applied to revolver side-arms and to the rifles and carbines issued to the cavalry for use in dismounted action.

By 1900, however, a question mark still hung over the most recent addition to the fire-power of infantry riflemen: the machine-gun. The breakthrough in machine-gun development had come with Maxim's successful use of recoil to produce the first single-barrelled machine-gun operated by trigger pressure rather than hand cranking (1885). The 'Maxim' had been adopted by Britain, Germany and Russia; France and Japan opted for the Hotch-kiss system, in which energy for automatic fire was provided by the cartridge gases released on firing. All experience showed that machine-guns were an invaluable aid for modern infantry engaging superior numbers in colonial warfare. There was, however, profound disagreement over their use against opposition enjoying comparable rifle and artillery fire-power, and this disagreement would not be dispelled until the First World War.

Though rapid-firing artillery and the machine-gun clearly ordained great care in its deployment and commitment, cavalry remained the standard mobile arm for reconnaissance, shock attack and pursuit, its supreme advantage still being the ability of horsed troops to cover difficult terrain at speed. There was nothing in 1900 to indicate the obsolescence of cavalry which the next 20 years would bring in its train.

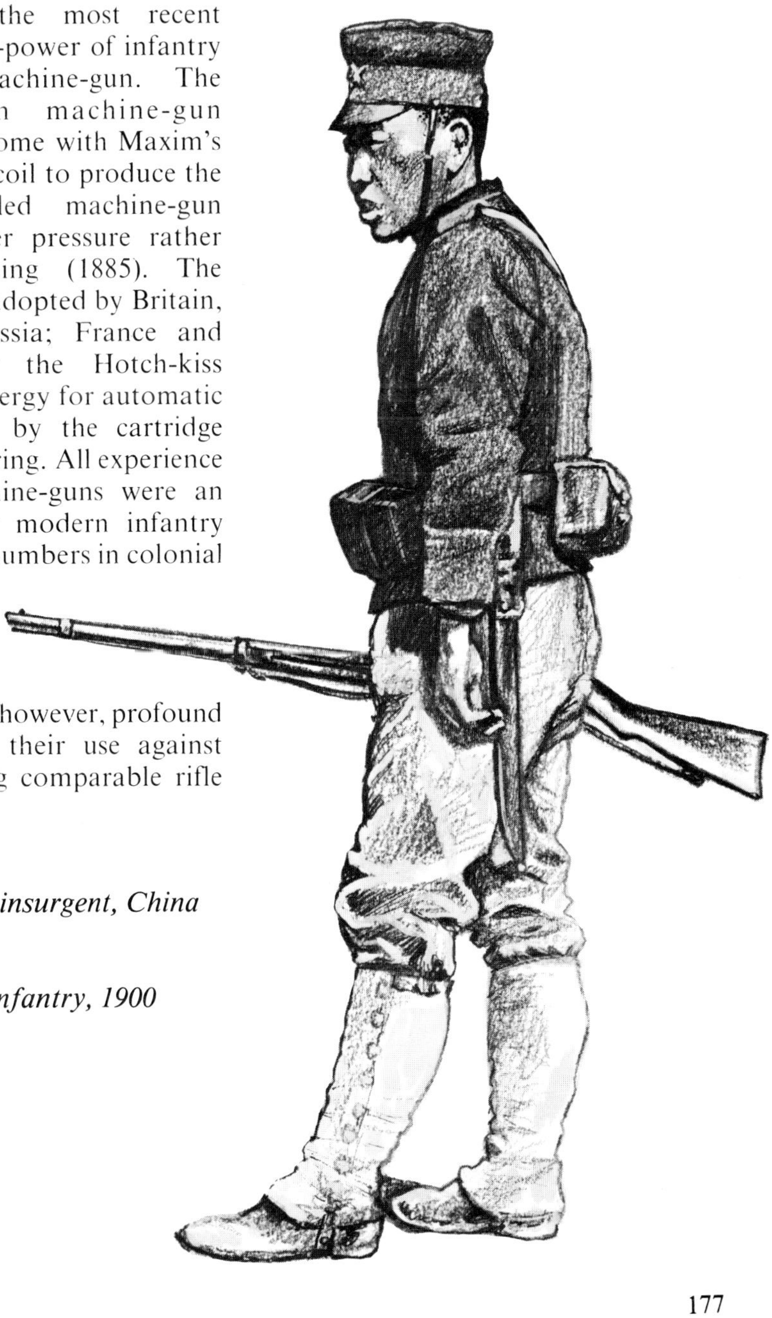

***OPPOSITE:** Boxer insurgent, China 1900*

***RIGHT:** Japanese infantry, 1900*

Ordeal in South Africa: the Boer War

ABOVE: Scourge of the British infantry in every battle of position - Boer marksman in secure firing position.

The South African or Boer War of 1899-1902 was a conflict of paradoxes. The British, seeking to defeat the Boer republics of the Orange Free State and Transvaal, had time on their side in the raising of overwhelming numbers, but no experience in bringing to action an enemy whose strength was mobility and fire-power which was virtually invisible due to superior fieldcraft. The Boers, though masters of defensive warfare and a constant threat to the vital British lines of communication, chose to squander most of their natural advantages in ventures for which their talents and resources were diametrically opposed.

At the outset of the war the Boers' advantages were formidable. They could raise over 60,000 mounted troops, all armed with Mauser rifles and possessed of marksmanship and fieldcraft infinitely superior to that of 14,750 British regulars opposing them; they had rifles and ammunition for 80,000, and planned to raise that number by enlisting Cape Dutch (who numbered two-thirds of the population of Cape Colony). But Boer 'grand strategy' was far too wasteful of these advantages. Their land-locked republics needed the Natal coastline and the port of Durban to enjoy any future as in independent nation, and this should have been the major Boer objective. They had the recent war in the Sudan to show them how the British would fight the war: use the railways from Capetown, Port Elizabeth and Durban to build up armies for an invasion of the Orange Free State and Transvaal from the west, south and east. But the Boers failed to sever these vital rail arteries while they had the chance; and by the time that the railways **were** marked down as a major objective, the early Boer advantage in numbers had been thrown away.

The Boer offensive, 1899-1900

The first month of the war, after the Boer rejection of the British ultimatum made hostilities inevitable on 11 October 1899, saw the predictable isolation of Mafeking, Kimberley and Ladysmith. But the expected rising of the Cape Dutch in support of the Boers did not occur and the Boer forces in the field, though unrivalled in mobility and individual marksmanship, proved to have little notion of how sieges should be prosecuted. With no immediate prospect of the Boers' capturing either of their three besieged objectives the initiative passed to the British.

By mid-November the British C-in-C, Buller, had been reinforced by a corps of three divisions. Buller promptly split this corps into three, ordering General Methuen to cross the Orange River and advance up the railway to relieve Kimberley; General Gatacre to chase the Boers out of the Stormberg region and advance up the East London railway to the Orange River; and General Cleary's division to proceed to Natal, where Buller took command of the main British push: the attempt to relieve Ladysmith.

The first battles were fought on the western sector, by Methuen's division: Belmont (23 November), Graspan (25 November) and Modder River (28 November). All three actions were fought along the axis of the railway, to which the British were tied; all featured frontal attacks, because Methuen had virtually no cavalry with which to bounce the Boers out of their positions with rapid encircling movements; and all three indicated that a new era in war had begun. Rapid rifle-fire from secure positions, supplemented by modern quick-firing artillery, meant that frontally attacking infantry took heavy losses from a virtually invisible foe. As soon as the attackers came dangerously near (thanks to high courage bolstered by regimental tradition) the Boers withdrew; dying where they stood was no part of their strategy.

Then, in December, came the triple shock of 'Black Week': Gatacre repulsed at Stormberg (10 December) with the loss of 135 killed and wounded and 600 prisoners; Methuen

1899-1902

halted at Magersfontein (11 December) with the loss of 910 killed and wounded, and obliged to dig in fewer than 20 miles from Kimberley; and finally Buller, abandoning not only his attack at Colenso (15 December) but ten guns, having lost 1,139 killed and wounded. Buller's subsequent willingness to abandon Ladysmith caused his replacement by Lord Roberts as C-in-C but before Roberts arrived Buller tried again, at Spion Kop (24 January 1900). This was the bloodiest British failure of the war, caused again by converging rifle and artillery fire which inflicted 1,700 casualties.

The British offensive, 1900

Spion Kop was, however, speedily reversed by the new strategy ordered by Roberts, who began the vital transformation from infantry to cavalry and mounted infantry. His first objective was the Boer army under Cronje which had foiled Methuen's attempt to relieve Kimberley. Roberts sent French's cavalry division to relieve Kimberley while the main force manoeuvered Cronje away from Magersfontein. French relieved Kimberley on 15 February, then returned to join in hounding of Cronje who surrendered with 4,000 men at Paardeberg on 27 February. Meanwhile, in Natal, Buller had attacked again across the Tugela and finally succeeded in relieving Ladysmith on 28 February.

The elimination of Cronje removed all obstacles to Robert's march on Bloemfontein, which fell on 13 March. It took several weeks to open the railway link south and contain the first chronic outbreak of disease (typhoid and dysentery) which caused the majority of British casualties in this war. The British advance to the north was resumed on 1 May, forcing the Boers to raise the siege of Mafeking after 217 days (17 May).

For his invasion of the Transvaall, Roberts directed an irresistible three-pronged advance from Kimberley, Bloemfontein and Ladysmith: 100,000 men in all, with contingents from every major Dominion of the Empire, against 30,000 Boers in scattered groupings. In conventional terms it was a runaway victory, with the enemy government put to flight and the enemy capital, Pretoria, occupied on 5 June. Two final victories were won over the rump of the Boer army in the Transvaal, at Diamond Hill and Belfast; by the end of September the last Boer rail outlet to Portuguese East Africa was sealed off with the capture of Komati Port.

The long guerrilla war

But by November 1900, when Kitchener took over from Roberts as C-in-C, it was clear that Boer resistance was far from over. It had entered its longest phase: that of mobile guerrilla warfare led by such adepts as de la Rey, de Wet, Botha and Herzog. Kitchener's reply was to deport the population supporting the elusive **commandos** into concentration camps and deny the raiders freedom of movement by means of chains of block-houses. Until the camps were transferred to civilian administration mortality (due to mismanagement rather than sadism) was appalling: 20,177 dead out of 117,871 by the end of 1901. The Boer leaders finally sued for peace in March 1902.

The Boer War lasted 31 months and cost the British 22,000 dead (over 16,000 of them of disease); Boer losses in the field were about 4,000. Altogether the British had committed some 45,000 troops.

BELOW: *British mounted infantry, 1901*

1914

THE FIRST WORLD WAR

-1918

The armies of Europe went to war in 1914 with planning based on experience culled from the Crimea, American Civil War and Franco-Prussian War of 1870: in fear of the terrifying power which entrenched riflemen and well-sited artillery could impart to the defender. War plans of 1914, on both sides, aimed at a quick decision in the open field to avoid battering at fixed lines, with the inevitable losses which this must entail. Once delivered to their frontier start-lines by railway during mobilization, armies depended as ever on horse-drawn transport, and on the marching endurance of infantry and cavalry.

Once the war had degenerated into trench stalemate from the Channel to the North Sea, the whole picture changed: the rival powers now had no chance but to resign themselves to frontal attacks of previously unknown prodigality. In these attacks conventional surprise was impossible; the decisive arms were artillery for the attack and the machine-gun – two men providing the fire-power of 20 – for the defence.

In the search for any means with which to break the deadlock, poison gas and flame-throwers made their hideous appearance; the demand for battlefield survivability re-introduced the steel helmet (after an absence of some 250 years) and the armoured fighting vehicle – the tank. This, too, was the first air war, with aerial reconnaissance 'spotting' for the guns and attempting to break enemy civilian morale by bombing cities.

Yet in the last analysis the decisive factor was the human one; the ability to keep pace with the prodigious expenditure of life on the battlefield. The great blood-letting of 1914-1918, with its traumatic effect on the belligerent powers, changed the nature of soldiering for ever.

Western Front, 1914: the short-lived

Supporting her ally Austria against Serbia and Russia, Germany went to war in 1914 with the intention of crushing Russia's ally France with a single mighty blow before railroading her armies east to settle accounts with Russia. But the Schlieffen Plan, aimed at trapping the French armies with a wide encircling sweep from the West, demanded the penetration of Belgium - accepting the risk that Britain would enter the war in defence of Belgian neutrality.

The execution of the Schlieffen Plan was delayed by the unexpected resistance of the Belgian fortresses around Liège (5-17 August) and at Antwerp. This slowed the great sweep of the German 1st and 2nd Armies through Belgium and allowed the British Expeditionary Force, despatched overseas by the most efficient mobilization ever experienced by the British Army, to join the westernmost French armies around Maubeuge.

As the German scythe began its southerly sweep through Belgium, the French 1st and 2nd Armies advanced to launch the long-awaited reconquest of Alsace and Lorraine, German provinces since 1870. The result was the first great infantry massacre of the war: the inaptly-named 'Battle of the Frontiers' which, in the fortnight beginning 19 August, cost the French Army over 300,000 killed, wounded and missing. No other army in Europe had retained so much 19th Century glamour in uniform, fatally obsolete in the age of the machine-gun. The red-trousered infantry and cuirassiers of the cavalry, viewed through the gunsight, would not have been out of place in the Crimea - even at Waterloo. Apart from being ridiculously conspicuous, French infantry doctrine was to rely on the flat-out bayonet charge, unsupported by medium or heavy artillery. It all added up to a recipe for slaughter.

This by no means implied that there was no scope for cavalry in 1914. Cavalry was still the natural reconnaissance medium, being both quicker and safer than aircraft in getting news of enemy movements back to where it was most immediately needed. The British cavalry - unlike the French, with its feeble Lebel carbine - carried the standard infantry Lee-Enfield rifle and was trained to give a good account of itself in dismounted action. This happened on 22 August: the first clash between British and German troops of the First World War. 'C' Squadron of the 4th

war of movement

FAR LEFT: *Obsolete relic of Napoleonic glory - French cavalry, 1914.*
CENTRE: *British cavalry, 1914 - far better suited to emergency dismounted action, with its troopers armed with the same excellent Lee-Enfield rifle as the infantry.*
BELOW: *German infantry, 1914 - marched to exhaustion in the great advance, yet still able to withdraw in good order.*

Dragoon Guards chased four German cuirassiers who retreated at the gallop, falling back on the rifle fire of the nearest infantry. Rapid, dismounted rifle fire enabled the British troopers to retire without loss, taking prisoners and trophies as they went.

Mons and after

This skirmish took place the day before the Battle of Mons, the German Army's first agonising encounter with British rapid rifle fire - but Mons was only a temporary if bloody check. The withdrawal of the French 5th Army on the British right flank obliged the British to retreat in order to avoid encirclement - the start of the long retreat to the Marne, punctuated by tough rearguard actions at Landrecies and Le Cateau (25-26 August).

By the last week of August the German Schlieffen Plan was beginning to break down, despite the fact that the Allies were in retreat on all fronts. The Plan had taken little account of the difficulties in maintaining communications between Army Supreme HQ at Koblenz and the fast-moving armies at the front. The German attempt to maintain communications via the new medium of radio was not a success and Army Chief of Staff Moltke (nephew of the great Prussian strategist of the previous century) had little idea where his leading troops were. Nor had the Schlieffen Plan taken account of the physical problems encountered by the German right-wing armies, the outermost of which (General von Kluck's 1st Army) was required to march 300 miles in three weeks, keeping up a marching pace of 15 miles a day without so much as a day's rest. By the end of August the scorching pace was beginning to tell and the Germans were suffering not only from fatigue but hunger, having out-marched their field kitchens and bakeries.

Most serious of all, the Schlieffen Plan - while attempting to provide for all eventualities - demanded a flexibility which the German military machine of 1914 simply did not have. There was no provision for unexpected setbacks such as the Belgian resistance at Liège and Antwerp or the delays imposed by the British at Mons and Le Cateau. In the event it was the French, not the Germans, who proved better at improvising an emergency strategy 'off the cuff' once the original plans had gone astray. By the 25th Moltke was beginning to panic at the danger on the Eastern Front posed by the Russian push into East Prussia. In the West he had already detached two corps to block Antwerp and one to attack Maubeuge, while two more were pinned down at Namur. As soon as Namur fell the latter two corps were withdrawn from the Western Front and railroaded east - at the moment that Joffre, the French C-in-C, was conjuring a new army into existence to cover the western flank of the German advance.

The ruin of the Schlieffen Plan was invisibly accomplished with the unexpected counter-attack of the French 5th Army against the German 2nd Army at Guise on 29 August. This led the German 1st Army to swing sharply to the east instead of continuing on course to outflank Paris from the west.

From the Marne to the sea

The upshot was the 'Miracle of the Marne' (6-9 September) in which the French and British armies turned about to counter-attack the German masses passing Paris to the east. The Marne counter-attack was spearheaded by a French Army (Maunoury's 6th) which had not existed at the outset of the campaign. It featured the rushing to the front of a French brigade carried by a fleet of Paris trucks and taxi-cabs - the first use of motorised troops in war, and another piece of improvisation which the Germans could not match.

But the Marne was not a German rout, the German armies fell back and held the Allies on the Aisne, both sides thereafter repeatedly hooking at each other's flanks until, in mid-October, the Channel was reached and the war of movement ended.

Stalemate at Gallipoli, 1915

***BELOW:** Australian infantry on Gallipoli, where the inexperienced Australian and New Zealand forces came nobly through their first baptism of fire.*
***OPPOSITE:** Turkish infantry. Long before the evacuation, 'Johnny Turk' had been accepted as a worthy and indeed chivalrous opponent by his attackers.*

Opened in April 1915, the Gallipoli campaign marked the first major expansion of the war outside the frontiers of Europe. It was brought about by Turkey's joining the war (30 October 1914) on the side of Germany and Austria, the Turkish Empire thereupon posing a triple threat to British Egypt, Britain's sea-borne communications with India, and the southern Russian frontier.

The notion of an offensive up the Gallipoli Peninsula was first discussed by the British War Council in late November 1914; it was presented as an ideal way of defending Egypt by dealing Turkey a 'blow at the heart'. The scheme envisaged a **coup de main** which, carried primarily by the British and French Mediterranean fleets, would thrust through the Narrows of the Dardanelles to take the Turkish capital, Constantinople. This would not only knock Turkey out of the war but enable the British and French to ship rapid aid to Russia. The supreme objective was to avoid duplicating the paralysis which had settled on the Western Front after the 'Race to the Sea' ended in October. As events turned out, what actually occurred was yet another trench-bound ordeal lasting from the first troop landings on Gallipoli (25 April 1915) to the last troop evacuations on 9 January 1916.

Apart from French naval support, Gallipoli was an all-British venture and it failed primarily because of the inability to reconcile the problems of the Army and the Royal Navy. There were no joint planning staffs to prepare such an amphibious venture at short notice (the rapid, trouble-free transfer of the British Expeditionary Force to France in August 1914 had been the result of years of meticulous staffwork). When Lord Kitchener protested that no troops could be spared for a Mediterranean offensive, Winston Churchill at the Admiralty insisted that the heavy guns of the fleet could silence the Turkish batteries protecting the Dardanelles.

The first naval bombardment began on 25 February 1915 and culminated in the attempt by an Anglo-French fleet to rush the Narrows on 18 March. It was a fiasco, with three old battleships sunk and four crippled out of 18. The culprits were mines which could not be swept because of Turkish gunfire from the heights above the Narrows. By this time Kitchener had reversed his opinion and despatched 70,000 troops to the Mediterranean to exploit the Navy's promised success. This Mediterranean Expeditionary force, however, arrived with its stores so lamentably packed that prompt landings were out of the question after the naval failure on 18 March. Not until the last week of April were the first troops ready to land on Gallipoli, and by then the original concept of a surprise assault was dead. The Turks were ready and waiting.

Failure of the first landings

The defence of Gallipoli was entrusted to the Turkish 5th Army, whose uncertain six infantry divisions were commanded by General Liman von Sanders, German military attaché at Constantinople. He deployed his troops (stiffened with German officers) in such a way as to command all high ground overlooking the likeliest invasion beaches on Gallipoli, and to prevent any British attempt to drive straight across the peninsula's narrowest point, at Bulair.

General Hamilton, the British commander, knew very well that the laborious preparations for the Gallipoli landing had forfeited surprise. His assault plan aimed at atoning for this by gaining **local** surprise over the waiting Turks: landing at six different beaches on Gallipoli with a feint landing to the north and a French corps landing on the Asian shore. He never knew how close this came to success. The great failure stemmed from the lack of accurate maps for the troops (while the Turks knew the terrain well), and from the inability of the supporting warships to provide accurate supporting fire. Liaison between the troops ashore and the warships remained bad throughout the vital first week of the Gallipoli venture.

The Australian and New Zealand Corps (ANZAC) landed virtually unopposed on the west coast of the peninsula but 2 miles north of their designated beach; they ended up penned in a triangular beach-head, forced back from the commanding heights by counter-attacks from the reserve Turkish divisions at Boghali. Further south, at Y and X Beaches, the landings had gone according to plan but on the two main beaches - W and V, at the tip of the peninsula - the result had been a shocking carnage. The Turks had abandoned their trenches during the naval bombardment, returning to savage the invaders, as they hit the beaches, with intense rifle and machine-gun fire. Just as the Western Front troops were finding in France, the bombardment left barbed-wire entanglements intact.

The net gain was two precarious beachheads: the ANZACs at Ari Burnu and the 29th Division across the tip of the peninsula, both dug in among deepening web of trenches with all prospect of a swift and steady advance on Constantinople gone. The Turks had managed to pin down an army 75,000 strong with barely 8,000 defenders, a situation impossible for the Allies to accept. Both sides settled down to reinforce, but in mid-May the arrival of German U-boats in the Aegean forced the Allied battleships to withdraw, depriving the troops ashore of their heaviest artillery support. Furious Turkish counter-attacks (the first wave sent in with unloaded rifles to ensure that the men charged home with the bayonet) were only painfully beaten off.

The last throw was the landing at Suvla Bay (6 August) which achieved nothing more than another hard-won beach-head. Ironically, the greatest Allied achievement on Gallipoli was the evacuation (18 December-8th January).

Carnage on the Somme, July-November 1916

British infantry, Somme 1916

The sequence of immensely costly attacks on the German trench line known as the 'Battle of the Somme' was the major British land effort on the Western Front in 1916. It was on the Somme that General Haig, the British C-in-C, sought to redress the failed British offensives of 1915 - Neuve Chapelle in March, Aubers Ridge in May, Loos in September-October. All these failures had been due to the same common factor: the loss of surprise to to preliminary artillery bombardment, the failure of even the heaviest shellfire to breach defensive belts of barbed wire, and the ability of the defenders to rush 'fire-brigade' reinforcements to any temporary breach which the attackers managed to force.

The military consensus was that the theory had been justified, but the means to carry it out had not been present in sufficient strength. It was, as C.S. Forester has written, almost 'like the debate of a group of savages on how to extract a screw from a piece of wood.- Accustomed only to nails, they had made one effort to pull out the screw by main force, and now that it had failed they were devising methods of applying more force still ... so that more men could bring their strength to bear. They could hardly be blamed for not guessing that by rotating the screw it would come out after the exertion of far less effort'. The British infantry attacked on 1 July in the belief that, after a week of the heaviest bombardment in the history of the world, the German front-line defenders would have been wiped out and the screening barbed wire cut to shreds. Neither was the case, and the result was the most appalling single day in the history of the British Army.

The terrible first day - 1 July 1916

One of the main reasons for selecting the Somme sector for the 'Big Push' of 1916 was that it was chalkland, excellent for cavalry exploitation once the vital breach had been made. The Germans, however, had succeeded in making their front-line infantry far more 'survivable' than the British ever dreamed. Under bombardment, they took shelter in deep dugouts, emerging with their machine-guns to savage the oncoming infantry when the barrage lifted. Only the French on the British right flank, with their huge 240mm and 400mm heavy mortars, had guns heavy enough to crack these defences; the 1,537 British guns used for the bombardment were spread evenly along an 18-mile front. It was therefore on the French sector that the deepest penetration was achieved on 1 July.

Weighed down under personal loads of 85-90 lbs, the British infantry could only advance at a steady walk. Total losses on 1 July came to 57,470 British - over double those of the entire Boer War - of which some 20,000 were killed. The tragedy was heightened by the fact that this was one of the finest armies which Britain has ever raised; 11 of the 14 British divisions committed to the Somme assault were made up of the volunteers of Kitchener's 'New Armies', recruited since the outbreak of war. In their enthusiasm and high average intelligence these New Army battalions deserved far better than the mincing-machine tactics in which they were trained.

French tactics on the Somme, as one British liaison officer sadly noted, were infinitely superior; 'the British rigid and slow, advancing as at an Aldershot parade in lines that were torn and ripped by the German guns, while the French tactical formations, quick and elastic, secured their objectives with trifling loss ... The German artillery, with targets no gunner could resist, neglected the more dangerous but invisible French groups and concentrated on the British ... As a display of bravery it was magnificent, as an example of tactics its very memory made one shudder'.

The German losses

But the inevitable decision to press on with the offensive, to keep up the pressure on the Germans regardless of the ever-mounting casualties, was more than mere wanton blood-letting. Since February the German 5th Army had been similarly battering the French defenders of Verdun **(pp.190-191)**, inflicting over 257,000 French casualties; the British had been repeatedly begged to bring forward the date of the Somme offensive to relieve the pressure on Verdun. But German losses at Verdun had also been horrific: some 226,000 between February and June. Abandoning the Somme offensive would not only have been a breach of faith with France. As the military statisticians saw it, the German Army could not sustain a continued offensive at Verdun combined with a defensive on the Somme. And despite their unforgivable complacency, as they continued with their new-found strategy of 'attrition', the statisticians were not so far off the mark.

The German losses on the Somme were far higher than they need have been because of the prevailing doctrine that not an inch of ground must be abandoned. The insistence of Chief-of-Staff Falkenhayn on 'counter-attack, even to the use of the last man' threw away the natural advantages of the defensive. By the time of the last British attack on the Somme (13-19 November) German losses were indeed higher than the British.

The reckoning

Insofar as an accurate count can be made, the Battle of the Somme cost the British about 420,000, the French 200,000 - and the Germans 450,000. The battle had lasted 141 days in all, and despite the cost can be counted an Allied victory, followed as it was by the German retreat (February 1917) to the powerful rear positions of the Hindenburg Line - the first German acknowledgement of defeat.

German machine-gunners, Somme 1916

The Alpine front: Italy and Austria 1915-1918

There was nothing altruistic about Italy's entry into the war on the Allied side in 1915. Italy's alliance was bought by Britain, France and Russia with promises of the Austrian-held lands - **Italia Irredenta,** to Italian patriots - which had not been won for the new kingdom of Italy during the **Risorgimento.** The most important of these lands were the South Tyrol, Trentino, Gorizia, Trieste and Istria. For some 200 years, enemies of the Austrian Empire had used North Italy as a remote-control 'second front' against Austria. Now for the first time Italian armies were fighting mountain campaigns on their own account.

When Italy declared war on Austria-Hungary in May 23 she had the 'youngest' army in the Allied coalition, with traditions barely 60 years old - all of **Risorgimento** vintage. The Italian Army's recent history had, moreover, included one of the most shattering defeats every suffered by a European army in Africa, by the Ethiopians at Adowa in 1896 (10,000 Italians killed or wounded out of a total strength of 14,000). With this chequered recent past the performance of the Italian Army between 1915 and 1918 appears all the more extraordinary. Viewed objectively, the endurance of the Italian soldier in these years certainly deserves to be ranked with that of the French at Verdun or the British on the Somme.

Italian strategy, 1915

General Cadorna, the Italian C-in-C, had his initial operations curtailed by Italy's unpreparedness for war and by the time it took her to reach full mobilization. He had to weigh the advantages and disadvantages of the two fronts along which operations against Austria promised any chance of success: the Trentino in the north, from which the Tagliamento and Brenta valleys led to the Adriatic coast on either side of Venice; and the Julian Alps in the east. Cardona's basic strategy remained defensive on the Trentino and unremitting offensives to the east, across the Isonzo River. Italy timed her declaration of war (23 May 1915) to coincide with promised offensives by Russia and Serbia against Austria, intended to draw off Austrian divisions from the Isonzo front; but this help never materialised. As a result the Austrians were able to reinforce their five divisions holding the Isonzo front with five from the Serbian front and three from Galicia, the Russian front. But this still left the Italian 1st and 2nd Armies with a numerical advantage of over two to one when Cadorna opened his first Isonzo offensive on 23 June 1915.

Stalemate in the mountains

The Alpine front perfectly demonstrated how much the First World War tended to favour the defensive. The nature of the mountain terrain ruled out the use of superior numbers in mass attacks; the eternal struggle for the high ground was not only for the best available artillery firing positions but for observation points from which the artillery depended for accurate fire. It was not enough to seize a peak, hill, or mountain with a determined rush; such gains had to be consolidated at once by moving up enough guns to silence the enemy artillery, which otherwise would massacre the exposed attacking troops. And such consolidation was impossible without constant improvisation on the supply-lines, pushing forward roads and ropeways and using manpower haulage where pack mules could not climb.

After preliminary indecisive skirmishing on the Trentino and Isonzo fronts in May, Cadorna's first main Isonzo offensive began on 23 June. It ended on 5 July with the Italians having gained barely a single mile for the loss of 1,500 prisoners. The Austrian casualty list, however, was no less high (8,800 killed and

OPPOSITE: *Italian **Bersagliere**, Isonzo, 1916. For the polyglot Austro-Hungarian Army the Italian theatre was only a sideshow; overall figures were for 1,200,000 dead and 3,620,000 wounded, most of them on the Eastern Front. But Italian figures for war dead only were a staggering 460,000, despite the fact that Italy entered the war nine months after Austria and that her operations were confined to Italian soil throughout. Nothing better illustrates the superb achievement of the Italian soldier in the First World War.*

BELOW: *Austrian infantry;*

wounded, and 1,150 captured or missing) when considered in proportion to the Italian superiority in numbers. The same factor was at work that cost the Germans so dear on the Somme in the following summer: the brutal cost of having to hurl reckless counter-attacks against every foothold won by the attackers.

Altogether Cadorna launched four offensives across the Isonzo in 1915 - the second from 18 July-10 August, the third from 18 October-3 November, and the fourth from 10 November-10 December. All resulted in negligible Italian gains; the Austrian front, with eight divisions and 350 guns against 18 Italian divisions and some 700 guns, held up well, profiting greatly from the greater destructiveness of its heavy artillery. The third and fourth Italian offensives were attempts to relieve Serbia from the great German-Austrian Bulgarian offensive, beginning on 6 October, which ground Serbia into total defeat in less than two months.

The battle of 1916

By the end of 1915 the four ill-fated Isonzo offensives had cost the Italians some 280,000 casualties, nearly double the Austrian loss; but Cadorna, faithfully imitating the 'nibbling' strategy then being pursued by General Joffre on the Western Front, launched a fifth and no more successful offensive from 15 February-17 March 1916.

The immense resilience of the Italian Army at this date was then revealed by the first Austrian offensive. This was the brainchild of the Austrian chief-of-staff, Conrad von Hötzendorff, who after the crushing of Serbia proposed a German-Austrian offensive to knock Italy out of the war as well. But his German opposite number, Falkenhayn, refused. Not only was Falkenhayn preparing for Germany's supreme attempt to break the French army at Verdun; he did not believe that there was any guarantee of achieving a decisive breakthrough on Hötzendorff's line of attack - the Trentino front. The Austrians nevertheless proceeded with their Trentino offensive (15 May-3 June) but as Falkenhayn had predicted failed to achieve more than a deep salient. Using reserves pulled out from the Isonzo front, Cadorna then counter-attacked (17 June-7 July) and recovered most of the ground lost - but it took another 150,000 Italian losses to do it.

Greatly aided by the 'knock-on' effect of the Austrian losses to the Brusilov offensive in southern Russia (June-August 1916) Cadorna's sixth Isonzo offensive finally took Gorizia (9 August) before the Italian attacks petered out on 17 August. There followed an eerie replay of the events of October-December 1915, prompted by Rumania's brief-lived entry into the war on the Allied side (27 August 1916). Commanded by Falkenhayn, an Austro-German army invaded and defeated Rumania (September-December 1916), while Cadorna launched his seventh, eighth and ninth assaults on the Isonzo front (14-18 September, 9-12 October and 31 October-4 November 1916).

In the spring of 1917 Cadorna proposed that the French and British should send powerful reinforcements to join the Italian Army in an offensive to knock Austria out of the war; but this was rejected by Generals Haig and Nivelle, still confident that a decisive breakthrough could be achieved in France. It was a near-fatal decision for the Italian Army, for the collapse of the Nivelle offensive (April 1917) and the results of the Russian Revolution enabled six German divisions to be sent to reinforce the nine Austrian divisions on the Isonzo front. Cadorna had meanwhile launched his tenth and eleventh Isonzo offensives (12 May-8 June and 17 August-12 September), thereafter preparing to withstand the coming German-Austrian attack.

Caporetto and after

The Caporetto offensive broke on 24 August with a short but ferocious bombardment completely severing the frontline Italian positions from the command areas. Cadorna's centre collapsed in rout, though he managed to save the flanking corps by ordering a headlong 70-mile retreat to the line of the Piave, leaving some 250,000 prisoners behind. Though Cadorna was sacked for the disaster his successor General Diaz changed none

of his dispositions and managed to hold the Austrians and Germans - who lacked the transport to keep pace with the Italian retreat - on the Piave. Bolstered by six French and two British divisions, the Italians repulsed the Austrians on the Piave (23-25 November). This splendid Italian recovery was crowned a year later when, having broken a final Austrian attack on the Piave (15-24 June 1918) Diaz attacked along the whole front, splitting the Austrian army at Vittorio Veneto (30 October) and finally advancing to take Trieste (3 November). The armistice requested by Austria was signed on 4 November.

Verdun and after:

ABOVE. *The French* ***poilu*** *('unshaven one') of 1916 wore a uniform and topcoat officially described as* ***horizon bleu,*** *the sight of which, coming pristine into battle-weary front areas, was a great boost to morale. When plastered with mud it provided quite as good camouflage as the khaki of the British or* ***feldgrau*** *of the Germans. The French light steel helmet helped deflect bullets, but was not much use against the massive fragments of burst shells.*

Verdun was the great exception to Germany's defensive strategy on the Western Front. It was conceived in late 1915, by German chief-of-staff General von Falkenhayn, as the corner-stone of German strategy for 1916: an offensive which was **not** intended to smash through the enemy line, break through into open country and win the war by Christmas with a triumphant entry into Paris. Falkenhayn chose Verdun as the German Army's main objective in 1916 because, as he rightly guessed, the French could not afford to lose it. Using an unparalleled concentration of artillery on a front barely 8 miles long, he planned to convert the Verdun sector into a mincing machine that would leave the French Army in shreds. The whole idea was to draw division after division into the deadly killing zone of the German guns, with a maximum economy of German infantry.

Verdun: threadbare fortress

Verdun was not a single fortress, but a garrison town surrounded by a chain of forts built after the Franco-Prussian War. These, however, after the crushing of the Belgian forts at Liège in 1915, had been stripped of many of their guns to reinforce the French Army's field artillery. The quietness of the Verdun sector since the 'Battle of the Frontiers' was to blame; instead of a tough, studded belt of self-contained fortresses, Verdun was screened to the north mainly by a flimsy skein of trenches with the largely disarmed forts behind it. When the German offensive broke on 21 February 1916, the French front-line positions were duly pulverised by the awesome concentration of German artillery,

crisis of the French Army, 1916-17

1,200 guns in all. Where Falkenhayn's plan began to break down was the unforeseen difficulty in moving the German big guns foward to keep up the pressure on the French rear areas.

Another advantage to the French throughout the battle was the terrain north of Verdun, with its cross-cut ridges interspersed with ravines. Above all there was the mistake, common to all armies in both world wars, of failing to realise that the survivors of an obliterated trench system could still put up an effective defence from shell-holes, from which they were even harder to dislodge by sustained artillery fire. The net result was that from the first week of the Verdun offensive German infantry had to be pushed forward to keep up the pressure on the French, exposing it to losses which eventually negated Falkenhayn's plan to 'bleed the French Army white'.

Pétain of Verdun

None of these advantages saved the French defenders of Verdun from being reduced to near breaking-point in the first week of the German offensive, even after General Pétain replaced the panicky General Herr on the morning of the fourth day (25 February).

Pétain's first objectives were to bolster the morale of the defenders and ensure the flow of reinforcements and ammunition. He achieved the first by insisting on revised artillery fire programmes, concentrating the fire of the French guns on to the most crucial sectors so that the hard-pressed infantry would never fear that their own guns had been silenced. The communications problem was, if anything, the most crucial of all. With the only available rail link to Verdun commanded by German 380mm fire there was nothing for it but to rely on the narrow road from Bar-le-Duc which, during the battle, earned the deathless title of **La Voie Sacrée** - the Sacred Way. With the organising genius of Major Richard, one of the truly unsung heroes of Verdun, the **Voie Sacrée** was kept open to road transport by the ceaseless labour of colonial troops. In the ten months of the battle, it was calculated that Richard's pick-and-shovel men had added three-quarters of a million tons of road surfacing to the vital lifeline. By June 1916, the crisis of the battle, trucks were moving up the **Voie Sacrée** at the rate of one every 14 seconds.

Pétain's appointment marked the true beginning of the French recovery at Verdun. The troops trusted him as a general who would not squander their lives on pointless counter-attacks; news of his arrival had an almost magical effect in stilling panic. This was vital, because on the very morning he took command Fort Douaumont, the strongest fort in the Verdun defences, was captured by the German 24th Brandenburg Regiment. (Douaumont's garrison consisted of a white-bearded warrant officer and 56 territorials). The news of Douaumont's fall was a great blow to French morale but it was Pétain who insisted that Verdun could be held without the Fort. Not the least of his achievements was directing the battle, for the first week, from his sick-bed, having gone down with double pneumonia within hours of taking command.

With one replacement corps already arrived and two more on the way (by December something like two-thirds of the French Army would have passed through Verdun), Pétain prepared to exploit the biggest error behind the German assault. This was created by the northerly meander of the Meuse out of Verdun, effectively dividing the battlefield into right-bank and left-bank sectors. Falkenhayn had concentrated his assault on the right bank, but the further the Germans advanced the more they came under flanking fire from the left bank. By the beginning of March, Falkenhayn had no choice but to agree to the extension of the battle to the left bank - only to find it defended by four French divisions and a fifth in reserve.

Three months of ferocious combat - March-May 1916 - established the Germans on the dominant ridge of the left bank: the aptly named **Mort Homme** - the Dead Man. But the cost was appalling. By the end of May French losses had risen to 257,000, but German losses were already up to 226,000. A last frantic offensive on the right bank in June was also held, despite the German use of the deadly new phosgene poison gas and the capture of Fort Vaux after a heroic siege; but it was too late. With the opening of the Russian Brusilov offensive on the Eastern Front and the British offensive on the Somme, Falkenhayn had no choice but to abandon the offensive at Verdun.

The last act at Verdun was the French counteroffensive of October-December 1916 which re-took Douaumont (24 October), Vaux (2 November) and pushed the front 2 miles north of Douaumont (15 December). Comparative losses for the ten months of the Verdun ordeal worked out at 315,000 for the French and over 282,000 for the Germans.

The U.S. Army, 1918

***BELOW:** 'Doughboy' - US infantryman, France, 1918. Even before the Americans proved themselves in action, the tonic effect of their confident arrival on the Western Front was an inestimable boon to the jaded French and British. From April to November 1918 US Army casualties totalled 325,876: 205,690 wounded, 48,909 killed in action, 4,526 prisoners or missing, and the rest victims of the great influenza pandemic.*

When the United States joined the Allies on 6 April 1917 its Army was completely incapable of bringing immediate effective aid to the Allied armies in Europe. Since the end of the Civil War 52 years before, the US Army had not only undergone a drastic reduction in size; the opposition which it had encountered in the Spanish-American War (1898) and Mexico (1914-17) bore little or no relationship to conditions on the Western Front.

It was true that the increasing possibility of American involvement in the war had had some effect. The National Defense Act of 1916 had provided for a regular Army of 288,000 men, backed by a National Guard - recruited from all able-bodied men between 18 and 45, called up in time of need by the Governors of the States - of 425,000. The snag was that this expansion was to spread over the next five years. In April 1917 the US Army consisted of 128,000 officers and men in the regular forces and 131,500 in the National Guard: a puny force by European standards. It lacked the manpower, its lacked the artillery, it lacked the experience and training to be of any use whatsoever in Europe. Only in its infantry weapons - the 1913 Springfield .30 rifle, and the .45 automatic pistol - did the US Army bear comparison to its European counterparts, but there were no stockpiles of these excellent weapons to assist a rapid expansion of the Army.

And yet, within the space of 18 months, a transformed US Army of 2 million men was conjured into being and sent overseas to play a full part in the final defeat of Germany. It was nothing less than a miracle of organisation surpassing Kitchener's transformation of the peacetime British Army between 1914 and 1916. But it is unlikely that this could have been achieved merely by the urgent need to create an army fit to face the Germans. The real challenge was presented by the French and British military chiefs who saw the American alliance in terms of a potential blood transfusion in manpower, making good the horrific losses sustained in 1916 and 1917. For President Wilson and the commander of the American Expeditionary Force, General Pershing, it was unthinkable that American troops should be injected piecemeal into the Allied bloodstream on the Western command, fighting beside the British and French instead of being shared out as Anglo-French cannon fodder; and their objective was triumphantly achieved.

Crisis and triumph, 1918

Amazing though it was a phenomenon, the build-up of American divisions in France was nevertheless only getting into its stride when the great German offensive broke in March 1918; by the beginning of February only five American divisions had arrived in France, and only two more complete divisions and elements of an eighth had joined by the beginning of May. Pershing nevertheless won the American Expeditionary Force's first battle during the desperate weeks of the German breakthrough: preventing the first American division from being dismembered to plug the gaps in the British front. On April 14, when General Foch was named generalissimo of the Allied armies, Pershing succeeded in retaining autonomy for his command. The American units rushed to the periphery of the German advance - the Lys (9-29 April) the Somme (6 April-28 May) and the Marne (27 May-5 June) did not prevent the formation of the US 1st Army under his own command.

It was in the dying phase of the German Marne offensive that the American Expeditionary Force won its spurs, with the defence of Château-Thierry (31 May-1 June) and the recapture of Belleau Wood (9-15 June). Four American divisions, with their huge complements of 17,000 rifles (average German divisional strength was 7,000 in 1918) took part in the Marne counter-offensive of 18 July-6 August. The American capture of the St. Mihiel salient (12-16 September) was the prelude to US 1st Army's northward drive through the Argonne (launched 26 September) which had captured over 16,000 prisoners and 468 guns by the time of the Armistice.

Revolution in Russia, 1917

Unlike the French Revolution of 1789-92, the Russian Revolution of 1917-18 did not leave the rank and file of the pre-revolutionary army substantially intact. Still less was the Russian Revolution saved from foreign and domestic enemies by the regular units of the pre-revolutionary army. Indeed, the circumstances of Russia in 1917-18 could hardly have been more different from those of France in 1792, when the French Revolutionary Wars began. At least the new masters of France in 1792 had had an army with which to fight. In October 1917, Lenin and the triumphant Bolsheviks were forced to start from scratch.

Lenin's original idea was to dissolve the remaining units of the old Tsarist Army (such as had not already collapsed in mutiny and mass desertion) and replace them with a people's militia based on the **Red Guards** - the motley, ill-disciplined gangs of soldiers, sailors and armed workers who had done all the fighting during the Bolshevik seizure of power. This plan soon proved impracticable, if only because the end of the German War guaranteed no safety for Russia against foreign intervention bent on restoring the monarchy. Moreover, there were only some 30,000 Red Guards in January 1918, of which only a third could be described as being in any condition of military readiness. As for the expected flood of volunteers for military service, this was too much to expect after the bloodbath losses since the outbreak of war back in 1914. By April 1 1918, only 153,678 men had joined up, and 40,000 of them were troops from former Tsarist units. On April 22, a decree proclaimed universal military training for the 'toiling masses', not only between the ages of 18 and 40 but for schoolchildren and teenagers as well.

Charged as People's Commisar for Military Affairs with building the new 'Red Army of Workers and Peasants', Leon Trotsky accepted that former Tsarist officers were essential, despite the prejudice against them harboured by hard-line revolutionaries. Another revolutionary ideal which went by the board was the election of officers from the ranks. This had also been attempted and abandoned by the French Republicans in the mustket-and-bayonet days of the 1790s but was wholly unrealistic for the demands of 20th Century warfare. The Bolshevik regime did, however, ensure virtually complete control of its officer corps by the appointment of commissars with authority to check and countersign every operational order written by all officers in any way politically suspect.

Even this clumsy and inefficient compromise, which enabled Trotsky to draw on the military skills of ex-Tsarist Army personnel, would hardly have been readily adopted without the outbreak of the Civil War in May 1918. This supreme crisis left the Bolshevik regime with no option but mass conscription and the recruiting of former Tsarist officers and NCOs. It was just enough, and just in time, to enable the fledgeling Red Army to beat off the White Russian and foreign army contingents which sought in vain to crush the Russian Revolution.

Fighting men of the Russian Revolution, 1917: Baltic Fleet Revolutionary sailor and 'Red Guard'.

Storm Troops and tanks:

OPPOSITE: *German infantry, March 1918*
BELOW: *British Whippet tank crew, Amiens, August 1918.*

Germany defeated, 1918

Massively reinforced by divisions released by the collapse of Russia, the German armies launched their bid for victory in the West on 21 March 1918. The plan was to use the new tactics employed with such success against the Italians at Caporetto **(p. 189)**. These tactics featured a hurricane bombardment to make the enemy front-line defenders take cover while at the same time cutting them off from their rear areas. Fast-moving parties of 'Storm Troops' **(sturmtruppen)** then pushed rapidly through the defended area, bypassing pockets of resistance and raising maximum havoc as far to the rear as possible.

Though these new tactics achieved a German breakthrough of up to 40 miles - unprecedented on the Western Front - they nevertheless had the same basic flaw as the modified Schlieffen Plan of 1914. Too much was asked of the endurance of the infantry 'at the sharp end', to whom insufficient reinforcements could be rushed to make the breakthroughs truly decisive. None of the anti-infantry 'horror weapons' - gas and flame-thrower - prevented the Allies from sealing off the German salients once the attackers had run out of steam. But when the Allies took the offensive in July-August 1918 they **did** have a master weapon - the tank.

Triumph of the tank, 1918

The British had developed the tank in 1915-16 as an antidote to the German trench system. It was designed as an armoured, tracked vehicle for machine-gunners which could traverse the broken ground of 'No-man's Land', crush the enemy wire, cross the enemy trenches and silence the enemy guns while the infantry came up. Though revealed prematurely and in insufficient numbers in the latter stages of the Somme battle in 1916, it had panicked the German infantry on the Flers-Courcelette sector. First used in mass at Cambrai in November 1917, the tank ripped open a 6-mile sector of the German line and pushed over 4,000 yards deep into the German rear areas. Cambrai, however, was little more than an experiment: the success gained there by the tanks was wholly unexpected and there were no reserves with which to exploit the breakthrough.

After the Somme battle the Germans frantically developed their own tank design, the lumbering, top-heavy A7V with a crew of 18. This took part in the 1918 offensive but proved too slow to keep up with the infantry; it performed indifferently in the first tank-versus-tank engagement at Villers-Bretonneux (24 April 1918). The Germans never did come up with a counter-part to the British medium tank, the Whippet, designed for the rapid deepening of breaches made by the slower Mk IVs and Mk Vs.

The last major single battle of the war, the British attack east of Amiens on 8 August 1918, was launched with only three weeks' preparation - purely due to the mobile fire-power and combat effectiveness of the tank. The attack spanned 14 miles and featured 324 fighting tanks, 96 Whippets to exploit the breakthrough, and a reserve force of 184 machines. The result was the savaging and collapse of six German divisions -. the 'Black Day' of the German Army. After Amiens the German soldier's morale could never be restored in full, and for this these tanks were largely responsible. From 8 August to 11 November 1918 - from Amiens across the Hindenburg Line to Mons in Belgium, where the first German offensive of 1918 had met with its first check - there was no single major engagement in which tanks did not continue to play a decisive role. The age of the armoured fighting vehicle had arrived.

1939

THE SECOND WORLD WAR

-1945

One of the most enduring myths about the two World Wars is that military butchery reached its peak between 1914 and 1918, and that on balance the Second World War was a softer option than the First. Nothing could be further from the truth; the scope of the Second World War was wider by far than that of the First, in which the worst fighting was restricted to the Western, Eastern, north-eastern Italian, and Balkan fronts. By 1945, however, the entire land-mass of Europe had become a battle-ground, from the Volga River to the Atlantic coast of France; so had the entire North African coastline from Morocco to Egypt, with the length of Italy from Sicily to the Alps. The war against Japan embraced the entire coastline of Asia from Korea to the Indian frontier, and the western Pacific from the Solomon Islands to the Japanese homeland. Small wonder, then, that Axis and Allied deaths between 1939 and 1945 topped 24.5 million, against only 8,634,000 Allied and Central Powers' military deaths between 1914 and 1918.

It is true that in the Second World War the rival alliances refrained from the use of poison gas, but this was only a modest 'plus' in a war which ended by producing the atomic bomb. At combat level, the machine-pistol or submachine-gun gave the infantryman more fire-power than he had ever known. Perhaps the biggest tactical innovation was not the use of tanks in massed armoured divisions: that had been the logical sequel to tank experience in 1918. It was the general mechanization of armies: the substitution of motor transport for the age-old reliance on horse-drawn transport, with the soldier riding rather than marching to his next battle, giving advancing armies unheard of range.

Above all, there was the newest element of warfare, air power, and its domination of ground warfare by 1945. From the invasion of Poland through to the Japanese surrender, the side which controlled the air over the battlefield controlled the battle.

Poland, 1939: the first blitzkrieg

One of the most misleading images of the Polish campaign of September 1939 is that of the German armoured colossus rolling forward to crush lemming-like waves of Polish cavalry. The truth is very different. Among the German generals there were far more who distrusted the new **panzer** (armoured) forces than believed in them. Moreover the Polish generals knew very well that attacking tanks with cavalry was a suicidal proceeding. Of such encounters which occurred (and these were rare) the normal pattern was one of German armour moving up to support infantry which had been badly shaken by unexpected cavalry attacks.

Of all the factors which sealed the doom of the Polish Army in 1939, three stood out. The first was the deployment of too many units up against the German frontier, inviting penetration and encirclement from the bastions of East Prussia to the north and German-occupied Slovakia to the south. The second was the rapid German acquisition of air supremacy over the battlefield, permitting the close integration of tactical air attacks with the movement of the ground forces. And the third, provided for by the notorious Nazi-Soviet Non-Aggression Pact of 23 August 1939, was the Soviet invasion of eastern Poland on 17 September, which brought the campaign to an end in less than four weeks.

Apart from the natural lie of the frontiers and the assistance provided by the Polish Army's dispositions, the invading German forces enjoyed several other crucial advantages. Polish mobilization, only partially ordered on 30 August, was still under way when the Germans invaded on 1 September; there were only 17 infantry divisions, three infantry brigades and six cavalry brigades to hold the entire front. Behind them another 13 divisions were moving up to the front along roads swept by German fighter dive-bomber attacks.

In weaponry, the German army was far better equipped than the Polish Army, which was only about one-fifth of the way into a modernisation programme. The Poles had 1,350 artillery pieces to the Germans' 4,300, 600 obsolete tanks to the Germans' 3,200, 842 equally obsolete aircraft to the Germans' 1,929 - all of which assisted the German objective, 'to disrupt, by a rapid invasion of Polish territory, the mobilisation and concentration of the Polish Army, and to destroy the bulk of troops stationed to the west of the Vistula-Narew line by converging attacks from Silesia, Pomerania, and East Prussia'.

Thanks to the sheer pace of the German advance, this objective had been achieved by the end of the first week of the campaign. Belated orders for the western Polish armies to fall back on the Vistula came too late to prevent the closing of the German 'inner pincers' west of Warsaw. The superior mobility conferred by the Germans' six panzer and four mechanised divisions permitted the switch of General Guderian's XIX Panzer Corps, after its first successes south of Danzig, across East Prussia to open a new offensive east of the Vistula. Guderian's drive south (10-16 September) finally made contact with advance units from the southern German Army group, closing a pair of 'outer pincers' round the Polish armies. Only an energetic break-out to the east could have enabled the Poles to carry on the struggle, but this was rendered impossible by the Soviet invasion on the 17th.

The Polish Army's performance during this shattering campaign was, in that time-honoured phrase, brave but baffled. For want of any alternative their encircled armies fell back on marching by night (free from air attacks by the **Luftwaffe)** and fighting by day. This enabled the trapped 'Pomorze' and 'Poznan' armies to catch the German 10th Army in flank as it drove towards Warsaw (10 September); but the crisis was soon resolved by **Luftwaffe** attacks 'taking out' the dangerous Polish bridgeheads over the Bzura River. In the south, two divisions of the Polish Carpathian army managed to fight their way through the tightening German net (15-18 September), capturing 20 guns and 180 vehicles from the German 14th Army. Warsaw's heroic 14-day resistance was, however, rendered vain by the German encirclement east of the capital; the German Army High Command wisely refrained from squandering troops on the siege of Warsaw and concentrated on tightening the bonds round the trapped Polish armies.

Such was the first **blitzkrieg** or 'lightning war', won by the revolutionary partnership of deep armoured penetration and encirclement sustained by tactical air supremacy - 'flying artillery' for the ground forces. This was the first war in modern history to end with the defeated army pinned down and trapped where it stood, rather than driven into retreat. Only troops from the southern Polish armies (about 100,000 all told) managed to escape to neutral countries to carry on the fight abroad. Accurate figures for Polish casualties do not exist but the Germans claimed 694,000 prisoners, while the Red army took about 217,000. Formal resistance ended with the flight of the Polish Government on 18 September, though Warsaw fought on until the 28th and the last trapped Polish force, at Polwysep Hel north of Danzig, did not surrender until 2 October. German casualties came to 10,572 killed, 30,322 wounded and 3,400 missing, believed killed; the **Luftwaffe** lost about 25% of the aircraft engaged (285 aircraft lost and 279 damaged beyond repair). These were by no means inconsiderable losses for so short a campaign (though derisory by First World War standards). The German losses would certainly have been far higher without the help of the Soviet invasion of eastern Poland.

OPPOSITE: *Polish cavalry, September 1939*

BELOW: *German infantry, Poland, 1939*

Western Front, 1940

Between 9 April and 25 June 1940 the German Army won the most extraordinary sequence of victories in the history of Europe, conquering not only the neutral countries of Denmark, Norway, Holland and Belgium but France as well, and forcing the British Army to quit the European mainland with the loss of all its heavy equipment.

The main reason for these German victories was the defensive mentality of the Allies, a direct legacy of the First World War and its fruitless offensives. This abandonment of the initiative to a better-armed and better-trained enemy was compounded by the Allied weakness both in air fighter defences and ground anti-aircraft armament, enabling the **Luftwaffe** to seize and retain air superiority over the battlefields of Scandinavia, the Low Countries and France. All German divisions moved with a lavish allocation of mobile anti-aircraft guns which took a heavy toll of Allied air attacks.

Apart from their weaknesses in tactical air cover and anti-aircraft fire-power, the Allied armies were fatally short of the two most effective weapons against massed tanks: mines and anti-tank guns. They soon learned how to contrive anti-tank defences - the heaviest German losses were inflicted during the final assault on metropolitan France in June 1940 - but not until the British had been driven out through Dunkirk and nearly a third of the French Army destroyed north of the Somme and the Aisne (10 May-3 June). And this first, decisive phase of the German offensive was won on the ground by the Germans' superior use of their tanks.

The panzer onrush

In terms of mere numbers the Allies actually had more tanks than the Germans in May 1940: 3,640 against the 2,690 in the ten panzer divisions used in the West. The vital difference was in the way they were used. The Allies employed their tanks in the same limited role of the First World War; infantry support first and foremost. But the panzer divisions advanced with their own field and anti-tank artillery, a strong infantry component and engineers for demolishing obstacles and building bridges. Their primary role was penetration in depth to panic the Allied rear areas, leaving the infantry divisions advancing in the rear to deal the **coup de grace**. Tank for tank, the best Allied machines had several advantages over the panzers, most notably in strength of armour and fire-power. But the Allied tank units were scattered piecemeal along the front, not massed in armoured corps on the German model. This guaranteed the panzer forces *local* superiority wherever they appeared, despite the overall Allied superiority in tank numbers.

Flaws of the French Army

The Allied array on 10 May 1940 consisted of nine Dutch, 22 Belgian, ten British and 94 French divisions - but that was only after the German invasion dragged neutral Holland and Belgium into the war. The ten British divisions were more than a match for the equivalent number of German infantry divisions, and had the advantage of being all-motorised. But 36 of the 72 French infantry divisions were reservists of far lower calibre, and no less than 43 French divisions were assigned to the fortified zone of the Maginot Line which the main German attack bypassed. Carried by seven of the ten panzer divisions, that attack came out of the Ardennes forest on 12 May and fell like a thunderbolt on the French 9th Army defending the upper Meuse - six of whose nine divisions were manned by these down-at-heel reservists. Their defeat permitted the German **panzergruppe** to drive west to the Channel. By 3 June 1,212,000 Dutch, Belgian, British and French prisoners had been taken, though 338,226 Allied troops escaped from Dunkirk.

Ironically, the resistance put up by the last 71 French divisions on the Somme (5-10 June) was far more effective: 95,300 Germans killed, wounded and missing between 4-25 June, against 61,242 between 10 May 3 June. French killed and wounded totalled some 342,000, Dutch 9,780, Belgian 13,350 and British 19,310.

OPPOSITE: *German paratrooper or* ***fallschirmjäger****, Holland, 1940. The Germans used airborne troops in their attacks on Denmark, Norway, Holland and Belgium with telling effect - paratroops, glider troops and units flown in by Junkers Ju.52 transports.* ***BELOW:*** *French infantry, 1940, of whom no less than 92,000 were killed (as against 3,457 British).*

The North African War,

BELOW: *An infantryman of the 4th Indian Division takes an Italian prisoner during the British attack at Sidi Barrani, Egypt (9 December 1940). The success of this attack led to the retreat of the Italian 10th Army from Egypt and a British pursuit into Libya, prompting the despatch of the* ***Afrika Korps*** *(February 1941) to save Tripoli.*

Though Italy entered the war as Germany's ally on 10 June 1940 it was not until September that the Italian 10th Army, based in Libya, launched its long-awaited invasion of British Egypt. By this time the British Western Desert Force had gained useful combat experience in spirited raids across the Libyan frontier south of Sollum.

The British commander in the Middle East, General Wavell, had barely 86,000 troops with which to defend Egypt, the Sudan, Palestine, Transjordan and Cyprus. Of these only 36,000 could be spared for the Western Desert, and they fell back before the invading Italians, who took four days to cover the 60 miles to Sidi Barrani (13-16 September).Marshal Graziani, the Italian commander, was determined not to advance further until the metalled coast road had been extended to Sidi Barrani, a water pipeline built and supplies concentrated for his next advance, on Alexandria. He was planning a methodical

June 1940-May 1943

advance on the lines of Kitchener's reconquest of the Sudan in 1896-98 (pp.174-5), having grossly overestimated the British strength in Egypt. On the night of 8-9 December 1940, Wavell launched his Western Desert Force - 4th Indian Division and 7th Armoured Division - against the Italian fortified camps around Sidi Barrani. He had planned for no more than a five-day raid which, if successful, could be extended, but which was aimed at little more than discouraging the Italians from making a further advance. The Italian stampede back to the Libyan frontier exceeded his expectations; in the first three days' fighting, Western Desert Force took 38,000 prisoners (including four generals), 237 guns and 73 light and medium tanks.

The Italian desert army

The shattering defeat sustained by the Italian Army in North Africa between December 1940 and February 1941 must be placed in context with its poor showing on other fronts: its repulse from eastern France (20-25 June 1940) and Greece (October-December 1940). Many calumnies have been heaped on the Italian soldier of the Second World War, but they tend to overlook the wretched failure of the Fascist regime in preparing the Italian Army for another major conflict. The threadbare Fascist economy had discouraged proper training and the provision of adequate weaponry, particularly in tanks and automatic weapons. The Italian soldier suffered from poor equipment, indifferent rations and generally abysmal leadership; in the field his interests were neglected in favour of maintaining the Italian officer corps in comparative luxury (such as motor caravan accommodation and the provision of bottled spa water, while the British and German desert forces both relied on local well water). When properly led the Italian soldier gave an excellent account of himself. Proof of this was given during the British conquest of Ethiopia in 1941, in the gallant and tenacious defensive battles fought by the Italians at Keren (February-March 1941) and Amba Alagi (May 1941).

In general, however, the Italian Army remained uncomfortable in the desert, in a sense which did not apply to the British and German forces which fought there. The Italians never tried any such expedients as the British Long Range Desert Group, with its ability to range far behind enemy positions.

Rommel's Afrika Korps

By the New Year of 1941 the pursuing British were advancing into eastern Libya, their advance speeded by captured Italian motor transport. Bardia fell on 3 January, Tobruk on the 22nd, Derna on the 30th. A daring advance across the desert trapped the rest of the retreating Italian forces at Beda Fomm (5-6 February). In two months, Western Desert Force with its two divisions had advanced 500 miles, crushed ten Italian divisions and taken some 130,000 prisoners for the cost of only 500 killed and 1,373 wounded. But there was to be no triumphant march on Tripoli; instead Western Desert Force was stripped to provide an expeditionary force for despatch to Greece, at the moment that the first German forces landed in Tripoli to bolster their sagging Italian allies.

For the next 18 months the two panzer divisions of Rommel's Afrika Korps remained the arbiters of the Desert War, the steel backbone of the predominantly Italian coalition army. Until the new American tanks (Grants and Shermans) arrived in the summer of 1942, the German combination of concentrated armour and forward anti-tank fire power dominated every major battle. To defeat Rommel's Italo-German army, the British 8th Army (formed 18 September 1941) needed more than mere reinforcements and better weapons. Its commanders had to learn, the hard way, to keep their armoured units concentrated for the decisive blow, channelling the enemy's movements by minefields, under the umbrella of the Desert Air Force.

BELOW:*Officer of the Afrika Korps, spring 1942. The German Army's tropical rig was as cumbersome as that of the peacetime British Army (including a massive solar helmet), but the troops soon opted for the informal lightweight rig favoured by the British. Apart from a constant fuel shortage caused by the fragile convoy link from Italy, ration quality and medical facilities were the worst deficiencies of the Afrika Korps.*

The Eastern Front, 1941-1945

Over 40 years after the German surrender of May 1945, there is still an instinctive British and American reluctance to admit that the defeat of the German Army was encompassed primarily by the Soviet Union. For the Eastern Front operations between the German invasion of 22 June 1941 and the surrender of Berlin on 2 May 1945 amounted to nothing less than the greatest and most destructive land battle in history. And the certainty that the struggle would end in Soviet victory was transparent long before the British and Americans re-opened the Western Front in June 1944.

'Barbarossa', the plan for the invasion and conquest of the Soviet Union, was Germany's supreme bid for victory in the Second World War. The invasion involved some 3,400,000 German troops, no less than 153 of the German Army's total of 208 divisions. These were pitted against some 4,700,000 Soviet troops (178 divisions). The three German army groups (North, Centre and South) included 17 of the German Army's 21 panzer divisions - 3,090 tanks in all. The German Army's motorised divisions were similarly committed to the Eastern Front: 12 out of 14. In the deployment of 'Barbarossa' the armour was massed in **panzergruppen** (subsequently up-graded in status to panzer armies). The flanking army groups, North and South, were allocated one **panzergruppe** apiece; Army Group Centre, carrying the main weight of the invasion on the Moscow axis, had two **panzergruppen.** Each of the army groups was also allocated the support and cover of a **Luftflotte** or 'air fleet', with a fifth operating from Norwegian bases in the Far North: 1,280 bombers, fighters and reconnaissance aircraft in all.

Flaws of the German plan

'Barbarossa' aimed at using the **blitzkrieg** technique, as mastered in Poland and the West in 1939-40, to carve up and massacre the Red Army where it stood, then push east past Leningrad and Moscow to a line connecting the White and Caspian Seas. The German planners were correct in their belief that sweeping advances could be made once air superiority had been seized in a surprise attack. Where they went fatally wrong was in their belief that Soviet military resistance could be permanently broken before the onset of the Russian winter. They failed to project the performance of the German Army in the West - where there were abundant metalled roads, airfields and roadside filling stations - to the expanses of Russia. They forgot that the German Army was still, in the second summer of the war, dependent on horse-drawn transport and the marching endurance of its infantry. And they wholly under-estimated the tenacity of Russian resistance, the quality of the Red Army's weaponry (particularly in heavy tanks) and the flexibility of the Soviet industrial base in conditions which would have wrecked any Western nation's war effort.

BELOW:** German infantry, Stalingrad, 1942-43.* ***OPPOSITE: *Soviet infantry, Stalingrad, 1942-43.*

The Red Army's ordeal

As with the Polish Army in 1939, the divisions of the four Soviet military districts between Leningrad and Odessa were deployed far too close to the German start-line. The predictable result was a massacre of Soviet aircraft (1,200 on 22 June alone, 800 of them on the ground) and deep, rapid penetrations by the German armour. The pockets of surrounded Soviet troops were enormous: 290,000 prisoners taken at Bialystok and Minsk, 300,000 at Smolensk, 103,000 south of Vinnitsa in the south. But it took time for the German infantry to close up and grind these pockets into surrender; the Smolensk pocket was not declared secure until 5 August. And German casualties were also heavy: 389,924 killed, wounded or missing by 13 August, compared with 218,109 suffered in the Polish, Norwegian, French, Balkan and North African campaigns put together (1 September 1939-31 May 1941). The southward sweep of Guderian's **panzergruppe** trapped another 500,000 at Kiev, but the time taken to reduce the Kiev pocket delayed the advance on Moscow until 2 October. It also permitted the evacuation of 1,523 Soviet industrial plants and 10 million people which, resuming weapons production in the Urals despite the appalling midwinter conditions, gave the Red Army the tools with which to continue to struggle in 1942.

'Typhoon', the German drive on Moscow, began with the German Army's last big encirclement victory in Russia: the double battle of

Vyazma/Bryansk (7-23 October). More vital time was lost during the reduction of these pockets, in which a claimed 600,000 prisoners were taken. The resumed advance was then bogged down in the Russian autumn **rasputitsa**, the season of torrential rains dissolving the terrain in mud. It was resumed with the first sub-zero frosts of early November when the mud froze solid - but all the German Army's winter equipment, belatedly ordered, was still in Poland, and a winter of appalling suffering began for the troops. It was augmented by weapons and engines freezing up and by immense mortality among the German Army's transport animals. By 4 December the German advance had ground to a halt and on 5-6 December, reinforced by divisions drawn from the quieter sectors and those rushed west from Siberia, the Soviet armies before Moscow went over to the offensive.

Even before this first Soviet winter offensive broke, it was obvious that 'Barbarossa' had failed to destroy the Red Army as a fighting force. The transfer of divisions from Siberia and Stalin's call-up of 15 million Soviet citizens had restored the Red Army's strength to 4,196,000 by 1 December, despite the terrible losses suffered since June. The Moscow counter-offensive not only secured the Soviet capital but came perilously close to destroying the German Army Group Centre. By the time it petered out in the mud of the spring **rasputitsa** (end March 1942) the German divisions of the Eastern Front had taken 1,073,006 casualties since 22 June 1941 - 240,000 of them since 1 January 1942.

The Stalingrad disaster

For 1942 Hitler sought a decision by reinforcing the southern army group for a drive to the Volga and Caucasus. Not only did this fail to win a single encirclement victory, but it exposed the German 6th Army to isolation and destruction at Stalingrad (November 1942-February 1943) for the loss of 171,200 casualties and 91,000 prisoners. By the late summer of 1943 the Red Army, larger and better equipped than ever before, had gained the initiative on the Eastern Front which it was never to lose.

Pacific island ordeal,

Considering the minute size of the land area contested, the island war in the Pacific was a conflict without parallel in the viciousness and high cost of its component campaigns. This was due primarily to the military ethos of the Imperial Japanese Army, to which surrender was the greatest disgrace imaginable. Unable to retreat from the islands which it had been charged with holding for the Emperor (with the sole exception of Guadalcanal in early 1943) the Japanese Army fought and died where it stood. The only mass surrenders in the Pacific theatre were Allied, during the surge of Japanese conquest between December 1941 and May 1942: 6,500 at Hong Kong, 130,000 at Singapore, 78,000 on Bataan and 15,000 at Corregidor in the Philippines. Throughout the two years of the Allied reconquest of the Pacific, from Guadalcanal to Okinawa, there were no such capitulations on the Japanese side; every Japanese garrison had to be wiped out by the attacking force before the objective could be declared secure. It was for this reason that the Americans developed the strategy of 'island-hopping', using their painfully-acquired naval and air superiority to isolate Japanese garrisons of secondary importance, and concentrating on objectives which **had** to be taken. Even so, the cost per head of troops involved was immense.

The Guadalcanal epic

The fight for Guadalcanal in the Solomons began with the establishment of 16,000 US Marines, whose supply and reinforcement was highly doubtful in the teeth of Japanese air and naval power, on 7 August 1942. The first Japanese attacks, in grossly inadequate numbers, were repelled with great loss but by mid October, when the Marines

1942-1945

had received only 7,000 Army reinforcements, the Japanese strength on the island had been raised to 20,000. Desperate fighting ensured before the Japanese abandoned their attempt to break the Marine perimeter screening the vital airfield (25-26 October), but the Japanese continued to run in reinforcements until the US Navy won night and day control of the sea approaches to the island. Eventually (7-8 February 1943) about 13,000 Japanese troops were evacuated, many unfit for further service; the Japanese had lost almost 24,000 killed in action or by disease, and 1,000 prisoners. American ground and air casualties came to 6,300, of which about 1,600 were dead.

Tarawa, Kwajalein and Eniwetok

American victory on Guadalcanal was the prelude to the slow advance up the Solomons island chain, while the Gilberts and Marshalls were attacked in the Central Pacific (November 1943-February 1944). Here again Japanese resistance had to be beaten down to the last man, particularly on 'Bloody Tarawa' in the Gilberts where only 146 prisoners (mostly Korean labourers) were taken out of a Japanese garrison 4,636 strong. The remainder died inflicting 3,119 American casualties - 17 per cent of the invading force. Improved American tactics halved casualties at Kwajalein in the Marshalls, where 7,870 Japanese died; and at Eniwetok, where 2,677 Japanese died out of a garrison of 2,741.

The Marianas, Iwo Jima, Okinawa

The battle for Saipan in the Marianas (16 June-6 July 1944) yielded less than a thousand Japanese prisoners from the 29,000 garrison, the US casualties being 16,525 - 12,934 suffered by the US Marines. On Iwo Jima (19 February 26 March 1945) the toll was even more horrific: 216 Japanese prisoners out of 21,000, for 5,931 Marines killed and 17,372 wounded. And it took nearly three months to capture Okinawa (1 April-22 July 1945), the bloodiest island battle of the Pacific War: 110,000 Japanese dead (regular troops and conscripted civilians) with only 7,400 prisoners, and total US battle casualties of 49,151.

To defend their home islands, the Japanese still had some 2,350,000 regular forces with a national militia estimated at 28 million. Had the Americans decided on invasion rather than nuclear bombardment, the resultant death toll defies imagination.

BELOW: *Japanese infantry, Guadalcanal, 1942.*
OPPOSITE: *US Marine, Guadalcanal.*

Victory in Burma, 1944-1945

BELOW: *14th Army infantry, Burma, 1945*

There had been two main motives for the Japanese invasion of Burma in January 1942, and both derived from the fact that Japan's main war front was that against China. It was to gain vital raw materials that Japan attacked Malaya and the South-East Indies; taking Burma would not only secure these gains against attack from India, but would sever the 'back-door' supply route into China - the Burma Road. By May 1942, when the survivors of Burma Corps and Chinese 5th Army completed their gruelling retreat across the Chindwin River into India, these objectives had been achieved.

The Allied plans for recovering Burma were necessarily delayed by the need to expel Rommel's Italo-German forces from North Africa before knocking Italy out of the war. Only when this had been accomplished (September 1943) was it possible to consider large-scale reinforcements for the Burma front. Prompt Japanese countermoves scotched an abortive attempt to reoccupy the Arakan coast and take Akyab (December 1942-May 1943). The main lesson of the Arakan setback was that the British and Indian forces on the Burma front had still to master the Japanese skills of jungle combat.

An important blow at the myth of Japanese invincibility was the first Chindit operation (February-March 1943). Masterminded by General Orde Wingate, this took the form of long-range columns operating deep in the area occupied by the Japanese 15th Army, supplied where possible by air. Though Wingate's first Chindit operation achieved little concrete in military terms, its moral effect was tremendous, prompting Japanese plans to forestall further offensive moves into Burma by taking the British frontier base at Imphal.

By the end of 1943 Burma had at last been promoted to the status of an active front in Allied grand strategy against Japan, and plans had been laid for a spring offensive in 1944. This included an advance by General Stilwell's American-Chinese force in the north, to take Myitkyina and permit the opening of a new land link to China; a second Chindit operation to disrupt the Japanese rear areas. Though the Arakan operations were jeopardised by an anticipatory Japanese offensive, the British managed to hold their positions by air supply - a moral turning-point in the Burmese campaign, on the eve of the Japanese assault on Imphal.

The battle of Imphal began with the Japanese crossing of the Chindwin on the night of 7-8 March 1944, and ended on 22 June with the land relief of the Imphal garrison. The Japanese defeat was compounded by the failure to take Kohima and so cut the only land link between Imphal and India. The British came through thanks to their attention to supply (predominantly by air) and medical services, sparing the triumphant 14th Army from the horrors which befell the retreating Japanese. Disease and starvation savaged the Japanese 15th Army as it fell back to the Chindwin; Japanese killed and missing were set as high as 53,000 out of 85,000. The sufferings of the Japanese survivors were augmented by the monsoon, which slowed 14th Army's pursuit to a crawl. On the northern sector, however, Stilwell's Chinese-American forces finally took Myitkyina after an 11-week blockade (3 August). And it was from the northern front, starting with the reopening of the land link to China (15 October 1944-27 January 1945) that the reconquest of Burma began.

The 14th Army's advance from the Chindwin to the Irrawaddy began in December 1944 and by the third week of February 1945 had seized four major bridgeheads across the Irrawaddy. Between 1 March and 20 March, in a battle brilliantly conceived by General Slim, 14th Army destroyed the Japanese 15th Army as a fighting force. Between Mandalay and Meiktila on 6 May, after a scorching advance, 14th Army's southernmost units met the force advancing from Rangoon (taken by amphibious landings on 2 May) blocking the escape route east of the Japanese 28th and 33rd Armies.

Victory in Germany, 1944-45

When the Western Front was re-opened with the invasion of 6 June 1944 the Eastern Front still lay deep in Russian soil. It was defended by some 157 German and Axis divisions, with only 59 deployed along the 'invasion coast' from Holland to the Pyrenees and the French Mediterranean coast.

The Western Allied 'Overlord' plan for the liberation of Western Europe had allowed 20 days for the breakout from Normandy but at the end of that period their armies were still struggling to take Caen (marked down for capture on the first day of the invasion). On 22 June, however (the third anniversary of the German invasion of Russia) the Red Army launched its second great summer offensive. This was aimed at the German Army Group Centre in White Russia with a crushing Soviet superiority in armour: some 4,000 Soviet tanks against 900 German.

By the beginning of August the German Army had suffered its worst defeat since Stalingrad: 28 divisions cut to pieces out of 37, with German losses of 285,000 killed and captured. Advancing some 375 miles in less than two months, the Red Army had reached the Vistula by the end of August. To this blow was added the Allied breakout from Normandy, launched on 25 July, which scythed east and north to trap two German armies at Falaise, with over 10,000 German dead and 50,000 prisoners. By the end of the month the British and Americans were across the Seine and Paris had been liberated. Headlong pursuit in September carried the Western Allies through Belgium to the Dutch/German frontier by the end of September, but there the pursuit stuck. Like the Red Army, the Western Allies had outrun their supplies, extensive demolitions in the captured Channel ports preventing their use for many weeks. The ensuing respite enabled Hitler to launch a powerful armoured counter-offensive in the Ardennes (16 December 1944) but its failure destroyed the German Army's last reserves of armour. On 12 January the Red Army attacked again, driving for the Oder and overunning East Prussia and Pomerania by the end of March. But while the Soviet forces closed up to the Oder and dressed their front for the final assault on Berlin, the British and Americans crossed the Rhine (23-26 March). In the first fortnight of April the greatest Allied encirclement victory of the war was won by the Americans, who by 18 April had captured 317,000 Germans in the Ruhr pocket. The Soviet drive on Berlin opened on 16 April, and met the Americans on the Elbe on the 25th **(below)**. Berlin surrendered on 2 May.

1945

THE MODERN ERA.

-1985

Hopes that the newly-discovered atomic bomb would render future wars impossible were short-lived after 1945; the 40 years since the end of the Second World War have seen repeated conventional wars in Asia, Africa, the Middle East and Central America. In the 1980s the international arms trade has never been more flourishing, not only for financial profit but for political manipulation of the customer powers.

Improved weaponry and technology have done little to change the basic experience of the Second World War. Despite repeated predictions, the tank is as vital a weapon as ever: a tool for enabling the soldier to fight and win in an impossible environment. Tactical air power is as vital as ever: no army of the 1980s has a hope of victory against an enemy supreme in the air. Speed of manoeuvre is as vital as ever, with troops rushed into action in armoured personnel carriers and that supremely versatile if vulnerable vehicle, the helicopter. There is, however, one ominous change. Though it was never used in the Second World War, chemicals and biological warfare are now back on the military menu. The armies of the two greatest rival power blocs, the North Atlantic Alliance and the Soviet Warsaw Pack, are both well stocked with chemical weaponry and no scenario for a 'conventional' (non-nuclear) Third World War can rule out the probability of its use.

Though the soldier of the 1980s has more fire-power and technology at his disposal than at any other age in history, study of the 'postwar' wars since 1945 shows that many military precepts, as enduring as war itself, still holds true. God does not always favour the big battalions; surprise, audacity, espirit de corps and professionalism still count for much, as proved by the Israelis in four wars of national survival (1948, 1956, 1967 and 1973) and by the British in the Falklands in 1982. On the other hand, as the French and Americans both discovered in Vietnam, superior technology and fire-power do not invariably guarantee victory against overwhelming numbers and the will to win.

Deadlock in Korea,

The Korean War remains the only conflict since the end of the Second World War in which member stat es of the United Nations have combined to meet and beat naked aggression. It was, however, the first of many 'proxy wars' between the superpowers, the Soviet Union on one side and the United States on the other. The Korean War was fought when the United States still enjoyed a virtual monopoly in nuclear weapons and the world's most powerful strategic bomber force. This underlying fact naturally combined with the geographical limitations of the Korean theatre (denying either side complete victory in a runaway offensive) to produce stalemate and drive both sides back to the conference table before the conflict went into disastrous escalation.

Origins of the war

The Korean War sprang from the attempt of the wartime Allies to manipulate the former possessions of defeated Japan to their own advantage. After its traumatic ordeal in the Second World War, the Soviet Union's immediate policy was to surround itself with as deep a belt of satellite and allied Communist states as possible - by force if need be. In Europe the process had begun with the purging of anti-Communist political parties and leaders in Bulgaria (October 1946), Hungary (February-May 1947), Rumania (July 1947) and Czechoslovakia (February 1948). In the Far East, 1949 saw the Communist triumph over Nationalist China despite massive American military aid, the relentless expulsion of the Nationalist armies from the Chinese mainland, and Mao tse-Tung's proclamation of the People's Republic of China at Peking (1 October). This was rapidly followed (14 February 1950) by a 'Treaty of Friendship, Alliance, and Mutual Assistance' between China and the Soviet Union.

Under the terms of the last 'Big Three' conferences of the Second World War, Yalta and Potsdam, Korea passed under Soviet occupation (north) and American occupation (south) after the Japanese surrender. The Soviet Union went along with the United Nations plan for the withdrawal of occupation forces from Korea and the establishment of a north-south Korean government, but refused point-blank to allow UN supervision of elections in the Soviet-occupied zone (January 1948). Elections thereupon went ahead in the south and in August 15 Syngman Rhee became the first President of the Republic of Korea, countered within three weeks by the proclamation of a People's Democratic Republic of Korea, on the Soviet Russian model, in the north. But though the Soviet Union announced the complete withdrawal of its forces in December 1948, six months before the United States followed suit in the south, training of the Communist North Korean 'People's Army' proceeded at a far greater pace than American training of the South Korean Army.

BELOW: *Duke of Wellington's Regiment (West Riding) Korea, 1953.*

North Korea invades, June 1950

The North Korean Army produced by its Soviet instructors was a rough but formidable force, provided with the weaponry which had carried the Soviet Army to victory in 1943-45: lavish artillery, mortars and automatic weapons for an extremely hardy, highly indoctrinated infantry. The accent in training was preparation for a storming offensive on land, to overrun South Korea before the vital factor of Western air power could be brought into play. This strategy came perilously close to success.

The war began on 25 June 1950 when the North Korean Army swarmed across the South Korean frontier, the 38th Parallel, at 11 points. The pace and ferocity of the North Korean advance, ignoring the UN Security Council's demand for withdrawal, overwhelmed the flimsy South Korean forces. With commendable speed, the Security Council called for members of the

1950-1953

United Nations to send immediate armed help to the South Korean Republic (27 June). The United States, from its vantage-point in occupied Japan, was naturally first in the field but throughout July and August 1950 the North Koreans had it all their own way, rolling up the South Korean troops and herding them south. By 5 September the South Korean Republic had, for all practical purposes, ceased to exist apart from an ominously small perimeter around Pusan, at the southern tip of the Korean peninsula.

As they pushed south, however, the North Koreans came under increasing pressure from the UN forces' trump card: carrier-based and land-based air power, including B-29 bombers able to attack civilian and industrial targets in North Korea itself.

In his plan to roll back the North Korean forces the UN commander, Pacific War hero General MacArthur, was able to use the 'triphibious' (air/sea/land) techniques which had speeded the defeat of Japan in 1944-45. His counter-offensive out of the Pusan beach-bead (13 September 1950) was followed two days later by an amphibious landing 200 miles up the Korean west coast, at Inchon. This recovered the line of the 38th Parallel by the end of September, but MacArthur's attempt to overrun North Korea as far as the Yalu River (9 October-1 November) prompted large-scale Chinese intervention on the North Korean side. On 1 November, as the Communist forces counter-attacked, the first Chinese prisoners were taken and Soviet-furnished MiG-15 jet fighters were encountered for the first time. By the end of the year the UN forces had been pushed back to the 38th Parallel.

From crisis to stalemate

1951 was the year of the heaviest fighting in Korea, with the Communists taking Seoul (4 January) only to lose it to a UN counter-offensive on 14 March. The fighting swayed back across the 38th Parallel (3 April), but by now it was becoming apparent that neither side could look for a conventional victory. UN forces, advancing out of the confines of the peninsula, were too vulnerable to enveloping Communist attacks in superior force; the further the Communists pushed south the more vulnerable they became to UN air power. On July 8 1951 the first armistice talks began at Kaesong on the 38th Parallel.

BELOW: *Chinese infantry, Korea, 1953.*

June 1967: the 'Six-Day War'

LEFT: *Israeli paratrooper, 1967*
RIGHT: *Egyptian infantry, 1967*

On 5 June 1967 the state of Israel was menaced on three fronts by the armed forces of Egypt, Jordan and Syria. Some 500,000 highly-equipped Arab troops, with 700-odd combat aircraft and over 2,000 tanks, were poised for the third Arab attempt to wipe Israel off the map of the Middle East. Six days later the Israeli army and air force had shattered the Arab opposition on all three fronts, destroyed over 400 aircraft and 1,000 tanks, and added 26,000 square miles to the territory under Israel's control. The events of June 1967 remain one of the most astonishing achievements in military history.

Israel's chances of victory in a conventional, prolonged war were slim, and non-existent if the Arab forces should seize and hold the initiative. The Israeli economy, already racked by the prodigious expenditure on modern weaponry, could not sustain the mass drain of labour needed to produce the fully-mobilized defence force of 2,365,000 (which in any event took three days to muster in full) and maintain it indefinitely. With wholly indefensible frontiers, Israel dared not wait to be attacked. The only chance was for a carefully-timed series of powerful pre-emptive blows at the Arab armies massing across the borders: in Sinai, the West Bank of the River Jordan, and behind the Syrian-held Golan Heights.

Arab air power destroyed

Israel's war plan involved tackling the Egyptian army in Sinai first, then turning successively on Jordan and Syria. The essential prerequisite was the annihilation of Arab air power, to be accomplished with minimal loss. This was achieved by a devastating series of perfectly-timed attacks launched at 18.45 Egyptian time on 5 June - after the Egyptian pilots had flown their normal dawn patrols - against ten Egyptian airfields simultaneously. Successive attack waves extended the damage to all 19 of Egypt's airfields. Follow-up attacks on 6 June raised the total of Arab aircraft destroyed to 418 - 309 of them Egyptian, 60 Syrian, 29 Jordanian, one Lebanese and 17 Iraqi. Of these no less than 393 were destroyed on the ground. Total Israeli air losses between 5-10 June came to 46 combat aircraft out of 266 - all but three shot down by ground fire. By the afternoon of 6 June, therefore, the Egyptian forces in Sinai were not only deprived of their own air cover but were exposed to the attacks of the Israeli air force.

The armoured battle

Though technically superior to the older British, French and American tanks in Israeli service, the bulk of Egypt 's Soviet-supplied tank force was ill prepared for a fast-moving encounter in the open desert. Much of it had only arrived over the 18 months before the war and training was by no means complete, particularly in the vital field of tank gunnery. Egypt's Soviet military advisers had also tended to concentrate on teaching 'fighting by the book' - leaden and inappropriate tactics mercilessly exploited by the Israeli tank crews. Concentrating on three main axis of advance - north, centre and south - the Israelis had cracked the front-line Egyptian positions by nightfall on the 6th and were plunging deep into Sinai, reaching the Suez Canal on 8-9 June. Over 500 Egyptian tanks were destroyed in battle, with 300 more captured intact; Egyptian casualties soared to about 11,500 killed and 5,500 captured.

West Bank and Golan Heights

The Israeli assault on West-Bank Jordan lasted three days (5-7 June) and gave the Israelis some of their toughest fighting: a total of 1,755 casualties, 1,326 of them in the fight for Jerusalem. The storming of the formidable defences created by the Syrians on the Golan Heights (9-10 June) could never have been achieved without massive Israeli air support, which knocked out over half the 265 Syrian guns on the plateau. For the Israeli ground forces, however, it was a hard-fought action, strongpoint by strongpoint, with over 100 Israeli tanks and half-tracks knocked out before Syrian resistance gave way on the afternoon of the 10th. Israeli casualties on the Golan came to 152 killed and 306 wounded; Syrian losses were estimated at about 1,000 killed and 3,000 wounded.

Vietnam:

For many the Vietnam War suggests a 20th Century replay of the War of American Independence: a world super-power trying in vain to crush an insurgent patriot militia, only to find its vastly superior military resources of no avail. In fact the Vietnam War was more like a replay of the Thirty Years War of the 17th Century than the War of Independence of the 18th. The American failure in Vietnam was only the latter phase of a conflict dating back to the end of the Second World War, and France's attempt to re-establish colonial rule in Indo-China.

French Indo-China consisted of Cochin-China and Cambodia in the south, with capitals at Saigon and Pnomh Penh; the central provinces of Annam (fronting the sea) and Laos (fronting the Thai border); and Tonkin in the north with its capital Hanoi.

Birth of the Viet Minh

When France fell in June 1940, real power in Indo-China passed to the Japanese; and it was under Japanese occupation that the Communist nationalist movement, destined for victory 30 years later, first became an active force. Its leader Ho Chi Minh was a lifelong opponent of French rule in Indo-China. He inspired his followers, the Viet Minh, with the dream of an independent Vietnam – Tonkin, Annam and Cochin-China – united under Communist rule after centuries of rivalry between north and south. With no prospect of friendly foreign aid, Ho accepted that conventional guerrilla warfare, even when stiffened by Communist ideology and discipline, would not be enough to overcome the formidable assets of Western mobility and fire-power. He and his military 'right arm', the brilliant Vo Nguyen Giap, developed a strategic blueprint for unassisted guerrilla victory which involved forcing the enemy occupation forces into an impossible dilemma.

Using the natural cover provided by terrain the Viet Minh must infiltrate the entire country, not try to extend its operations from a fixed base where it

the long agony, 1945-1975

could be trapped and destroyed. When the enemy concentrated his forces to make sure of the ground he stood on, he would abandon the bulk of the country to the Viet Minh's influence; when he advanced to grapple with the Viet Minh his forces would become dispersed and vulnerable to counter-attack. To the ceaseless battle for the support of the Vietnamese people must be added an international psychological offensive. The aim here was to make the peoples of the western powers seeking to dominate Vietnam feel that decisive military victory was impossible and the cost of striving for it too high. The latter aim was perfectly achieved both with France and the United States, in each case yielding victory.

The road to Dienbienphu

For the Viet Minh the most dangerous years were 1946-49, before the victory of the Red Chinese provided an arsenal for their fellow Communists in Vietnam. In 1945 Giap's forces were barely 50,000 strong, armed with a motley collection of Japanese, French and American weapons. Fortunately the French returned in 1946 with only 40,000 troops; insufficient to crush the Viet Minh, but enough to induce the French Government to authorise offensive operations. The French troops were veterans from the European war and their trump card was unchallenged air superiority. Operating from Hanoi, they were able to strike at Viet Minh communications with China; but in the early years the French wasted their assets by relying on anti-guerrilla tactics of cordoning-off and combing selected areas. The time taken to establish the cordon enabled large Viet Minh units to slip away and small ones to go to ground and vanish. By 1952, with ever-growing assistance from China, Giap had raised the Viet Minh to a regular establishment of 100,000 troops, plus 120,000 provincial guerrillas and over 300,000 local volunteers.

The French, however, had discovered that sudden strikes at Viet Minh rear areas and supply dumps, using paratroops, were highly effective. The result was the 'Castor' plan to drop a powerful paratroop force deep in Viet Minh territory, luring the Viet Minh tod annihilation against superior French fire power. Dienbienphu was elected as the target, 140 miles from Hanoi but only 80 miles from the Chinese border.

'Castor' took no account of the tremendous increase in Viet Minh artillery fire-power, which encouraged Giap to take up the French challenge. Against the 16,544 paratroops dropped at Dienbienphu in November-December 1953, Giap massed 70,000 regular Viet Minh plus 60,000 male and female labour battalions, with a mass of ground and AA artillery - a superiority of 8 to 1. Massive attacks from 12 March cost the Viet Minh 8,000 dead and 15,000 wounded but crushed the French garrison after 55 days. Seven months after the Dienbienphu disaster, France had not only concluded an armistice along the line of the 17th Parallel, but ceded independence to Laos, Cambodia and the new republic of South Vietnam.

American nightmare, 1961-75

By the tenth anniversary of Dienbienphu it was clear that American cash, military aid and encouragement were not going to be enough to stop the North Vietnamese forces - now styled Viet Cong or 'Vietnamese Liberation Front' - from undermining South Vietnam. A horrific new element in the American war, however, was the use of strategic bombing, napalm and defoliating attacks causing massive civilian casualties. From January 1961 to the last American evacuations in Saigon in April 1975, these were estimated at 5,773,190 with 2,122,224 dead, 56,231 of them American. Though American helicopter-borne attacks on Vietcong concentrations proved highly effective in the first three years they did not avert Giap's morale-shattering Tet offensive of 1968, which hit over 80 major centres and dispelled American illusions that the war was being won.

OPPOSITE: *US Marine, Vietnam, 1966*

BELOW: *Woman soldier of Viet Cong, Saigon, 1975*

Falklands 1982

The British reconquest of the Falkland Islands, seized by Argentina on 2 April, 1982, was an extraordinary feat of arms if only for the unique chapter it wrote in the history of amphibious warfare. For the first time in modern warfare an invasion force was required to land without the superior strength hitherto considered essential, and without absolute superiority in the air to protect the invasion fleet while the troops went ashore.

The bulk of the Argentinian garrison was held back for the defence of Port Stanley, where the airfield was a vital prize to be denied to the British. Though there were no 'obvious' sites for an invasion on East Falkland before an overland drive on Stanley, two of the likeliest candidates were San Carlos in the north-west and the southerly peninsula of Lafonia. The Argentinian commander General Menendez deployed his main reserve, the 12th Regiment, on the wasp-waist of land which connects Lafonia to mainland East Falkland, at Darwin and Goose Green. From there it would present a flank threat to a British advance from whatever direction it might come.

The main hope of the defending Argentines, however, was that their vastly superior air strength would massacre the British invasion fleet before enough troops and supplies could be landed for a British land offensive to get under way. If this could be achieved, Menendez had ample forces with which to succeed where Rommel had failed against the British and Americans in Normandy 38 years before. Until Rapier SAMs (surface-to-air missiles) could be set up ashore, defence of the invasion fleet would devolve upon the warships of the Royal Navy.

Fortunately for the British the Argentinian pilots, though more than willing to press home their attacks, failed to solve the dilemma facing them. This was how to co-ordinate attacks so as to draw the fire of the warships while the all-important troopships and storeships were attacked. For four days after the

ABOVE: *British Para with full kit.*
OPPOSITE: *Marine Commando with Argentinian prisoners.*

landings at San Carlos on 21 May recurrent air attacks concentrated on taking out the warships, sinking HMS **Ardent, Antelope** and **Coventry** and damaging four others. The troops and stores were nevertheless landed and by 26 May were poised to break out from the beach-head area.

A serious loss was the destruction of **Atlantic Conveyor** by Exocet missile on 25 May. She had managed to fly off the squadron of RAF GR3 Harriers embarked to supplement the hard-pressed Sea Harriers flown by the Fleet Air Arm - but not the vital transport helicopters (three Chinooks and a squadron of Wessex) intended to speed the overland advance. The pace of this advance would now depend on the marching powers of the troops, with the handful of Lynx and Sea King helicopters working overtime to bring up ammunition and supplies.

From Goose Green to Stanley

By 26 May the San Carlos beach-head had been deepened and consolidated for the breakout. This was accomplished between 27-29 May and was notable for the hard-fought victory of 2 Para at Darwin and Goose Green (28-29 May) against unexpectedly tenacious Argentinian resistance. Despite heavy losses, 2 Para's victory eliminated the Argentinian blocking force to a southern approach to the approaches of Stanley, while in the north 3rd Commando Brigade (3 Para and 45 Royal Marine Commando) made an epic 50-mile march, in all weathers and across appalling terrain, carrying full kit weighing up to 120 lbs.

This third or build-up phase lasted from 30 May to 10 June and saw the arrival of 3,300 men of 5th Brigade, trans-shipped and landed after their long voyage from Britain in the liner **Queen Elizabeth 2.** On 8 June the supply ship **Sir Galahad**, carrying the Welsh Guards forward to Bluff Cove, was bombed and set ablaze in Fitzroy inlet with heavy losses. By nightfall on 11 June, however, General Moore's two brigades were poised to storm the heights west of Stanley: first Mount Longdon, Mount Harriet and Two Sisters, then Wireless Ridge, Mount Tumbledown and Mount William. It took two days of intense fighting to clear the Argentinian defenders off these vital peaks, with a prodigious expenditure of small-arms, mortar and artillery ammunition - far more than the over-stretched British helicopters could replace. But the loss of Tumbledown by dawn on 14 June knocked the heart out of General Menendez's troops. As the weary British prepared for the last battle to take Sapper Hill and fight their way into Stanley, the white flags started to go up. Menendez surrendered at 09.00 that morning.

Accomplished in 24 days from the first landings at San Carlos, the reconquest of the Falklands was a brilliant feat of endurance and improvisation, underpinned by sheer professionalism - at 8,000 miles the most extended amphibious operation ever mounted against superior odds.

The Afghan War, 1979-

It has become commonplace to refer to Afghanistan, occupied by the Soviet Army since December 1979, as 'Russia's Vietnam': yet another example of a superpower bogged down in a guerrilla war of national resistance which it has no way of winning by conventional means. But the parallel is not an exact one. The Vietnamese armies which defeated the French and American forces between 1946-54 and 1965-75 were massively armed and politically sustained by the two Communist superpowers, China and the Soviet Union. As far as military material was concerned, the two phases of the Vietnamese struggle amounted to proxy wars between East and West. This does not apply to the Afghan war, in which the defending **mujahedin** ('holy warriors') are, by comparison with Giap's Viet Minh and Viet Cong, on their own against the Soviet Army and Air Force.

Parallels with Vietnam

Though the **mujahedin** are forced to survive and fight largely on their own resources without superpower assistance from outside, there are nevertheless many parallels with the Vietnamese guerrilla conflict. The most obvious is the use of the country's terrain against the invaders. Though the bare mountain terrain of Afghanistan is as different from the swamp and jungle of Vietnam as it could be, the same vital principle applies: the success of the guerrillas lies in converting the whole country into a hostile 'sea' through which the enemy 'fish' swim in fear and with maximum difficulty. The Soviet garrisons - like their French and American counterparts in Vietnam - are never immune from hit-and-run attack even in the towns they hold. And to keep open the vital roads along the valley floors, heavily-escorted convoys have become a way of life for the Soviet occupation army.

Soviet master weapon: the helicopter

As in Vietnam, the principal bane of the guerrillas is the enemy's air power and above all his helicopter gunships, adopted by the Soviet Army in direct emulation of the success achieved by the 'imperialists' with these potent weapons in Vietnam. This is the only vehicle of mobile fire-power which can find and hit the guerrillas and their people in the mountain fastnesses; when a Soviet helicopter appears, the **mujahedin** go to ground. Even so, foreign observers have noted a significant shift in the 'helicopter war'; the increasing acquisition of anti-aircraft weaponry by the **mujahedin** (most importantly one-man missile launchers) has enforced caution on the Soviet Air Force. Soviet helicopters now embark on search-and-strike missions with a copious supply of decoy flares with which to 'fox' **mujahedin** AA missiles.

Soviet losses in helicopter gunships (mostly the huge Mi-24 'Hind') have been high; up to 250 were lost in the first 18 months after the Soviet invasion. Not all were shot down; the **mujahedin** are helped by the limitations on helicopter flying imposed by bad weather and the thin mountain air, in which no Soviet helicopter was designed to operate. The **mujahedin** have learned to go for the three weak spots: the tail rotor assembly, the turbine air intakes and (neatly situated right under the massive red star fuselage insignia) an oil intake. Another serious failing in 'Hind' design is the aircraft's massive main rotor span; if the pilot attempts too violent a turning manoeuvre, the main rotor blades can collide with the tail rotor assembly with disastrous results.

Soviet training ground

The biggest Soviet asset in Afghanistan is the diplomatic vacuum which leaves the **mujahedin** without an active ally. This offers the Soviet Union the ability to maintain its original objective in invading the place: preventing the overthrow of an anti-Soviet regime. For the rest there are obvious advantages to be extracted from the war with Afghan guerrillas: a training-ground with live ammunition for the Soviet Army and Air Force.

From the point of view of the West,

BELOW: Soviet soldier, Kabul 1982.

there are definite grounds for optimism. There is, for example, no indication of any significant change in the lack of flexibility in Soviet tactics. The biggest symptom of this inflexibility is a sad lack of initiative at combat level, a paralysis when the crisis breaks and conditions do not match those of the training manual. One reason why the **mujahedin** are still in being, and fighting, has been the tendency of convoy-escort troops riding in armoured personnel-carriers to stick with their vehicles when ambushed, rather than disperse by platoons to counter-attack at once.

A classic instance of this Soviet inflexibility was the decision to invade with a full complement of mobile AA artillery and AA missiles, regardless of the fact that the enemy at which the invasion was aimed had, and still has, no aviation at all. These weapons promptly became a prime target for Afghan raids and ambushes. Captured Soviet weaponry of all kinds have greatly raised the fire-power of the **mujahedin**; by summer 1984 foreign observers were particularly struck by the rapid availability of captured Soviet automatic rifles over the past two years.

On the morale front, the **mujahedin** have one positive advantage. They are up against conscript troops, virtually unsustained by regimental tradition, who hate the country and the anonymous nature of this war against a largely invisible enemy. As with the Americans in Vietnam, drugs provide another morale-sapper in the ranks of the Soviet Army and the longer the Afghan War continues the worse the problem is likely to get.

RIGHT: *Mujahedin warrior.*

'Brushfire' wars of the 1980s

In the 1980s, armies of the front-rank military powers continue to develop ever more sophisticated weaponry, equipment and training. Yet none of this increased combat potential is a guarantee of automatic victory over nominally weaker para-military forces, recruited and maintained by nationalist and separatist movements, with or without superpower backing. Since the first telling example of the 1807-13 Peninsular War, the most difficult of all military tasks has been a guerrilla war with little or no prospect of a clear-cut solution.

'Professionals' v. 'Amateurs'

Apart from guerrilla warfare, there has never been a time when armies of military 'professionals' (judged by the quality of their equipment and experience) have not been subject to the occasional surprise defeat by 'amateurs'. The 19th Century was replete with such surprise reverses. Many of them were British, as witness the disastrous retreat from Afghanistan in 1842, the Zulus' triumph at Isandhlwana in 1879, and Boer victories not only in 1881 but in the humiliating 'Black Week' of 1899. Then there were Garibaldi's defeat of the regular Neapolitan Army in 1860-61, the Dervish annihilation of Hicks Pasha at El Obeid in 1883, and the shattering Ethiopian defeat of the invading Italians at Adowa in 1896.

Most of these surprise defeats of 'professionals' were the result of over-confidence, poor generalship, weak morale, or a host of other military flaws which could be traced, diagnosed, put right, and avenged with an 'attack as it should be delivered'. The shock of Isandhlwana, for instance, was dispelled within months by the destruction of the Zulu Army at Ulundi. It took barely a year after 'Black Week' before the last Boer field army was beaten. But in other instances there was no speedy reversal of an initial defeat. In the Sudan it took the British 15 years to avenge El Obeid at Omdurman, while in Afghanistan 40 years separated Elphinstone's disastrous retreat from Kabul in the 1st Afghan War from the successes of Roberts in the 2nd Afghan War.

LEFT: Embattled against Yasser Arafat's PLO and the Syrian 'peace-keeping' regular army in Lebanon: Israeli-backed Christian Phalangist guerrilla, Beirut, 1982.

The scales swing back

As the 19th Century drew to its close, however, it did seem that the ever-improving weaponry and technology were tipping the balance more and more in favour of the 'professionals'. In the 1890s, a good example was Kitchener's use of gunboats and railway to sustain his methodical reconquest of the Sudan. By 1914 there were clear signs that when the 'professionals' got their act together and made full use of the resources at their disposal, 'amateur' forces stood little chance in a stand-up fight.

Spain, 1936-39; first of the 'wars by proxy'

On the surface, this trend was confirmed by the outcome of the Spanish Civil War of 1936-39: a defeat for the Republican 'amateurs' at the hands of the Fascist 'professionals'. But this view, still to be heard occasionally, is superficial and obscures the fact that the Spanish Civil War was really the first 'war by proxy', fought by superpowers - a prototype Vietnam. Without foreign involvement the war between Franco's Nationalists and the Communist Republic would probably have dragged on interminably; but the assistance of Franco by Nazi Germany and Fascist Italy proved quicker and far more effective than the Soviet Russian aid supplied to the Republic. Nor was the Fascist-backed Nationalist victory a result solely of the circumstances of the Spanish War. Within a year, the causes of the Republican defeat had been demonstrated again with the Soviet defeats in Finland and the German victories in Poland and the West.

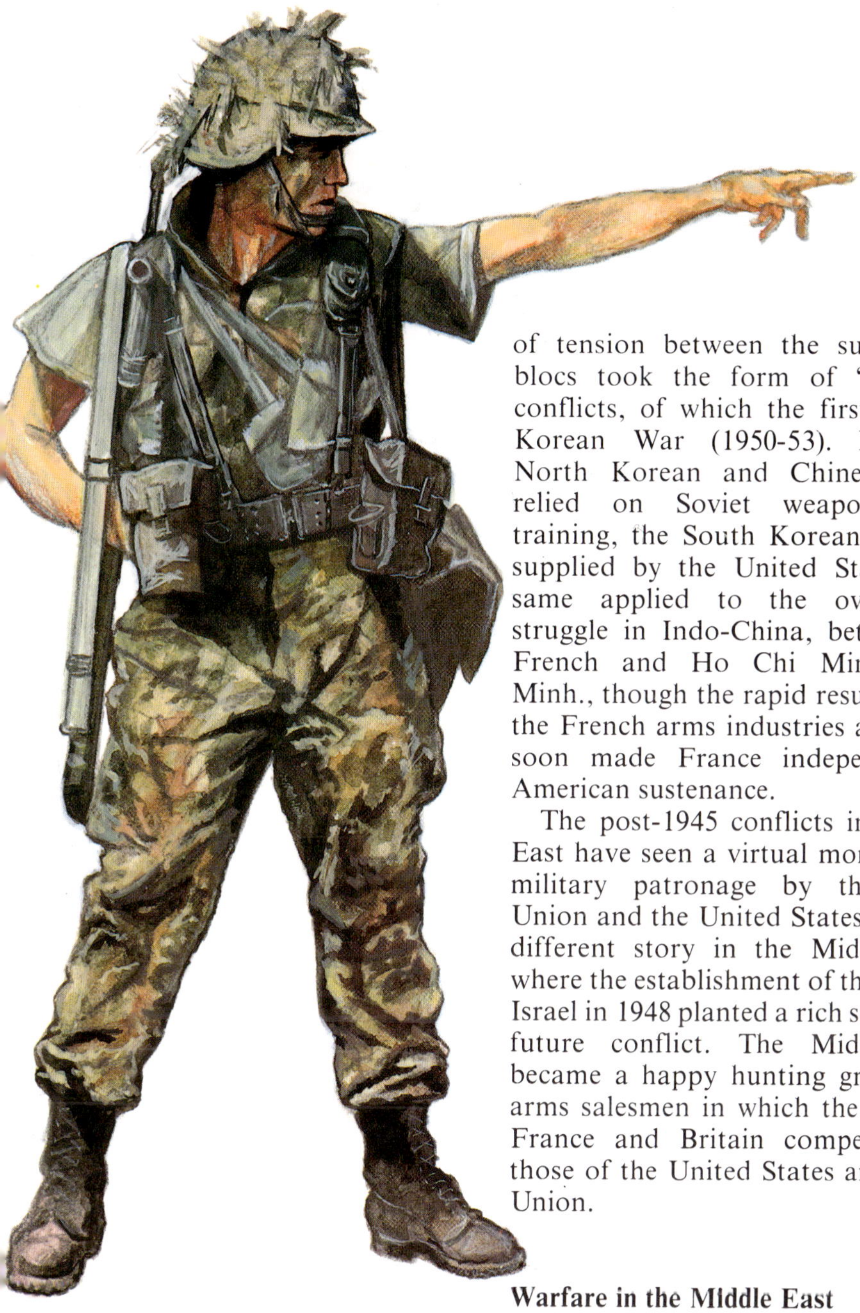

ABOVE: *Spearhead of rapid amphibious intervention by the United States - US Ranger, Grenada, 1983.*

After 1945: 'cloned' client armies

With the onset of the Cold War after 1945, the rival superpowers set about establishing client armies in the nominally independent states along the ideological frontier between the Soviet Union and the Free World. These armies were - at least as far as their equipment and training were concerned - 'cloned' replicas of the main superpower armies.

As the nuclear arms race haltingly gathered pace after the first Soviet atomic explosion in 1949, the resolution of tension between the superpower blocs took the form of 'brushfire' conflicts, of which the first was the Korean War (1950-53). Both the North Korean and Chinese forces relied on Soviet weaponry and training, the South Koreans on that supplied by the United States. The same applied to the overlapping struggle in Indo-China, between the French and Ho Chi Minh's Viet Minh., though the rapid resurgence of the French arms industries after 1945 soon made France independent of American sustenance.

The post-1945 conflicts in the Far East have seen a virtual monopoly of military patronage by the Soviet Union and the United States. It was a different story in the Middle East, where the establishment of the State of Israel in 1948 planted a rich seedbed of future conflict. The Middle East became a happy hunting ground for arms salesmen in which the wares of France and Britain competed with those of the United States and Soviet Union.

Warfare in the Middle East

In the Arab-Israeli wars of 1956, 1967 and 1973, desert warfare in the most 'naked' combat conditions offered both superpower blocs invaluable chances to assess new weapons and systems. These wars also revealed the hopelessly rigid nature of the Soviet training in the armies of Egypt and Syria. Time and again, delighted Israeli soldiers came upon copies of the weighty, Soviet-written 'combat manuals', intended to give commanders stock solutions to the myriad crises of battle.

After the hard-won Israeli victory in the 'Yom Kippur War' of 1973, Arab pressure on Israel was maintained by Yasser Arafat's 'Palestine Liberation Organisation', Soviet-equipped and operating from nominally independent Lebanon. This hapless border state, jammed between the frontiers of Syria and Israel, became a battle ground long before the Israeli invasion of 1982. For nearly a decade Lebanon's capital, Beirut, was battered by recurrent fighting between the Israeli-backed Christian Phalangists and the Syrian-backed PLO.

The Israeli invasion of Lebanon in June 1982 brought about the ejection of Arafat's PLO from invested Beirut, under international supervision. But the 'peace-keeping forces' hastily pushed into Beirut by the United States, France and Britain themselves became the target for fanatical attacks, and were withdrawn after the French and American 'peace-keepers' had suffered heavy loss. Israel was left with the immensely costly occupation of southern Lebanon, having failed to eliminate the powerful Syrian presence in the east of the country.

From Cuba to Grenada, 1962-83

In the Western hemisphere the United States has consistently opposed the proliferation of Communist regimes in Central America and the Caribbean. This policy has been intensified since Fidel Castro became effective dictator of Cuba after ousting the American-backed Batista regime in 1959. Once premier, Castro accepted prolific Soviet aid and in 1962 nuclear war was threatened by the Soviet attempt to emplace medium-range ballistic missiles on Cuba. The missiles were withdrawn after President Kennedy's 'quarantine' blockade of Cuba.

Since the Cuba Crisis of 1962, American heavy-handedness has only encouraged the establishment of Communist movements in Central American states with American-backed repressive regimes. In December 1983, strong American forces landed on the Caribbean island of Grenada to overthrow the Marxist regime which, ostensibly with Cuban aid, was building an airfield big enough to permit Soviet air reconnaissance of the southern United States.

INDEX - GENERAL

CHRONOLOGY AND THEMATIC INDEX

1709 - Russia defeats Sweden at Poltava (Great Northern War, 1699-1721) - **pp.108-9**
1740 - Prussia defeat Austria at Mollwitz (War of Austrian Succession, 1740-48) - **pp.110-111**
1745 - Scots Jacobite defeat English at Prestonpans; Jacobite Rising crushed at Culloden (April 1746) - **pp.113-114**
1775 - Outbreak of War of American Independence - **pp.114-123**
1777 - Americans defeat British at Saratoga
1781 - Fleeting British victory at Guilford Court House - **pp.118-119, 122-3**
1781 (Oct.) - British defeat at Yorktown seals loss of American colonies
1789 - Summoning of French States General, fall of Bastille herald French Revolution
1792 - outbreak of Revolutionary War; initial French defeats retrieved at Valmy - **pp.126-7**
1793-1796 - French Republic defeats 1st Coalition, conquers Belgium & Holland
1796-1797 - Napoleon's 1st Italian campaign
1798-1800 - War of 2nd Coalition; Russian participation against France in Italy, Holland - **pp.128-9**
1798-1800 - Napoleon's expedition to Egypt & Syria; French victories at Pyramids, Aboukir - **pp.130-1**
1800 - Austrian defeat at Marengo seals collapse of 2nd Coalition - **pp.132-3**
1804-1805 - Napoleon proclaims French Empire, defeats Austria & Russia at Austerlitz
1808-1813 - Peninsular War, opened with French defeat at Baylen - **pp.136-7**
1809 - British return to Spain after retreat to Corunna - **pp.138-9**
1812 - Napoleon's **Grande Armée** destroyed in Russia - **pp.140-1**
1813 - Napoleon defeated in Germany at Leipzig; France invaded (1814) - **pp.142-3**
1815 - Final defeat of Napoleon by British & Prussians at Waterloo - **pp.146-151**
1830 - French invasion of Algeria - **pp.154-5**
1818-1828 - Foundation of Zulu Empire by Shaka - **pp.156-7**
1834-1846 - Repeated Kaffir Wars in South Africa - **pp.156-7**
1848-1861 - **Risorgimento** achieves union of Italy - **pp.158-9**
1846-1848 - British victories in Sikh Wars - **pp.160-1**
1854-1855 - Crimean War - **pp.162-3**
1857-1858 - British crush Indian Mutiny - **pp.164-5**
1861-1865 - American Civil War - **pp.166-7**
1879 - Zulu War (battles of Isandhlwana, Rorke's Drift, Ulundi) - **pp.168-9**
1870 - Franco-Prussian War - **pp.170-1**
1878-1880 - 2nd Afghan War - **pp.172-3**
1896-1898 - British reconquer Sudan in River War (Dervish defeat at Omdurman, 1898) - **pp.174-5**
1899-1902 - 2nd or Great Boer War - **pp.178-9**
1900 - Chinese 'Boxer Rising' crushed by international intervention - **pp.176-7**
1914 - Outbreak of First World War
1914 - French & British repel German invasion after retreat to Marne - **pp.182-3**
1915 - Failure of British attempt to seize Gallipoli - **pp.184-5**
1916 - British offensive on Somme - **pp.186-7;** French defence of Verdun - **pp.190-1**
1917 - Collapse of Italians at Caporetto - **pp.188-9;** United States enters war - **pp.192-3;** outbreak of Russian Revolution - **pp.193**
1918 - Failure of German offensive heralds Allied victory on Western Front - **pp.194-5**
1939 - 1st German **panzer** victory in Poland - **pp.198-9**
1940 - Germany conquers Scandinavia, Low Countries, France - **pp.200-201**
1940-1941 - Italian defeat, German intervention opens Desert War in North Africa (1940-43) - **pp.202-3**
1941 - Germany invades Soviet Union; Japan attacks United States at Pearl Harbor
1941-1943 - Germany fails to take Moscow, loses 6th Army at Stalingrad - **pp.204-5;** American victory on Guadalcanal opens 'island war' in Pacific - **pp.206-7**
1944-1945 - failure of Japanese offensive against Imphal, Kohima heralds Allied victory in Burma - **p.208;** Anglo-American landings in Normandy commence liberation of Western Europe - **p.209**
1948-1949 - 1st Arab-Israeli War **1950** - outbreak of Korean War (1950-3) - **pp.212-213**
1954 - French defeat at Dienbienphu ends 1st Vietnamese war - **pp.216-17**
1956 - Anglo-French landings at Suez; 2nd Arab-Israeli War
1965-1966 - Mass American troop landings escalate 2nd Vietnam War
1967 - 3rd Arab-Israeli or 'Six-Day' War - **pp.214-215**
1968 - Vietnamese 'Tet Offensive' shatters American illusions of imminent victory - **pp.216-217**
1975 - Final American withdrawal from Saigon
1979 - Outbreak of Iraqi-Iranian 'Gulf War'
1979-1980 - Soviet Union invades Afghanistan - **pp.220-221**
1982 - British-Argentinian war in Falklands - **pp.218-219**
1983 - United States intervention in Grenada - **pp.222-223**

BIBLIOGRAPHY

'Men-at-Arms' series **(Osprey, London)**

The Ancient World
(109) **Ancient Armies of the Middle East**
(69) **The Greek and Persian Wars, 500-323 BC**
(121) **Armies of the Carthaginian Wars**
(46) **The Roman Army from Caesar to Trajan**
(93) **The Roman Army from Hadrian to Constantine**
(129) **Rome's Enemies: Germanics and Dacians**

The Middle Ages
(125) **The Armies of Islam, 7th-11th Centuries**
(89) **Byzantine Armies, 886-1118**
(85) Saxon, Viking and Norman
(75) **Armies of the Crusades**
(50) **Medieval European Armies 1300-1500**
(105) **The Mongols**
(111) **Armies of Crecy and Poitiers**
(113) **Armies of Agincourt**
(94) **The Swiss at War, 1300-1500**
(99) **Medieval Heraldry**

The 16th and 17th Centuries
(58) **The Landsknechts**
(101) **The Conquistadores**
(86) **The Samurai Armies, 1550-1615**
(14) **English Civil War Armies**
(110) **New Model Army, 1645-1660**

The 18th Century
(97) **Marlborough's Army, 1702-11**
(118) **The Jacobite Rebellions, 1689-1745**
(6) **The Austro-Hungarian Army of the Seven Years War**
(48) **Wolfe's Army**
(1) **The American Provincial Corps**
(18) **George Washington's Army**
(39) **The British Army in North America, 1775-83**

Revolutionary and Napoleonic Wars
(96) Artillery Equipments of the Napoleonic Wars
(97) **Dutch-Belgian Troops of the Napoleonic Wars**
(77) **Flags of the Napoleonic Wars** (1)
(78) **Flags of the Napoleonic Wars** (2)
(115) **Flags of the Napoleonic Wars** (3)
(64) **Napoleon's Cuirassiers and Carabiniers**
(55) **Napoleon's Dragoons and Lancers**
(44) **Napoleon's German Allies** (1)
(90) **Napoleon's German Allies** (3)
(106) **Napoleon's German Allies** (4)
(122) **Napoleon's German Allies** (5)
(83) **Napoleon's Guard Cavalry**
(76) **Napoleon's Hussars**
(88) **Napoleon's Italian and Neapolitan Troops**
(68) **Napoleon's Line Chasseurs**
(87) **Napoleon's Marshals**
(51) **Spanish Armies of the Napoleonic Wars**
(84) **Wellington's Infantry** (1)
(114) **Wellington's Infantry** (2)
(126) **Wellington's Light Cavalry**
(130) **Wellington's Heavy Cavalry**

The 19th Century
(107) **British Infantry Regiments, 1808-1908**
(67) **The Indian Mutiny**
(91) **The Bengal Cavalry Regiments, 1857-1914**
(92) **Indian Infantry Regiments, 1860-1914**
(38) **The Army of the Potomac**
(4) **The Army of the German Empire, 1870-88**
(57) **The Zulu War**
(59) **The Sudan Campaigns, 1881-98**
(82) **The U.S. Army, 1890-1920**
(95) **The Boxer Rebellion**

The 20th Century
(123) **The Australian Army at War, 1899-1975**
(81) **The British Army, 1914-18**
(80) **The German Army, 1914-18**
(108) **British Infantry Equipments, 1908-80**
(14) **The Panzer Divisions** (revised)
(117) **The Polish Army, 1939-45**
(70) **The U.S. Army, 1941-45**
(131) **Germany's Eastern Front Allies, 1941-45**
(54) **Rommel's Desert Army**
(103) **Germany's Spanish Volunteers, 1941-45**
(128) **Arab Armies of the Middle East Wars, 1948-73**
(127) **The Israeli Army in the Middle East Wars, 1948-73**
(132) **The Malayan Campaign, 1948-60**
(104) **Armies of the Vietnam War, 1962-75**
(133) **Battle for the Falklands Land Forces** (1)

Particular thanks are given to th
following for the loan of Artwork fo
this publication.

Roger Baker
Peter Barnacle
Joan Bingham
Alec Gee
Andy Statham
Charles Goodwin
Trevor Hopkins
David Mitchell
Angela Osborn
Mrs Rice